STATION BUILDIN...
MARTLESHAM HEATH

1. Main Road.
2. Officers' Married Quarters.
3. "B" Flight Road (Portal Avenue).
4. "B" Flight Offices.
5. No. 15 Squadron "A" and "B" Flight Hangar until 1929. "A" only after.
6. No. 15 Squadron "A" Flight Offices.
7. Latrines.
8. Oil and Dope Store.
9. No. 15 Squadron Hangar (after 1929) "B" Flight.
10. Mill Cottages.
11. Woodbridge-Felixstowe Road.
12. Old Sports Ground.
13. No. 1 "22" Runway. (After 1943)
14. Parachute Section.
15. Armoury.
16. No. 22 "C" Flight Hangar.
17. Aircraft Firing Butts.
18. Petrol Dump.
19. Airmen's Married Quarters.
20. Halton Road.
21. Coal Dump.
22. No. 22 Squadron "A" Flight Hangar.
23. M.T. Yard.
24. Main Stores.
25. Latrines.
26. No. 22 Squadron "B" Flight Hangar.
27. Duty Pilot's Hut.
28. Fire Tender.
29. Fire Picquet Room.
30. Guard Room.
31. Pyrotechnics Room.
32. Station Workshops. (Carpenters, Doping, Fabric Workers and Coppersmiths.)
33. Rifle Ranges.
34.
35. Power House.
36. Engine Maintenance and Test Shop.
37. Accounts Section.
38. Maintenance Hangar.
39. Photographic Section.
40. Headquarters and Orderly Room.
41. No. 2 "30" Runway. (After 1943)
42. New Sports Ground.
43. Workshops Barrack Room.
44. Headquarters Barrack Room.
45. Bread and Meat Store.
46. Cookhouse.
47. Dining Hall.
48. Barrack Square. (Memorial after 1945)
49. Gymnasium.
50. No. 15 Squadron Barrack Room.
51. No. 22 Squadron Barrack Room.
52. Meteorological Hut.
53. Band Room.
54. Single Officers' Sleeping Quarters.
55. Church.
56. N.A.A.F.I. Store and Shop.
57. N.A.A.F.I.
58. Shoemaker's Shop.
59. Sports Store.
60. Sergeants' Mess and Quarters.
61. Disused Coal Dump.
62. Airmen's Quarters and Motor Cycle Store.
63. Station Sick Quarters.
64. Officers' Mess.
65. Sewerage Farm.
66. Waldringfield Road.
67. Foxhall Road.
68. Spratt's Plantation.
69. Swale Plantation.

MARTLESHAM HEATH

MARTLESHAM HEATH

The Story of the Royal Air Force Station 1917—1973

by

GORDON KINSEY

Foreword by

Air Vice Marshal John Gray, R.A.F. (Retired)
and
Air Commodore H. F. V. Battle, R.A.F. (Retired)

TERENCE DALTON LIMITED
LAVENHAM . SUFFOLK
1975

Published by
TERENCE DALTON LIMITED
ISBN 0 86138 023 1

First published 1975
Second impression 1979
Revised edition 1983

Text set in 11/12pt Baskerville Typeface

Printed in Great Britain at
THE LAVENHAM PRESS LIMITED
LAVENHAM   SUFFOLK

Contents

Index of Illustrations

Dedicated to all who through seasons and years faced the
wind on the Heath and especially those who lifted from it
to their Greatest Flight.

Acknowledgement

My special thanks to the "flying men" of Martlesham, Air Commodore H. F. V. Battle, who searching through his log-book came up with a feast of information on types tested in the early 1920's—Wing Commander A. R. Boeree for his information on First World War flight testing and the use of his wonderful photograph album—Group Captain Stuart Culley, D.S.O. for his testing experiences, and as a bonus, his recollections of destroying the Zeppelin L.53—the late Major R. H. Carr A.F.C., D.F.C., for his exciting letters describing his days as the first Commanding Officer, Flying, Aeroplane Experimental Squadron, Martlesham —Mr Jack Easedown for stories of Martlesham and as a pilot with Sir Alan Cobham's Flying Air Circus—Mr R. M. McGlasson for his log-book records of life with No. 15 Squadron—Mr V. C. Gaunt, F.R.Ae.S, of Westlands who as a "civvy rep" saw life from the non-Service angle and recalled many incidents—Air Vice Marshal John Gray for unlimited assistance with aircraft types and great encouragement for this project—Mr H. B. Haward, who as a Chief Technical Officer saw many changes to note—the late Mrs Anne Hammond, whose husband, Captain Walden Hammond was a pioneer of aerial photography, and her recorded memories of life in the early days on the Station—Wing Commander W. Hinckley for flying days of not so long ago—Wing Commander John Jewell of Martin-Bakers Ltd for memories of his days with Corporal East and Leading Air-craftsman "Brainey" Dobbs—Wing Commander C. Hole for recalling his adventures on the stern of a 2-seat fighter during test—Group Captain J. Noakes and the first flight of the Beardmore Inflexible and his near-fatal crash in the Parnall Pippit—Group Captain P. J. R. King for his visits and recollections as a test-pilot and later as Commanding Officer of No. 64 Squadron, both at Martlesham Heath—Wing Commander Royle-Bantoft for recalling post-war flying days at the Heath—Mr H. L. Stevens, C.B.E. and Mr E. T. Jones, who, as Chief Technical Officers, saw it from all sides and recalled their days at the A & A.E.E.—Group Captain R. R. Stanford-Tuck for his Battle of Britain days and use of extracts from his book, also Group Captain D. R. S. Bader for writing to me of his Battle days spent at the Heath—Mr A. J. "Bill" Pegg of Bristols for use of his book *Sent Flying* and help with aircraft types—Harald Penrose O.B.E. a tower of strength in several ways with help in all directions— Mr W. H. E. Thomas for his most interesting letters describing the early days and recalling names and incidents.

On the ground and fortunately still living in the locality, many served who knew and loved the Station and have given freely of their memories, Mr W. J. Brown with an illuminating photograph album—Mr W. Begbie who provided many contacts of latter days—Mr Bishop who also came to grief with the C.O.W. Gun—Mr A. G. Cooke, Station Engineer for providing details of the runway construction—Mr W. W. Harvey also for use of his photographs and notes—Miss F. E. Jermyn for the use of her unique Visitors' Book from *Black Tiles* and her memories of Second World War days—Mr G. F. Kitchen for his information on post-war activities—Mr K. Leighton for sources of local interest and general help—Mr H. Lee for interesting talks and use of his extensive photograph album—Wing Commander Mumford for memories of between the wars days—Mr M. H. Matheson for information about the site before the Station was built—Mr E. Prescott for almost everything about life on the ground and the exploits of the Station Concert Party—Mr and Mrs R. J. Pratt for help and encouragement in several directions—Flight Lieutenant R. G. Pike of No. 56 Squadron, Royal Air Force, for information on his Unit—Mr Powling for local knowledge—Mr J. Trower for providing many contacts—Mr S. R. Wigg for talking at length about things Martlesham—Canon Trevor Waller of Waldringfield for his recollections of the very early days and the construction of the Station—and Mrs Hervey of Little Bealings for her memories, and the photographs of the Martlesham Heath Memorial and the Book of Honour.

Of great help in the project has been Mr Christopher Elliott of Wimbledon, a fellow East Anglian and kindred lover of all things "air", who provided copy and sources of information—the "Air Historians" who have helped wittingly and unwittingly in so many ways and have made available to me their photographs and anything else requested, Messrs C. F. Andrews, C. H. Barnes, J. M. Bruce, D. L. Brown, A. J. Jackson, J. N. James, H. F. King, P. Lewis, F K. Mason, O. Tapper, H. A. Taylor and O. Thetford—together with Mr Frank Cheeseman for help with early aircraft types, Mr Roger Freeman for assistance with the 8th Air Force on which he is the acknowledged expert, and Mr Bob Malster for his help in many ways.

On the photographic side many of the older prints would not have been possible without the skills of Mr A. R. J. Frost, A.I.I.P., A.R.P.S., M.I.R.T., who with limitless patience brought these precious, ageing prints back to life for a permanent record. Mrs Mollie Martin and her daughter Miss Victoria Martin for their great help with the priceless photographs of the late Captain Walden Hammond and for being able to loan these for close examination. Also, in this field, Mr L. S. Armandias helped with the French aircraft—Mrs Olive Baker with the St Francis photographs—the late Mr A. R. Fairweather with the Royal visit portraits and Mr Stuart Leslie of Scarborough with a never ending flow of photographs of early aircraft from his wonderful collection. Mr Ian McLachlan and Mr Stuart Evans for prints of the salved Hurricane of Flying Officer Czernin,

Flight Lieutenant Tim Mason for visiting me and helping with various items, Mr C. E. Powell of Dublin for contact help, Miss Anne Tilbury, Photographic Librarian of *Flight International,* who, in spite of a departmental move, still managed to hunt out some of the less familiar specimens, and of course the many private albums that were so readily made available for my use.

Last but by no means least, the Trade, the Aircraft Manufacturers and their Publicity Departments who helped in such a kind hearted manner with stacks of photographs and information. The Air Historical Branch, The British Motor Corporation (Mr Peter Burdon M.A.I.E.) British Aircraft Corporation through all its branches, with Mr N. A. Barfield at Weybridge, British Airways, formerly British Overseas Airways Corporation, and British European Airways, (Mr W. Oliver), Messrs William Beardmore of Glasgow, Bristol Siddeley Engines of Filton, Coventry and Leavesden, Hawker Siddeley Aviation Limited, Hatfield (O. J. Tapper), Kingston-on-Thames (G. Anderson) Manchester (G. Allen) and Brough (E. Barker), the former Handley-Page Aircraft Company Limited (A. C. Morris), Headquarters of the Third Air Force, U.S.A.F., South Ruislip, Middlesex, Ministry of Defence (Air), Ministry of Public Building and Works, Ministry of Technology—R.A.E. Bedford and A & A.E.E., Boscombe Down Short Brothers and Harland Limited, Office of the Secretary of Defence, Washington, U.S.A. (Lieutenant Colonel Daniel M. Hill), Post Office Research Department, Dollis Hill and Martlesham Heath (Dr H. H. Daglish, C.Eng.), Qantas International Airways (C. Walmsley), Parnalls of Yate, Royal Aeronautical Society and their Librarian, Rolls-Royce Limited (Aero-Engine Division—M. H. Evans), South African Airways, Skyfame Air Museum, Public Relations Officer, United States Air Force, R.A.F. Bentwaters, Suffolk, Ransomes, Sims and Jefferies Limited, Ipswich and Vickers Limited.

Mr Cooper of Horham helped with helicopter information, Squadron Leader D. H. Clarke with useful suggestions on many subjects, the *East Anglian Daily Times* and its associated newspapers with records, *Flight International* for use of photographs, Mr W. Garrod of Greenford for his help with early radar information, Mr Hall of Ipswich who kept such a wonderful and informative diary during the War years and made it freely available, Mr T. Heffernan of Boscombe Down with information on the present-day A & A.E.E., the Ipswich and District Historical Transport Society for help from its many members, Miss Wood and Miss King of the Ipswich Borough Library for their keen help and ability to get almost any book for my reference.

For quiet encouragement, patience and help at all stages, my wife Margaret, and daughters Sallie, Carolyn and Margot who all helped with many items.

Gordon Kinsey,
Ipswich, Suffolk.
1975.

Foreword

THIS is a valuable and interesting record of the work done at the Royal Air Force Station, Martlesham Heath, Suffolk, in peace and war from the time the Royal Flying Corps established an experimental flying unit there in 1917 until the R.A.F. left it in 1972.

In peace it was primarily engaged in the testing of civil and service aircraft and armament and in war as a fighter station. As one can imagine both these roles provided a story of exceptional interest and at times of great courage and sacrifice.

The author lived as a boy close to Martlesham airfield and spent many hours watching numerous British and foreign aircraft being tested. Later he was to serve in the Royal Air Force as an aircrew member in the Second World War.

During all these years he has never lost his interest in the activities of Martlesham Heath and has been at great pains to record in these pages the many and varied aspects of life on this station which will undoubtedly prove of great value to those interested in the development of aviation in this country.

John A. Gray.   H. F. V. Battle.
Air Vice Marshal R.A.F. (Retd)   Air Commodore R.A.F. (Retd)

Introduction

MARTLESHAM Heath is situated approximately four miles east of Ipswich on the south side of the main coastal road, the A.12, and midway between Ipswich and Woodbridge. The flat heathland plateau is characteristic of the countryside of this part of East Anglia, with the rivers and estuaries cutting inroads into the windswept salting and water meadows. It is bounded on the south-west by the River Orwell some four miles distant, and to the east by the River Deben only some two miles away; and the restless, grey North Sea lies ten miles to the south-east. The village bearing the name Martlesham nestles in the valley of the River Finn some distance to the north-east and boasts a fine old coaching inn, *The Red Lion*, which proudly displays for its sign a grand figurehead from a ship wrecked in the middle of the eighteenth century. The colour of this unique inn-sign has prompted East Anglians over the years to quote "as red as Martlesham Lion" when describing anything of a bight reddish hue. The medieval church of St Mary stands some distance from the community high on a tree-shrouded promontory overlooking Martlesham Creek and the River Deben.

Tree-covered tumuli bear evidence to the burial places of ancient people on the 830 acres of the Heath, and in fact England's greatest treasure trove in the form of an East Anglian king's burial ship was unearthed during the late 1930's just across the Deben at Sutton Hoo. Parts of the Heath are still a haven among modern activities and extend succour and habitation to all kinds of wild life and flora. Heather and ling cover the surface, and in late summer nature displays wonderful shades of pinks and purples.

Spring brings forth the tall unfolding bracken fronds, known locally as "brakes", which deepen in shade through the long days into a waving sea of gold and russet browns before being struck down by the early frosts of winter. Intervening gaps are covered with rough grasses and small silver birches, while tiny sand-loving plants carpet the ground with bright yellows and whites. Tall spikes of willow-herb thrust above the bracken in colourful pyramids and flowering gorse or "whin" grows in great clumps in tangled confusion: its march over the open stretches is only halted by occasional cutting and by the summer fires from which it returns phoenix-like, with pale green spikes on blackened stems and masses of brilliant yellow flowers, the following year.

The site is ringed by dark pines, gaunt and twisted, through which the warm breezes gently sigh with a fragrant scent, but the bitter easterlies of winter roar and hiss. A breeze of any strength whips up the loose dusty top surface causing miniature sand-storms, and indeed in former years some test-pilots remarked that if an aircraft's engine filters withstood the Martlesham dust the machine was definitely suitable for desert operations.

Partridges and pheasants burst up in the path of the walker. Plovers or peewits start their departure run before flapping upwards to lure the intruder away from their stoney nests, and the spring air is filled with the song of ascending skylarks. Rabbits sport on the grassy patches and burrow their way into the easily worked sandy soil, while lizards bask in the sun with the occasional snake during the hotter days.

The airfield is now bisected by the eastern end of a new by-pass which will enable traffic to avoid Ipswich, and this includes among its works the graceful new Orwell bridge. To the western side of the road the daily growth of new residences rises in multi shades of brick, weatherboard and tile, hip-roofed, non-regimental and styled to the Suffolk scene. Small windows peer out from under deep eaves, and the distant viewer is hard pressed to find two examples the same colour and shape.

On the other side of the road, the old hangars still stand erect, housing modern merchandise in their role as units of the industrial estate whose roads are designated with names once so familiar to the site, Hawker, Gloster and others. Barrack blocks still guard the former parade square where stands the memorial, now under the excellent care of the Woodbridge squadron of the Air Training Corps, whose weekly attention keeps the names of lost American airmen ever bright.

The wartime Control Tower is the home of the Martlesham Heath Aviation Historic Society whose aim is to perpetuate the memory of the Station in all its aspects over the years. Watching out over runways no longer visible, its interior will still be warmed by the talk and feel of things Martlesham. Ex-"residents" from over the years make the Heath a place of pilgrimage and the talk goes on long into the night, not always about aeroplanes, but of men, men from Empire and Allies, with Australian twang and Texan drawl. These are all the ingredients that made up the life and times of this most famous and respected of Royal Air Force stations.

Unit Badge of the Aeroplane and Armament Experimental Establishment.   *Ministry of Defence*

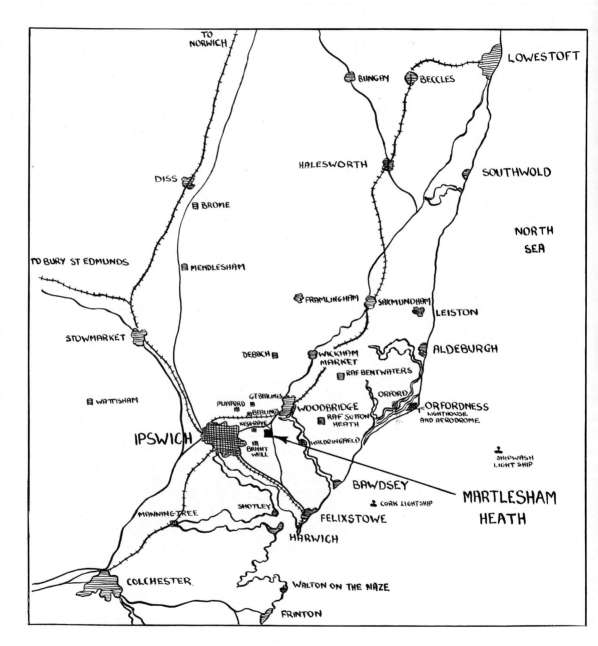

Location of Martlesham Heath showing places named in book.

CHAPTER ONE

In the Beginning. 1917—1925

> "There's something at Martlesham people declare,
> Which is found on the ground and is felt in the air.
> It's a spirit of Homeliness, Friendliness and Fun,
> And it's free to all-comers, like the warmth of the Sun."
> *Black Tiles* Visitors' Book, 1943.

MARTLESHAM Heath was first officially mentioned during May 1916, as on the 17th of that month, an interesting experiment was carried out at the nearby established Royal Naval Air Service Station at Felixstowe. A large Porte flying-boat piloted by its designer, Squadron-Commander John Porte, took-off from Felixstowe carrying attached to its upper main-plane, a Bristol Scout, No. 3028, piloted by Flight Lieutenant M. J. Day. When a height of 1,000 feet had been attained over Harwich Harbour, the Scout pilot switched on his motor, activated the release gear and climbed away safely to land on the Heath at Martlesham. This experiment, which was designed to carry fighter aircraft out over the North Sea in order to attack raiding Zeppelins, was not repeated and unfortunately Flight Lieutenant Day was killed shortly afterwards in France.

Many people wonder why one of the prime experimental stations of the British Air Industry was situated in this locality far from the manufacturing centres and a quick look back into the early days of the Royal Flying Corps gives the answer.

During the autumn of 1915 it was decided that the Experimental Flying Section of the Central Flying School at Upavon, Wiltshire, which had been formed during November 1914 with Captain A. H. L. Soames M.C. as Flight Commander, a regular officer from the 3rd Hussars, was occupying too much of the flying training time of the School, and therefore aggravating the already short supply of instructors and machines. It was therefore decided to move the Armament Experimental Flight of the Experimental Squadron to Orfordness, in Suffolk, its new home being situated on the island opposite the town of Orford, skirted by the River Ore on the landward side and the North Sea on the others. At that time the sole occupants of this low-lying, barely above sea level, land and saltings were the keepers of the light-house on the Ness and the occasional shepherd tending his wandering flock grazing on the salty grasses.

The only Martinsyde F-1, A.3933, at Orfordness late 1916. Note the canvas aeroplane hangar in the background and the canvas covers over the airscrew. *Mrs M. Martin*

Thus the Armament Flight took up residence in somewhat primitive conditions, carrying out their experimentation with guns and bombing gear, the aircraft participating in the work being housed in canvas hangars and flying from a crude landing strip in the centre of the island.

After the first few months, and further thought, it became apparent and deemed expedient that the Aircraft Testing Flight, still at Upavon, should be sited nearer to the Armament Flight, and therefore a survey was carried out to find a new home in East Anglia for the other half of the Unit. It was in this connection, therefore, that during the autumn of 1916, Captain Bertram Hopkinson and Lieutenant Henry Tizard visited Ipswich, and using the town as a base, examined various likely looking sites in the district. Their travels eventually brought them to the heather-covered stretches of Martlesham Heath, where occasional flying was taking place by aircraft based at Felixstowe and Orfordness. After discussions and consultations, a decision was made, naming Martlesham as the suitable site with its nearness to a large town, road facilities and nearby Bealings railway station.

During the winter of 1916 work started on the Heath by removing an avenue of pine-trees which ran across from east to west and the more prominent hillocks and hollows levelled. Huts were erected for living accommodation together with sheds for the aircraft and their equipment, whilst at Upavon dismantling of the Unit's equipment took place, some of the larger pieces being the two camera-obscura which were used for testing aircraft speeds over the ground.

The transfer of the Experimental Aircraft Flight from Upavon was carried out by the second week of January, 1917, and Martlesham Heath was officially opened on the 16th January, 1917, under the command of Major (later Lieutenant-Colonel) H. L. Cooper. Shortly before the commissioning of Martlesham Heath, a Squadron, No. 37, had been formed at Orfordness to carry out Armament Experiments, but this Unit was short-lived and "A" Flight of this Squadron was absorbed into the newly arrived Martlesham formation.

The Unit soon settled down and Major G. D. Mills replaced Major Cooper in command, with the newly-promoted Captain Henry Tizard in charge of the technical side, as Scientific Officer. The early days of the Squadron were described to the author by the first Commanding Officer (Flying), the late Major R. H. Carr, A.F.C., D.F.C., who was an early pre-First World War aviator with Mr Claude Grahame-White at Hendon.

"I was there from January 1917 until the end of the War, first as a test-pilot and then promoted to Major and ran the flying side of the business. There were then two large built hangars for the machines, and wooden huts for the Mess, Quarters and Flight Offices. We soon settled down and made ourselves comfortable. Our food was rationed and at times consisted of a box of Australian rabbits, frozen, complete with skins, which when removed, had to be returned to Luton in Bedfordshire to be made into flying helmets, gloves, etc. The cooks usually made a hash and all were well satisfied.

We were sent to Martlesham to test and report on the aeroplanes and I think we did a good job at that. Every type of machine and engine was sent to us for test, single-seater scouts to four-engined bombers. Monoplanes, biplanes, triplanes and quadruplanes: single-engine, twin-engine and multi-engined: in-line, and Vee-water cooled, rotary and radial air-cooled engines as well as all the associated

A unique line-up of Sopwith aircraft of the Armament Flight, Orfordness, during 1916. Right to left—Triplane, Pup, Camel, Pup and 1½ Strutter.
Mrs M. Martin

Captured German Albatross Scout flying over Martlesham village during 1918. The Ipswich-Lowestoft railway line crosses from left to right whilst the Woodbridge-Ipswich road runs from top to bottom.

Mrs M. Martin

equipment for these aircraft and engines. We also tested various types of captured German machines, the flying of which we found very interesting.

Machines were tested at ground-level for speed and at various heights, rate of climb, ceiling, petrol consumption, load carried and the calibration of instruments. The top speed of the fastest machine was around 125 m.p.h. and very few had a ceiling, absolute obtainable height of much above 18,000 feet. I once went up to 20,000 feet in a Sopwith Camel, no oxygen in those days, but this was very exceptional.

Our first Commanding Officer was Major Mills and Captain Tizard was in charge of all trades and tests. One could never have had a better man to work under. Lieutenants Inton and Gore worked out the mathematics, Lieutenant Chilvers was in charge of the instruments and Lieutenant Pearson looked after the Workshops. Pilots were Captain Mayo (later inventor of the Mayo pick-a-back aircraft), Carr, Palethorpe, Orde and Lewis. Captain Mayo also invented a system which we built in our Workshops for flying a machine using the feet only, leaving the hands free for cocking guns, throttle, control column, etc., and it was tested at Martlesham. Testing at this time was carried out by what was known as the "density" method where the speed and climb of an aircraft was used as the standard basis for performance rating of all types.

Major Mills left and was replaced by Major T. B. O'Hubbard, always known as "Mother," whilst more pilots, Boeree, Gathergood and Muspratt arrived and very good they were. Austin Hopkinson, a leading scientist, was often there and Churchill came once or twice."

The day to day test flying was carried out by operational pilots posted for one reason or another from the squadrons in France, "on rest," but with the somewhat unreliable nature of the new machines and engines of this period, testing must have been only slightly less hazardous than being engaged in mortal combat over the Western Front.

By the autumn of 1917 the Unit had really bedded down and in October its name was changed to the Aeroplane Experimental Unit, Royal Flying Corps. During this early period, Captain Tizard commenced his research work and trials conducted into improving the efficiency of aircraft fuels, and it was the long range result of his experimentations that played such a great part in the latter day performance of Royal Air Force aircraft. Investigation was also carried out into the problem of cloud-flying, or blind-flying as we now know it, common enough nowadays, but at that time a dangerous and not often indulged-in exercise. Tizard was also actively engaged in developing and carrying out trials of a new bomb sight and the techniques for its use. In this connection he would often position himself in the target-area in order to observe more fully the fall of the missile after it had left the aircraft. Witnesses have stated that on many occasions he instructed the pilot of the aircraft engaged in the tests to aim at him

Officers of the Aeroplane Experimental Squadron, Martlesham Heath, 1918. Major Carr is fourth from the left, front row, whilst Colonel Tizard is seventh.   *Wing Commander A. Boeree*

in the target area. He is quoted at this time as saying, "Aeroplane testing like all other work connected with aeroplanes is only in its infancy and as time goes on and knowledge accumulates better methods and instruments will be evolved."

The Vicar of nearby Waldringfield, Canon Trevor Waller, remembers the early days of the aerodrome when the Royal Flying Corps arrived, as he drove over it in a pony and trap on his way to Woodbridge School. At other times he cycled to school and remembers seeing the first aircraft to arrive, a F.E. pusher. For many months after this a daily sight on the road from Woodbridge were groups of German prisoners-of-war marching from their camp at Barrack Corner, Woodbridge to Martlesham Heath where they were constructing the hangars and laying hard-standings. Others worked at Waldringfield, demolishing Mason's old Cement Works which had moved to Claydon on the other side of Ipswich, and the bricks and rubble were carted to Martlesham and used for the aerodrome works. Among his recollections are that of a Sopwith Scout landing in a flock of sheep in Newbourn village killing about a dozen as it turned over amongst them. The pilot escaped injury although soaked from head to foot in petrol from the ruptured fuel tank, and bruised from being bounced from sheep to sheep as he landed on their backs.

Mr W. H. E. Thomas who, as an officer, served at the Aeroplane Experimental Unit remembers some of his fellow officers: the Commanding Officer, Major O'Hubbard, had a "private" captured German Fokker D.VII which was considered, by him, a safe means of transport in the face of the anti-aircraft guns of those days.

Captain Palethorpe who won a Military Cross for shooting down a German aeroplane whilst on a testing flight from Martlesham. Captain Boeree who was the author of a most spectacular crash.

Major R. H. "Reggie" Carr who was called "Crikey" after his favourite expression. Captain Gathergood was Officer Commanding "B" Flight and later practised as a dentist in Weymouth. Mr Thomas remembered going on a harassing flight with him in the back seat of a monumental triplane called the Bristol Braemar, "the tail of which appeared to twist through a terrible lot of degrees."

General view of the wartime aerodrome with a captured German Fokker D.VII in foreground. A D.H.4 and F.E.2B pose in the background. *Stuart Leslie*

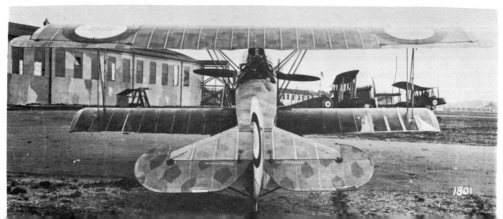

Captain Palethorpe M.C., A.F.C., who encountered the raiding German squadron whilst on a test flight.

W. J. Brown

Major O. M. Sutton and Captain Gathergood in jolly mood. Major Sutton was killed at Martlesham during 1921 in the Braemar crash.

Mrs M. Martin

Lieutenant Thornton, later Sir Gerald Thornton. Captain Barlow was Chief Technical Officer and later a Director of Fairey Aviation. Captain Geddes was in charge of the Photographic Section and was chiefly responsible for the development of the first camera gun.

Captain Wallwork and Mr Thomas shared a room together all the time Mr Thomas was at Martlesham Heath; Captain Wallwork was unfortunately killed during 1922 whilst flying a Sopwith Snipe from the airfield at Brockworth, Gloucestershire.

Captain Woodhouse was another wonderful character (two or three D.S.O's) whose main work during the War was landing and picking up British spies from behind the German lines. On one occasion he burnt the seat of his pants out sitting on the hot engine of an R.E.8 aircraft that would not start-up again, while he had a spy aboard and the Germans approaching all around.

Group Captain Stuart Culley, who as a Lieutenant was the victor over the Zeppelin LZ.53, remembers that he kept a Sopwith Camel at Martlesham from August 1918 until he left during March 1919 when his Flight at Felixstowe was disbanded. This aircraft was to keep his "hand in" as Felixstowe being a flying-boat station there was no opportunity for flying land-planes, although on one occasion he did take a newly-erected Sopwith Camel off the slip-way at Felixstowe to deliver it to Martlesham, "that being, of course, the simplest way in which to deliver the aircraft after erection." Group Captain Culley was in later years the Station Adjutant at Martlesham Heath, but it is interesting to recall his previous notable achievement, the destruction of the LZ.53. This took place on the morning of 11th August, 1918, when after being towed across the North Sea on a lighter behind the destroyer *Redoubt,* the Sopwith Camel's engine was started, and Lieutenant Culley took the aircraft off the extremely restricted deck of the lighter, climbed to altitude and destroyed the airship off the Dutch island of Terschelling. Admiral Turwhitt observing the action instructed his Flag Officer to make the following signal. "Flag-General. Your attention is called to Hymn No. 224, Verse 7."*

*O happy band of pilgrims,
  Look upward to the skies,
Where such a light affliction,
  Shall win so great a prize.

The cottage at Waldringfield in which Captain and Mrs Hammond lived during their stay at Martlesham Heath. Photographed from the air 1918.   *Mrs M. Martin*

Group of Technical Officers with Major Barlow seated in centre and Captain Hammond with stick.   *V. H. E. Thomas*

The late Mrs Anne Hammond, whose husband Captain Waldon Hammond was one of the aerial photographic pioneers recalled their early days at Martlesham. "We knew Major Tim Barlow and his wife quite well as they had rooms in Waldringfield where we had half the cottage of the village dress-maker. When I was there in 1967, I visited Miss Lankester, then Mrs Thompson, who was living in the same cottage, aged eighty-nine years." With Major and Mrs Barlow the Hammonds spent quite a lot of time on the River Deben with an Ipswich dentist and his wife, Mr and Mrs Gordon Stewart. Captain Lindemann, who later became Lord Cherwell and Mr Winston Churchill's right-hand man when he left the Air Force, often flew Captain Hammond on his experimental work over the sea. When the Hammonds first arrived on Christmas Eve 1917 they took the only place available and this was a cottage on the end of the aerodrome and Major and Mrs Thomas lived in the next door cottage. Mrs Hammond said it was snowing hard and when they were moving in the Reverend Doughty, Vicar of Martlesham, called and asked if they had all the furniture they wanted. The next day he sent chairs, table, a coal bucket and a number of other things. After a short time the Hammonds moved to Miss Lankester's in Waldringfield. Mrs Hammond said "I well remember the day Lieutenant Muspratt was killed — he was such a charming youth. Unfortunately we got used to fatalities it being an experimental station."

Distinguished Officers of the A.E.S., 1918

Captain Lindemann	Captain Griffith	Captain Mumford	Major Tim	Major "Reggie"
Later		U.S.A.S. Officer	Barlow	Carr
Lord Cherwell			C.T.O.	1st O.C. Flying

De Havilland 6 biplane in background.

V. H. E. Thomas

The architect for the aerodrome in its early form was Mr Walter Henry Bulloch of the Barrack Construction Department of the War Office, seconded to the Air Board. He was born in 1870 in Aberdeen and died in 1932.

At this time, Martlesham was the only aerodrome of any size in the district, the nearest operational airfields being to the west, one situated at Elmswell between Ipswich and Bury St Edmunds, and the other at Hadleigh, between Ipswich and Sudbury. Bristol Fighters of No. 75 Squadron were stationed at these two aerodromes, with "A" Flight at Hadleigh, and "B" and "C" Flights at Elmswell.

With the cessation of hostilities, the tempo of the work at the Station eased somewhat, the hustle and bustle of the war years and their new prototypes now being a thing of the past, the majority of the aircraft on the Unit being, in the main, "left-overs" which had been developed as far as it was expedient to carry on with them. The urgency to get aircraft into operational service as soon as possible no longer existed, and so many of the test aircraft became residents and included such types as the Vickers Vimy and the giant Handley-Page V.1500 bombers which had only just missed active service. Events of note, did however still occur, like the 7,000 mile trip of the Handley-Page V.1500, Serial No. J.1936 and named "Old Carthusian" which flew from Martlesham to Lahore in India. Leaving Martlesham on the 13th December, 1919, it made the journey in stages, but what must seem strange today, is the fact that during the middle of January it broke down a few miles from Karachi, and a warship was sent to its assistance. After repairs it continued on its way and eventually reached Lahore where it was given an enthusiastic reception after circling the city twice.

Martlesham pilots figured in the 1919 Civil Air Races, Captain G. W. Gathergood flying a De Havilland 4R, K-141, being placed first and Major R. H. Carr flying a Grahame-White Bantam, K-153, doing well until he was forced down with mechanical trouble.

On 21st March, 1920, Martlesham was the venue for a successful attempt on the World's Air Speed Record, when Mr F. P. Raynham flying the Martinsyde Semiquaver G-EAPX, fitted with a 300 h.p. Hispano-Suiza engine, set up a new record of 161.434 m.p.h. over one kilometre.

The British Air Speed Record was raised on 17th June, 1920, when Major L. H. Tait-Cox flew the A.B.C. Dragonfly 320 h.p. engined Nieuport Goshawk, G-EASK at a speed of 166.5 m.p.h.

Another record was achieved on 19th December, 1921, when Mr J. H. James flew the Gloucestershire Mars Bamel I, G-EAXE to a new British Speed Record of 194.6 m.p.h.

The Gloucestershire Mars Bamel I, G-EAXZ, in which Mr J. H. James created a new British Speed Record of 194·6 mph on 19th December, 1921.   *Flight No. 2063*

At the Royal Air Force Pageant held on 24th June, 1922, a Martlesham Heath pilot, Flying Officer C. E. Horrox won the Handicap Race in the large Avro Aldershot, J.6852. Also taking part in this race were several Martlesham-based aircraft including the two Westland Weasels, K.2918 and J.6577, a Sopwith Snipe, the Martinsyde Buzzard F.4, a Sopwith Pup, Two De Havilland 9a's, a S.E.5a, Bristol F2B, an Avro 504K and a Vickers Vimy.

During the night of 6th October, 1922, an event of a different nature occurred, when a fierce unaccounted-for fire raged through and totally destroyed the wooden "C" Flight Hangar alongside the road running through the Camp. This was one of the prisoner-of-war erected buildings and was particularly dangerously placed, it being the middle hangar of three and contained many stores as well as the collection of captured enemy aircraft, both erected and crated. A variety of engines and tool-boxes were also lost and the Station Fire-Section did extremely well to prevent the fire spreading to the adjoining hangars. Woodbridge Fire Brigade arrived with a horse-drawn engine and a horse cab, the Fire Chief giving his orders by calls on a bugle!

View looking north through the Camp with Station Headquarters on the left and the Guardroom on the right.   *W. J. Brown*

Hangar on fire 5 a.m., 6th October, 1922. It is the second one in the previous illustration.

W. J. Brown

Surveying the damage the morning after the fire. Wreckage of an aircraft can be discerned by its engine and wire-spoked wheels and appears to be one of the German "captures". *W. J. Brown*

Some of the German aircraft destroyed in the hangar fire.
a. L.V.G. No. G/5BDE/18 2-seat observation aircraft.
b. Rumpler CV. C8500/16. 2-seat observation aircraft. G.117.
c. Pfalz D.III Scout G141 4184/17a 828.
d. Fokker D.VIII. Note mixed German and R.A.F. markings.

Wing Commander A. Boeree
Stuart Leslie

At this time various local bye-laws were brought into being, the most important being those connected with the Aircraft Speed Range which at this time crossed the Woodbridge-Felixstowe road within the aerodrome boundary. A flag-pole was erected, and during speed tests a red flag was flown from it and a sentry posted in order to protect the public, by stopping any persons wandering on to the course and being struck by low-flying aircraft. Much discussion ensued as to whether or not Service personnel should be used for this purpose, or whether or not it was the responsibility of the civil powers. The latter pleaded lack of sufficient men so the Service personnel carried on with the duty.

Right of way on the road through the aerodrome also came up for discussion and meetings were held in connection with this problem, and at one time it looked as if this road would be closed to the general public altogether. Plans were drawn up for a new road to be constructed, around the aerodrome, but lack of finance and other circumstances shelved this project. The public were still allowed the use of the road for vehicular traffic, but stopping and watching was strictly prohibited, and speed limits were imposed. The use of cameras was also illegal both on this road and on the A12 road running alongside the aerodrome and large notice-boards warned of the restrictions and the penalties which could be imposed on conviction. It is reported that in several instances cameras were confiscated, the films developed by the authorities, and, if they had proved not to be a security risk, both film and camera were returned to their owners with a letter of caution. Some of the illustrations in this book were obtained in this manner by various over-keen but well-meaning people.

Avro 504 biplane flying low along original Speed Course. This illustration was confiscated by the Air Ministry after it was taken and then returned to its owner.

No. 15 Squadron, "B" Flight hangar, which replaced the wooden one destroyed in the fire.

A. R. J. Frost

Rights-of-way on the aerodrome field itself were also a matter of prolonged legislation. Arrangements were made for a new connecting road to be constructed from the A12 originally called "B" Flight Road but now Portal Avenue, and further bye-laws were established providing for its use by the general public on the same basis as the existing aerodrome road. At the north-western or Ipswich end of the new "B" Flight Road, detached and semi-detached houses were built for the accommodation of the Officer Commanding and Senior Officers. Further hangars were also erected, permanent buildings for testing equipment, and barrack-blocks for non-commissioned officers and other ranks. New Messes, both Officers' and N.C.O's were also built, although a number of the old war-time structures were still used and continued to be for some years to come. A feature of the single officer's accommodation at Martlesham Heath was the fact that the quarters with their bedrooms, which were in the form of bungalows, were on one side of the road, and the bathrooms on the other side. It was not therefore unusual to see officers at various times of the day strolling across the road clad only in dressing gowns or with just a towel round their waists.

The Armament Experimental Flight which had left Orfordness during 1921 to take up residence at the Isle of Grain, moved to Martlesham Heath during 1924, and on the 20th March, 1924, the name of the Station changed once again to the Aeroplane and Armament Experimental Establishment, the A & A.E.E., a name it still bears to this day at Boscombe Down, Hampshire. The two flying units remained separate under their respective Squadron Leaders, (Flying). The personnel were told that they would be formed into two squadrons, each with its own special establishment of personnel, but that they would be equipped only in an emergency with De Havilland 9a's. The Armament Unit thus became No. 15 Squadron under the command of Squadron Leader P. C. Sherren and the Aeroplane Unit became No. 22 Squadron under the command of Squadron Leader C. H. Nicholas. The Station retained its title and special personnel under the command of Wing Commander N. J. Gill. This was an admirable arrangement as the Government could say at any time that they had formed two more bomber squadrons at no extra cost to the tax-payer. These aircraft would have been under the control of No. 3 Group, Spittlegate, Grantham, and incorporated under a bombing wing. Political subterfuge or not, the duties of the Units on the Station were plain enough.

In the case of No. 15 its duties were to test all new types of armaments and bombs and bombing gear, and in order to carry out these tasks a number of established types of "hack" aircraft were housed. These could be fitted with bomb-dropping gear or guns, the testing of which usually took place off Orfordness, the airfield of which still operated as a satellite to Martlesham.

No. 22 Squadron was responsible for testing and reporting on all new types of aircraft, both military and civil, and covered all aspects of flight-testing and acceptance trials as the Air Ministry was the authority for the issue of Certificates of Airworthiness. For this purpose the Squadron was divided into three Flights, a normal procedure at this period, and named "A", "B", and "C" Flights.

"A" Flight was responsible for testing fighter types and light civil aircraft, "B" Flight tested and reported on bomber types and large civil passenger carrying machines, whilst "C" Flight dealt with all aircraft which did not fall into the above categories, such as the aircraft intended for the Fleet Air Arm and Army Co-operation, and in general anything regarded as odd. This Squadron was housed in the large hip-roofed hangar on the left-hand side of "B" Flight Road, "A" and "B" Flights being accommodated there, whilst "C" Flight lived in the brick hangar on the other side of the road. In latter days, after the large steel hangar was erected alongside "A" Flight hangar, "B" Flight moved into the new building.

No. 15 Squadron worked basically in the same manner and was accommodated in the wooden round-topped hangars alongside the Woodbridge-Felixstowe Road, and the large steel hangar set back from the road alongside the site of the hangar burnt down and described previously. Fighter aircraft engaged in armament trials were housed in the wooden hangar whilst the bombers lived in the steel hangar.

A De Havilland 9A of No. 15 Squadron taxiing-out and it can be seen that the rough aerodrome surface called for assistance by the ground crews.

During the summer of 1924 the Commoners of Martlesham presented a petition to the Air Ministry pleading the loss of grazing rights on land at the north-east corner of the aerodrome. On the 3rd September, 1924, the Air Ministry agreed, after much discussion, to meet the Commoners at Woodbridge and, as a result of this meeting, a sum of £5 per year was granted as compensation. The Commoners at that time numbered some 300.

On 12th August, 1924, the King's Cup Air Race started from Martlesham and the following interesting aircraft took part.

De Havilland 37	G - E B D O
Vickers Vixen III	G - E B I P
Armstrong-Whitworth Siskin III's	G - E B J G and G - E B J S
De Havilland 50's	G - E B E N and G - E B F P
Fairey IIID	N.9777
Martinsyde F.6	G - E B D K
Supermarine Seagull III	

This was the only race in the series open to both landplanes and seaplanes. The landplanes started from Martlesham Heath and the seaplanes from Felixstowe, the route being Martlesham Heath — Leith Harbour — Dumbarton Castle — Pendennis Castle, near Falmouth, with the finish at Lee-on-Solent, Hampshire. The course mileage was 950 miles, and the winner was Alan J. Cobham flying a De Havilland 50 (240 h.p. Siddeley Puma) at an average speed of 106 m.p.h.

Life on the Station in the mid 1920s is best told in the words of those who served there, one such being Mr McGlasson, ex-Managing Director of Constant Speed Airscrews, but then a sergeant-pilot.

"I joined No. 15 Squadron as a sergeant-pilot to assist armament testing. The Station was commanded by Wing-Commanders John Napier Gill and Harold Blackburn in that order, and our Squadron was commanded by Squadron Leader Sherren, a Canadian and an ex-R.A.F. boxer. He was a 1914—1918 vintage pilot, a real tough nut who disliked all forms of "bull" intensely.

It should be borne in mind that this was a time of intense National depression being in the time of Mr Ramsey MacDonald and the Royal Air Force including places like Martlesham Heath suffered as a result of low Air Ministry Estimates. Reforming squadrons like No. 15 was marked by the dual work of having to carry out armament experiments as well as the normal squadron work, and slowly, as personnel became available, the unit was evolved. As a further result of this financial cramp, promotion suffered and in the general sense was nil for several years. The large Armament Section was run by Flight Sergeants Garner, Hannah and Sergeant Whalen, under Flight Lieutenant "Dizzie" Davis. Orfordness was used as the testing ground for work on bombs, guns and gun-sights, notably the Wimperis. We at No. 15 worked in close co-operation with Farnborough and I had the job of shooting off the blades of the then new metal fixed-pitch airscrew fitted to the D.H.9a, blasting it with a Vickers gun.

I vividly recall when the wicker-seat of my D.H.9a caught fire at 2,000 feet and as I was sitting on an auxiliary fuel tank, I kept my gloved hand on the flame and landed by side-slipping the aircraft. It only smouldered on the ground as the seat was smartly "whipped-out", the fire being traced to the exhaust pipes which had not been de-scaled during overhaul.

Speed tests were carried out with two camera obscura and I've often done "Paper Speeds" in one of these when the Fairey Fox was tested and helped to convert the "paper speeds" to actual speeds.

Occasionally during mad moments we would fly over to Felixstowe and "shoot-up" the beach and pier and then fly low over the River Deben in order to give the local yachts "a blow". The local police visited us and put an end to our capers!

On another occasion we visited Larkhill on Salisbury Plain as a partly formed squadron for the Annual Bombing Exercises, after which we called in at Northolt on the way home. We were a formation of five, led by Whitworth-Jones, and we landed as such. R.A.F. Northolt always had a lot of unpredictable sheep on it and the result was that four machines crashed, undercarriages and tail-up etc. As I fortunately knew the aerodrome well I put on throttle and went round again for a safe landing. The "Northolt crowd" were derisive and abusive, but nothing to what Squadron Leader Sherren said when he arrived from Larkhill with "Hoppy" Wray in a Virginia. The air was blue and I was sent back by air to Martlesham Heath alone, in my glory — the rest by train.

"G" Flight, No. 22 Squadron hangar, the original home of the Parachute Section with a Vickers Vanguard standing outside. This hangar was partially destroyed by the Luftwaffe during 1942.

An early type of parachute worn by a D.H. 9A pilot, showing the static-line used to open the canopy. *Stuart Leslie*

The Parachute Section came under the A & A.E.E., and was headed by Flight Lieutenant John Potter, inventor of the Potter Parachute. Other personnel were Sergeant Hawkings M.M., Corporal East and ten men who rejoiced in the name of "loonies." Leading Aircraftsman Ernest "Brainy" Dobbs was one of these and he was a very remarkable "body," being tall, practically bald, described as scruffy in appearance, without any sense of discipline, and although he had made more free falls I would say than any other man in the world, was not really ready for promotion. Corporal East and Dobbs did all the air experiments on what some years later pilots and aircrews were fitted out with — parachutes. They jumped with Guardian Angel, Potter and Irvine types. "Brainy" had ideas as an inventor when he made an aquaplane which crashed on the banks of the River Deben. He also possessed an American Indian motor-cycle to which he fitted a handle-bar locking device. On this machine he would career up and down the road through the Camp, doing appalling acrobatics with everyone expecting him to be killed at any moment. He would also try a parachute jump at any time, and pilots such as I with whom he was friendly had to ascertain he had no parachute with him before embarking on a flight. This was because the machines of those days were mostly nose-heavy and if he had jumped from the back cockpit without due notice, this would have had a serious result on landing.

A jump which had been detailed or one on the spur of the moment were all the same to Dobbs. He was killed a few years later, "in civvy street," demonstrating jumping with huge balloons over obstacles, and unfortunately failed to clear some electric pylons near Hendon.

Shortly after this the Parachute Section moved to R.A.F. Henlow. Corporal East, also a notable experimentor with parachutes was killed a little later whilst carrying out a delayed jump over Biggin Hill, the pilot of the Vickers Vimy aircraft, Flight Sergeant Harry "Timber" Woods, also being an ex-Martlesham pilot. The inventor of the Irvine Parachute, American Mr Leslie Irvine, visited the Station and to demonstrate his faith in his invention, literally stuffed his 'chute into its pack, climbed aboard an aircraft and took-off. Having reached the necessary altitude, he baled-out and landed safely to show that his parachute was so good that it did not have to be packed in any particular fashion.

Whilst at Martlesham I also had great fun in starting, skippering and playing all over the country with the Martlesham Heath Rugby Football Club."

The high spirits in the Camp were only equalled by those in Ipswich, when off duty, in the *Grand Hotel,* now demolished, as it was owned by a very good friend of the Royal Air Force, Mr Bill Reed. This hostelry, together with the *Salutation,* still standing in Carr Street, were the haunts which could cater for all needs.

Mr W. J. Brown, now living in retirement in the district was with "A" Flight at this period and many of the fine photographs in this book originated from him. He often flew with and was a friend of Squadron Leader Orlebar and Captain Rollo de Haga Haig. Whilst airborne one day with Squadron Leader Orlebar in a Bristol F2B biplane, the wooden seat in the rear cockpit, which was occupied by Mr Brown collapsed and slid from its retaining rails. He was then deposited heavily on the cockpit floor with only crossed piano-wire bracing and doped fabric between him and the ground, which fortunately they both reached safely a little later. Another recollection is also one of how a certain Corporal Ball who had been in the Royal Flying Corps and the Royal Air Force for some years was due for demobilization and the day before his departure from the Service was prompted repeatedly by his fellow airmen to make what was to be his first flight ever, as so far he had always resisted the temptation to do. However, on this occasion he weakened and was taken aloft by Flight Lieutenant Bird in a Short Springbok, an all-metal two-seat biplane. Unfortunately, whilst airborne at some altitude over the aerodrome, the aircraft suffered a structural failure and plunged to the ground. Both occupants were killed instantly, the pilot being buried in the churchyard at nearby Stowmarket.

Wing Commander J. Jewell, O.B.E., A.F.R.Ae.S, Service Manager for Martin-Baker Aircraft and still very much in the air safety business remembers his days at Martlesham.

"I went to the Aeroplane and Armament Experimental Establishment, Martlesham Heath and was posted to "C" Flight. Now this is a very long time ago but I well remember Corporal East and Leading Aircraftsman Dobbs, as well as Flight Lieutenant John Potter and Flying Officer Sidney Webster with whom I flew on a number of occasions. When I joined "C" Flight as a very young and green airman, Flight Lieutenant Potter was its Flight Commander and he was at that time one of the R.A.F's most experienced parachute specialists, having himself designed a parachute which I believe was in competition with both the Guardian Angel and Irvine parachutes. John Potter was a quiet unassuming and very likeable officer for whom one had the greatest respect and I think he took to me somehow, because at that time I was also quiet, but it was largely fostered by my timidity and inexperience. I flew with John Potter on many occasions and was with him in the Avro Bison when it crash-landed at Martlesham. It was at this time that I became passionately interested in parachutes and it was this fact that brought me into close association with both Corporal East, who joined "C" Flight after myself, and particularly "Brainy" Dobbs. I was not a close friend of Corporal East but liked and respected him as a very skilful and accomplished parachutist, whose particular speciality was long delayed drops which, as we know, ultimately led to his tragic death in a delayed exhibition drop at Biggin Hill some years later.

"Brainy" Dobbs on the other hand was a real and close friend and I spent much time with him, helping him with a number of his hare-brained schemes. I call to mind particularly his two-wheeled car, which at that time he felt had something of a future. At that time I was not an experienced motorist or motor-cyclist and one or two of my runs in the two-wheeler car, this is when we could get the engine started, which was not too often, were hair-raising in the extreme. I maintained a close friendship with "Brainy" until I went abroad in 1927 when my other youthful interests intervened, so I had no direct contract with him after that. I was pained and grieved, as all his friends were, when he was tragically killed flying into some high-tension cables in his balloons.

Ex-Flight Sergeant Harry Woods was another Martlesham man that I knew well and flew with him quite often. "Timber" Woods was in fact the pilot of the Vickers Vimy from which I made my first parachute descent."

It will be seen that in the mid 1920s the Station had settled down well in its new home and both the business side and the social field were expanding as the establishment increased. The post-war decline had been halted and now several new and interesting types of aircraft were presented for testing and evaluation, together with a good sprinkling of the new civil types as this was the new industry, and it was Martlesham's task to ascertain that they would meet the stipulated requirements and safety standards.

36

CHAPTER TWO

The Golden Years. 1926—1939

THE Aeroplane and Armament Experimental Establishment, Martlesham Heath, was now a well-known and much respected Unit, and its fame reached out to all sections of the aeronautical industry both at home and overseas. The pilots who were posted to the A & A.E.E. were duly proud of their appointments, because to be a Martlesham test-pilot was to be one of the élite of the profession, and one could justly feel the respect which was so rightly deserved by this band of devoted and skilful men. The word of a Martlesham test-pilot was listened to by all members of the "trade" and suggestions and ideas were readily noted and often incorporated as modifications without extensive investigation. Nevertheless life on the Station was still in the light-hearted state and Mr V. C. Gaunt, F.R.Ae.S and a Westland "Civvy Rep" (Aircraft Company Civilian Technical Representative) for a number of years at Martlesham recalls happy and full days.

"As an Aeronautical Engineer since 1915, I first came into contact, as a visitor, around 1926, and for some ten years I was the Westland Aircraft Representative chosen to make regular liaison visits and to introduce our new aircraft designs. My first landing at Martlesham Heath was with Major Openshaw, as pilot, in the Westland Westbury, a twin-engined "fighter" carrying a 1½ lb Coventry Ordnance Works gun in the forward open gun position and a similar gun mounted at an angle of elevation of around 55° to fire over the centre-section of the top mainplane. It was like landing on open moor-land, similar to the heather-clad, bog-bespattered surface of my native Yorkshire. As we already know there were in those days two Squadrons, the one dealing with Armaments and the other with the aerodynamic testing. Sometimes planes were directed first to one, and then to the other, there being a healthy spirit of competition between the two as to which should get the new aircraft first. The firm's test-pilot was often ex-R.A.F., and usually well-known to some of the Martlesham pilots, who appeared to be allowed to try the new types before others had the chance. Their first comments were often very illuminating and went far to help one's assessment of how and what the pilots would like. If, however, the type was accepted for R.A.F. service, one's main concern on arrival was to hand over the aircraft by checking carefully the inventory and getting the necessary forms signed so that payments due, if contracted, could be claimed.

We who were accepted as Honorary Members of the Officers' Mess found ourselves caught up in a virile and lively atmosphere. Good fellowship amongst all the Staff of the Station enabled them to work hard and play hard. Guest Nights often ended in a game of Tanks, wherein the large wheeled chairs and settees were usually damaged as the result of a series of spine-jarring collisions. Flight Lieutenant Jenkins was noted for his stunt of biting-off and eating a wine-glass bowl; Bobbie (Lewis-Roberts) specialised in sticking pins in his arm up to their heads with no apparent pain or bleeding. Many an early morning test followed such nights and I marvelled at the fitness of most of the pilots under the strain.

When the Annual Hendon Air Pageant was held the latest aircraft were displayed and demonstrated there by Martlesham pilots, it being an R.A.F. show, and these were the only pilots with enough experience of such new and sometimes novel types. The Aircraft Companies each tried to have a new aircraft at Martlesham each year for the valuable publicity which ensued from his yearly show.

On my first visit to the A & A.E.E., Squadron Leader Pynches (nicknamed "Nippers") was the Gunnery expert whilst Flight Lieutenant Garnome B. Williams was the senior pilot in the Armament Flight and he was nick-named "Garney-Bill." Around this time Squadron Leader T. H. England (Tom-Harry) had charge of the Flight Tests but a little later he joined Messrs Handley-Page Limited as their chief test-pilot. "Batchy" Carr was "on the strength" and we sometimes met him and his wife on his Thames barge which he kept moored at nearby Waldringfield from where he occasionally sailed. The Medical Officer who replaced Dr White, Squadron Leader H. F. Haytherthwaite, had a German canvas-covered canoe with lee-boards and a sail, and in this we had occasional trips on a Wednesday afternoon and at the week-ends. This Doctor was nicknamed "Oswald-

The Westland Westbury C.O.W. Gun Fighter in which Mr V. C. Gaunt made his first acquaintance with Martlesham Heath. *Westland Aircraft Co.*

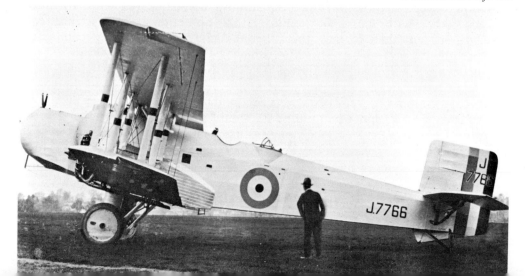

The Officers' Mess with tennis courts in foreground. This building was the scene of the Contractors' Nights, and in later days many of the famous and "the Few" messed within its walls which have now disappeared under the G.P.O. Research Station.   *A. J. R. Frost*

thistle" by some, but to his enemies he was plain "Fits." He and his wife Mary contributed to the social life of the Station by organising slides and swings and similar recreational facilities for the kiddies of the Station. They also arranged and presented programmes of music for the adults.

In those days there was a happy "family" atmosphere about the place which I am sure served to lay the foundations for efficiency and helped those visitors whose business took them there to improve the breed of aircraft by trial and error. In this connection I must pay my tribute to Chief Technical Officers Stevens, Rowe and Scott-Hall and to the Chief Engineer, Squadron Leader McKenna, particularly. The latter's gruff exterior and dour manner hid a sound knowledge and long experience, so that it was very instructive to discuss maintenance and other problems with him in order to sift evidence to help elucidate the reasons for crashes and minor failures.

The Annual Dinner to the Trade, first held in 1923, was one occasion when the chief representatives of the various firms visited in a social mood and met those who were testing their products. These personnel, in many cases, were thereafter taken on as test-pilots, engineers and liaison staff on quitting the R.A.F., for here undoubtedly the elite were gathered and trained. At one such dinner I recall the great "H.P" (Sir Frederick Handley-Page) in his speech, prompted by the Commanding Officer, Wing Commander Blackburn, mentioning De Havilland's test pilot, Mr Hubert Broad, who was not "broad" and Westland's representative, Mr Gaunt, who was not, and is not "gaunt" for Broad was a thin, almost puny and wiry man, whilst I am short and stout. "H.P's" witty sallies were always appreciated and often had a biblical tinge.

As illustrating the friendly rivalry, I remember two parties being given at Felixstowe, one by Oliver Vickers and the other by Squadron Leader Bennett-Baggs, to which I was invited. Many social events were held — some in conjunction with the Marine Aircraft Experimental Establishment at Felixstowe, at one of which, a blonde lady, being fed winkles by a certain Wing Commander, christened him "Winkle Commander." A party of us often visited the *Great White Horse* (a Pickwickian inn) at Ipswich, which was mis-named "The Pig" for some obscure reason, and I remember a newcomer searching the town on his first visit there for this hostelry under its nickname. There were several officers whose names flash across the pages of memory — Menzies, D'Arcy Greig, Wheatley, Horrox and one, who when I introduced the Westland Wizard fighter to Martlesham, nicknamed me "Baron Wizard of Westland."

Visits of inspection by Air Vice Marshal "Stuffy" Dowding and "Boom" Trenchard and other brass hats (hat decoration also referred to as "scrambled egg") called for a smartening-up of the aircraft and the Station in general, so we civilians kept well out of sight and deprecated the delay in testing."

At this time, the Speed Course was moved from its existing position which crossed the Woodbridge-Felixstowe Road and thence straight across the aerodrome. It now ran in a line from east to west from the Waldringfield Heath, crossing the road just south of the Station Headquarters, along the southern side of the airfield itself towards Dobb's Lane Corner and then across the Foxhall Heath to the bottom of Bell Lane. Observers' huts were erected with time gear and airmen were posted on the road to control traffic whilst tests were in progress. Permanent engine test beds were constructed so that the new and re-built engines could be run for long periods under varying load and altitude conditions. Butts were erected for the ground testing of aircraft guns, these being behind the Station Workshops on the other side of the road from the hangars. Larger aircraft required more fuel and this necessitated the construction of larger fuel and oil installations. This increase in the size of aircraft also called for larger accommodation for them, and so Martlesham's largest building was erected, the all-metal "B" Flight hangar. Whilst on the subject of hangars, they too were a cosmopolitan group, no two really being the same, except the small wooden ones, as their shape and size differed; also the materials of construction consisted of all-wood, through brick and wood, to all brick and finally all-metal.

As was the common practise at the time, Martlesham Heath was an unsurfaced aerodrome consisting of a large field of turf and close cropped heather and aircraft could, generally speaking, take-off and land virtually from any direction to suit wind conditions. As the prevailing wind was south-westerly, the majority of take-offs were in the direction of Dobb's Lane Corner, landing approaches being made from the direction of Martlesham village and thence across the aerodrome road. Flying Control used a left-hand circuit, but as all landings were visual, the circuit was for the most part within the aerodrome perimeter. Taxiing was a long slow job after touch-down, as the aircraft's wooden or metal tail-skid invariably picked up quantities of turf and heather, but this was obviated to some extent with the coming of the tail-wheel. As mentioned previously, the summer months also brought the miniature dust-storms forcing the ground-crews to take shelter in the lee of the hangars after each take-off.

The next buildings to be erected were the Airmen's Married Quarters, on the eastern side close to Spratt's Plantation, and were approached by a road, now known as Hilton Road, after Flight Lieutenant Hilton, running from the junction of the Woodbridge—Felixstowe Road and "B" Flight Road. These were modern in concept, each with its own front and rear garden. Quite a number of the married personnel lived in their own or rented houses in the neighbouring villages and, as at this time the period of service at any particular Station was known within limits, this was a suitable arrangement.

Martlesham was a staging-post for the 1926 King's Cup Air Race which was held on the 9th and 10th July of that year.

Another memorable Martlesham event was the Station Concert Party which gave regular performances both at home and away and a typical programme ran as under:—

THE "HUSH-HUSH" PARTY AND JAZZ BAND

At Martlesham Heath Aerodrome
(By kind permission of Wing Commander H. Blackburn M.C.)
In aid of the Royal Air Force Memorial Fund
Thursday, 14th October, 1926
at 8.00 o'clock

Manager	Flying Officer R. Vaughan-Fowler
Producer	Flight Sergeant F. W. Harris
At the Piano	Corporal Markham
Bandmaster	Corporal Munro
Property Master	Leading Aircraftsman E. C. King
Lighting	Leading Aircraftsman Bishop
General Assistant	Leading Aircraftsman H. E. Rous

PART ONE

Selections by the "Hush-Hush" Band	
Prologue	Flying Officer Vaughan-Fowler
"Laughter Land"	The Party

"Red, Red Robin"	W. A. Daniel
"Oh Sarah!	A. Rudd,
Oh 'Enery"	E. Prescott
"When it was June"	H. M. King
"Summerzet Fair"	A. Rudd,
	R. Scrimger,
	F. W. Harris
"Since I walked out	E. Prescott
with an Airman"	
Stars of the Summer	H. M. King,
Night	H. Walters
"A Silly Ass"	Flying Officer
	Vaughan-Fowler
"Eat Bananas"	A. Rudd
"The Cutter	The Party
Merchants"	

A member of the "Hush-Hush" Concert Party.

PART TWO

"The Cup Tie"	The Party
Monologue	F. W. Harris
"The Pirates"	H. M. King,
	E. Prescott,
	R. Scrimger
Banjo Selections	A. Pitt, T. Morris
"Wanna go back	R. Scrimger
again"	
Ideas	H. M. King,
	W. A. Daniel
Songs Selected	H. Walters
Our Music Hall	The Party
(Including the famous Melo-Drama)	

"DARKNESS TO DAWN"

Gilbert Goodman	H. Walters
Gwendoline	F. W. Harris
(his wife)	
Jasper Strangeways	H. M. King
The Stranger	R. Scrimger
P. C. Padsfeet	E. Prescott
Scene — The Goodmans' House	

On the 18th June, 1927, a Hawker Horsley II, Serial No. J.8608, piloted by Flight Lieutenant C. R. Carr and Flight Lieutenant P. H. Hackworth, whilst attempting a long distance record flight, suffered oil leakage and force-landed at Martlesham whilst carrying a tremendous load of petrol, some 1,000 gallons in all, which, at that time could not be jettisoned, making it a brilliant feat of airmanship. The aircraft had taken-off from Cranwell, in Lincolnshire and was heading for the Persian Gulf when it ran into trouble.

During November 1928, a Martlesham test-pilot, Squadron Leader Jack Noakes was selected to be the pilot of the Fairey Long Range Monoplane Mk.1, J.9479, which was to be used to make an attempt on the World's Long Range Flight Record, but owing to an unfortune crash in a Parnall Plover at Martlesham just previous to the event, he was replaced by Squadron Leader A. G. Jones-Williams, who with another Martlesham pilot Flight Lieutenant N. H. Jenkins, had already made a long-distance flight of 4,130 miles from Cranwell to Karachi.

Unfortunately this second attempt ended in disaster for the two Martlesham men, when the Fairey Long Range Monoplane in which they were attempting to fly to Cape Town, South Africa, non-stop, flew into a mountain-side whilst crossing the Atlas Range in North Africa and crashed near the village of St Marie de Kit, both Squadron Leader Jones-Williams and Flight Lieutenant Jenkins being killed instantly. Flight Lieutenant Jenkins' body was brought back to England and was buried in Ipswich Cemetery.

The Fairey Long Range Monoplane Mk.I J.9479 in which Squadron Leader A. G. Jones-Williams and Flight Lieutenant N. H. Jenkins were killed in North Africa.   *Westland Aircraft Co.*

A good idea of the select group of officer test-pilots who resided at the A & A.E.E. at this time can be gathered from an account in the local paper of the funeral arrangements for Flying Officer G. V. Wheatley who was killed whilst carrying out terminal velocity dives in a Gloster Gamecock fighter. The deceased was a very popular member of the Mess at Martlesham, in the social life of which he took a prominent part, and it was to do honour to one who earned the respect and esteem of all ranks that a special memorial service was held in the Men's Dining Hall, which, in the absence of a regularly constituted place of worship, was the most appropriate building for such a purpose.

Attending the service were all the 450 Officers, N.C.O's, and men of the Establishment, and representatives from the R.A.F. Marine Aircraft Experimental Establishment, Felixstowe, and the Shotley Royal Navy Training Establishment.

The service was conducted by the three Padres of the Camp, The Reverend R. W. Green (Wesleyan) of Woodbridge, reading the opening sentences, the lessons being read by the Reverend J. Doughty, Vicar of Martlesham, and the Reverend W. J. Nunn (Baptist) Woodbridge. The service was of a simple nature, the hymns being the first two and final verses of "O God, our help in ages past" and the first and last verses of "Rock of Ages."

At the conclusion of the service, the cortege lined up on the Aerodrome Road, headed by personnel of No. 22 Squadron to which the deceased belonged, under Flying Officer P. J. R. King. Then came the firing squad under Flight Sergeant Hanna, which was followed by the band of the Felixstowe R.A.F., behind which came the motor-hearse and the bearers, Flying Officers Webster, Summers, Wilson, Vaughan-Fowler, Alliot and Sayers. The rear of the procession was brought up by the remaining Officers, N.C.O's and men. The coffin, draped with an Union Jack, was buried in a mass of beautiful floral tributes. Among these was one from the members of the kitchen staff, the deceased having held the appointment of Mess-Secretary, which took the form of a two-bladed propeller, about 6 ft in length, composed of yellow chrysanthemums.

To the strains of the "Dead March" and the "March Funèbre", the cortege wended its way to the Main Road, where all traffic was stopped as a mark of respect.

Bill Pegg in latter years gained fame as the Bristol Aeroplane Company's Chief Test Pilot in taking aloft for the first time the giant Brabazon and Britannia aircraft. His autobiography, which includes details of his early Martlesham days, was called *Sent Flying,* and it is from this excellent book that he suggested I should obtain the details.

He was granted a General Duties Branch Commission in 1930 and was posted to the A & A.E.E. at Martlesham Heath during the same year. As an Acting Pilot

Officer, the pay was 14/10d (74p) a day out of which he had to pay 4/6d (22½p) a day messing fee. This fee was not, generally speaking, a regular feature of mess life in the R.A.F. at that time, and if the letter of the rule-book should have been enforced, they should have been messed for the regular allowance of some 1/- (5p) per day. However, the fee was charged and varied from Station to Station, the amount being in accordance with the standard of messing required by officers at the various Stations. Martlesham must have had about the highest standard of any R.A.F. Mess, the reason being of course, the number of high-ranking Officers on the Station Establishment, coupled with the number of distinguished visitors and guests from the Aeronautical Industry who visited the Station.

On the first morning he had a rather embarrassing experience, brought about by procedures in the Officers' Mess. Having arrived in the dining-room ready for breakfast, he found that he was much too early, and having asked the Head-Waiter the breakfast-time, was informed that it would be served in precisely thirty minutes. Retiring to the ante-room in order to listen for the steps of fellow officers making for the dining-room, he surprised the cleaners who were making the place ship-shape from the previous evening's revels. Not wishing to go back to his room and facing the ordeal of meeting his batman again, he sat down to await the appointed time. After satisfying himself that the dining-room now had a small gathering, he proceeded in to find a dozen or so officers all sitting at a long table with newspapers in front of them, supported on large wire frames. The place was in complete silence, so he sat down and grabbing a paper conveniently lying on the table, ordered breakfast when the waiter appeared, all the time hoping that he had not sat down in the Commanding-Officer's chair, or for that matter anyone else's. Adding still further to this already embarrassing situation, was the dress of the day, for at that time the No. 1 uniform was breeches and puttees, with slacks and tunics as every day working dress. He had arrived in his No. 1 uniform, and must have felt like arriving at a tea-party dressed for dinner.

Being posted to "B" Flight he reported to the Flight Commander, and received a shock, yes, a real shock after the interview, as taking hold of the brass door handle he got a severe electric shock. This was the "old, old Martlesham welcome", brought about by connecting up the door handle to a hand-starter magneto, and on a given signal the fellow conspirator cranked the handle vigorously to create the necessary current. Work started at 7.30 a.m. and finished at 3.45 p.m. with Wednesday afternoon devoted to sports or recreation, this in the summer months including trips to Orfordness for bathing in the sea.

Pilot Officer A. J. "Bill" Pegg at Martlesham Heath, 1930.   *A. J. Pegg*

The large fire on the Heath during August 1930. The Airmen's Married Quarters can be seen centre left, the photograph being taken from the roof of "B" Flight No. 22 Squadron hangar.

A feature of Martlesham between the wars were the large fires which broke out on the Heath during the hot days of summer, the largest of which occurred during August, 1930. It started on a Friday and burned fiercely for over a fortnight. Airmen were called out to keep the fire from approaching the Station buildings, but the outbreaks which smouldered through the deep bone-dry heathland could not be completely contained, and sprang up over the 'drome. A 24-hour guard was mounted on the perimeter of the airfield, the guards being armed with spades and fire-brooms to smother outbreaks as they occurred. All leave was stopped and the fire finally died down after some 21 days. One contributory factor was the fact that the outskirts of the airfield were riddled with rabbit warrens and the fire travelled through these underground passages and the overall thick covering of dead heather and bracken. Rabbits and other small animals caught up in the inferno ran blazing from one spot to another thereby starting fresh fires and thick black smoke could be seen ascending into the sky from considerable distances. A local family named Powling, who farmed from the Mill Farm on the edge of the airfield, ploughed the fire-belt round the aerodrome, and they were called out urgently whenever one of these blazes broke out, to plough a belt around the blazing area in order to prevent the spread of fire across the Heath.

A fine Old English Sheepdog roamed the Station, and it is believed that it originally came from this farm, and although no one on the Station owned the dog, everybody loved it and cared for it.

Two incidents in lighter vein: the six ground staff airmen with the most flying time each month were paid a shilling a day for the month concerned and great rivalry was afoot in order to gain this added pay, and there were never any lack of volunteers for ballast or other airborne duties, such as crew-assistance on test flights, in both the squadrons. Two Vickers Virginias, Nos. J.7558 and J.7717 were wheeled out for an armament test-flight to Orfordness and the rival crews and their airmen ballast jockeyed for position to take part in the flight, it being near the end of the month, and only one aircraft was being used for this test. The Flight Sergeant in charge directed that J.7717 be started up, much to the disappointment of J.7558's crew who watched dejectedly as the twin Napier Lions of the "lucky" machine warmed up. Suddenly, with a loud report, the airscrew on the strut-mounted generator of J.7717, turning in the slipstream of the port airscrew, flew off, and passing through the top of the fuselage, carried on to crash through the centre-section of the upper mainplane. J.7717 switched-off, and with joy unbeheld, J.7558 started-up, its crew and passengers gaining the vital times to get the coveted extra flying pay.

One Hallowe'en Eve, the N.C.O. Guard Commander took a recently arrived airman on his guard rounds and posted him on a deserted section of the airfield near the Powlings' Farm. On his way to the post, the N.C.O. had explained to the somewhat apprehensive airman that the site was one on which had stood a Roman Camp and that at mid-night on Hallowe'en night, the legions marched again, all dressed in white and accompanied by the sounds of clanking chains and the rattle of side-arms. Just before mid-night, the N.C.O's joke almost came true, as a large white apparition appeared, complete with the clanking of chains, and this hit the unfortunate airman fair and square in the stern, knocking him down, and necessitating his removal to Station Sick Quarters. The cause of the trouble was a large white goat, which had slipped its leash, and living up to its name, had gone on the rampage, butting anything in sight!

It was not only the shape of the aircraft arriving at the Heath which changed but also the appearance of the personnel, as about this time the familiar monkey-jacket, fastened tight up to the neck, with its attendant riding-breeches and puttees, was replaced by the belted jacket and trousers. The peaked cap or "cheese-cutter" still lived on and was only out-moded during the late 30's by the now familiar forage-cap, a combination of cap and flying helmet, for general wear. The "cheese-cutter" was used for ceremonial purposes as it is to this very day. With the monkey-jacket and breeches outfit, a polished black swagger stick with an ornamental knob was carried and it was not unusual to find one or two of these lying by the road-side having been dropped by some revelling airman returning home from one of the near-by towns.

Airmen's uniform before the introduction of jackets and trousers. The peaked cap remains to the present day for ceremonial occasions.

Further buildings were erected in order to carry out the increased research work in new fields created by the various items coming along for test, and one of these buildings was the refrigerator block used for testing engines at altitude and temperature.

The various Station sporting teams, rugger, hockey and football participated in local leagues, entertaining and playing away, and were usually well placed in their respective spheres. Indeed, in the early days, Flight Lieutenant Sidney Webster was the Captain of Ipswich Town Football Club, which played at this time in the Southern League. To mention a few more names, Corporal Hudson was a champion runner, Corporal Timms, a regular champion "miler" and Suffolk Champion six years running, whilst Leading Aircraftsman Prescott excelled as an outstanding hurdler. Boxing was also well attended, in fact, most of the sports had a fair following. Wednesday afternoons were devoted to sporting and recreational activities and with the nearness of the River Deben, boating and swimming figured well to the fore, if somewhat seasonal.

To bring back memories for pre-Second World War airmen a Daily Routine Order for 1936 will revive those days:—

547.   QUARTERLY AUDIT BOARD

An Audit Board composed as under will assemble at a time and place convenient to the President to audit the non-public accounts of the Royal Air Force Station, Martlesham Heath.

President:—   Squadron Leader E. D. Davis
Members:—   Flight Lieutenant E. D. M. Hopkins
Captain L. Ritson (Retd)

543.   ROMAN CATHOLICS VOLUNTARY SERVICE

There will be a voluntary service in the Roman Catholic Church, St John's Street, Woodbridge, on Sunday 3.5.36. Airmen wishing to attend are to hand their names to the Station Warrant Officer by 09.00 hours on Saturday 2.5.36 in order that transport may be arranged. They are to report at the Guard Room at 07.45 hours on Sunday. 3.5.36 in best blue uniforms. The wives of airmen wishing to attend may travel by service transport provided there is sufficient accommodation. The Messing N.C.O. is to arrange for late breakfasts to be available.

530.   CHURCH PARADE

The undermentioned officers are detailed for Church Parade on Sunday next 3.5.36.

Squadron Leader E. G. Hilton D.F.C. A.F.C. (In Command)
Flight Lieutenant E. G. Granville.   (Adjutant)

The undermentioned N.C.O's are detailed for Church Parade on Sunday next 3.5.36.

Flight Sergeant French.   Sergeant Wright.
Sergeant Wroath.   Sergeant Northrop.

531.   PAY PARADES

Civilians.   Accounts Office at 11.15 hours.
Airmen.   A.R.S. Hangar at 11.45 hours.

Special Supplementary Pay Parade in Accounts Office at 14.00 hours.

During 1936 a new event occurred at selected R.A.F. Stations, Empire Air Day, this being a day, a Saturday, when the Station was thrown open to the general public for them to inspect the latest "wares" purchased with their tax payments. The local paper reported this in some detail, and their photographer attended a rehearsal prior to the event, and reported how they had seen the Station at work, and its many and varied aircraft, and that the public should be in for a real treat on the forthcoming 23rd May.

Just prior to this event, history was made again at Martlesham when Squadron Leader E. G. Hilton took off from the Station for a flight to South Africa. The paper reported this as being a holiday trip for Squadron Leader Hilton, as well as testing the new engines installed in the Airspeed Envoy aircraft which he was piloting, and which had been built for the previous year's Mildenhall—Melbourne Air Race. Many brother officers, relatives and friends were there to wish the airman bon-voyage. Among them were Mrs Hilton and her father, Mr H. J. Martin of Yoxford, Group Captain A. C. Maund (Commanding Officer, Martlesham) and Squadron Leader D. F. Anderson, who was to have flown the machine in the race to Australia. Mrs Hilton had planned to accompany her husband but to her great disappointment the plane would have been over-weighted, so Squadron Leader Hilton was therefore only accompanied by a mechanic, Mr H. A. Lacroix. Originally the take-off time was set for 9.00 a.m. but there was a delay owing to the necessity of sending another aircraft to Henlow for parachutes for the pilot and his mechanic.

The trip, taken during six week's leave, by Squadron Leader Hilton, was not to break records, but to proceed by easy stages, noting the performance of the plane for the Wolseley Company who had loaned it to him for this purpose. His route was by way of Marseilles, Sardinia, Tunis, along the north coast of Africa to Cairo, and then by way of the eastern route, via Khartoum, Malakao and Nairobi to the Cape.

Squadron Leader Hilton, whose home was at Felixstowe, had had considerable flying experience on the African Continent, since during 1919 he had been flying in Egypt and later commanded the "West African Cruise" from Cairo to the Gold Coast. His luggage for this trip included, in addition to spare propellers and emergency rations, a small collapsible boat.

On the return trip Squadron Leader Hilton took-off from Cape Town on 30th May, 1936, to attack the South Africa-England record, but unfortunately met with considerable delay at Athens and had to forsake the idea of a record-breaking flight.

In mentioning the Mildenhall—Melbourne Air Race previously, it is interesting to note that several of the aircraft participating were weighed at Martlesham, one of the most interesting being the American Boeing 24TD, Serial NR 257Y, later NC 13369, which was flown into third place by Roscoe Turner and Clyde Pangborn. The American Douglas DC.2 PH-AJU, belonging to the Dutch K.L.M. airline and named "Ulver" was also weighed, this aircraft being flown into second place by Captains Parmenter and Moll. The reason for this weighing procedure at Martlesham was the fact that the aircraft were too large for the scales at Mildenhall.

Martlesham Heath was visited by Royalty during this year when H.R.H. the Duke of York and H.R.H. the Prince of Wales came to inspect the new prototypes being tested and evaluated as forerunners of the new expansion schemes. Lined up alongside the wooden hangars of No. 15 Squadron, they made a colourful spectacle and to those only used to seeing biplanes an unusual one, since all the aircraft involved were monoplanes. Being in natural metal finish, several of them, the only ones to ever appear as such, gleamed in the sunlight, the only paintwork on their surfaces being the national markings and the aircraft serial numbers. The line-up consisted of the following prototypes:— Armstrong-Vickers Wellesley medium bomber monoplane, Fairey Battle light bomber, Hawker Hurricane interceptor, Bristol Blenheim medium bomber, Westland Lysander Army-Cooperation monoplane and the Supermarine Vickers Spitfire. Wives and families were invited to attend this event and they lined the hangar walls to the rear of the aircraft, the Service personnel being paraded in front of the machines. The Royal brothers had arrived in the colourful Airspeed Envoy, G-AEXX, which was painted in the colours of the Household Cavalry, and after the parade they took afternoon tea in the Officers Mess before departing later for London. To return to the aircraft and their natural finish, they were unique in this respect because during their construction period, camouflage finish of brown and green for upper surfaces of all aircraft was instituted, and all successive machines produced were in this finish. It will be noted from the illustration that the Royal brothers are wearing broad black armbands, as this was during the period of Court Mourning for the late King George V.

The Royal Party inspect the new aircraft of the Expansion Scheme, Westland Lysander K.6127.

A. R. Fairweather

Hawker Demon K.4527 of No. 64 Squadron, Squadron Leader P. J. R. King's aircraft. It was in such an aircraft that Pilot Officer Vickery and Leading Aircraftsman Hutchinson were killed on the 28th May, 1937.

P. J. R. King

During 1937, Martlesham Heath extended its role somewhat, and became partly operational by virtue of the fact that it now housed an operational unit, No. 64 (F) Squadron.

This Squadron, which had just returned to Home duties after a spell in Egypt, was commanded by a former Martlesham officer, Squadron Leader P. J. R. King, and was equipped with the Hawker Demon, 2-seater turret fighter, a development of the Hart bomber. The Unit was housed in canvas hangars alongside the "A" Flight Hangar of No. 22 Squadron, and the aircraft brought a touch of colour to the Station with their bright Unit Markings and Squadron badge which embodied the sacred Egyptian scarab beetle. This Unit stayed at Martlesham until 1938, when it re-equipped and moved to Church Fenton, in Yorkshire. It made its mark during its stay, with its then new dive-bombing techniques, as the usual flying routines for testing did not employ this manoeuvre, and the descending aircraft were watched with some awe by passing spectators. Unfortunately, accidents do happen, and one such occurred on 28th May, 1937, when a Demon flown by Flying Officer P. C. Vickery, failed to pull out of a spin and crashed in the centre of the aerodrome, killing the pilot and his gunner, Leading Aircraftsman J. Hutchinson. This was the first fatal accident since the Squadron had been reformed in Egypt during March, 1936.

Two more Martlesham men were killed during the course of the 1937 King's Cup Air Race, when Wing Commander P. C. Sherren and Wing Commander E. G. Hilton were flying in the Miles M.3A Falcon Major G-AENC. Whilst rounding Flamborough Head in Yorkshire, they ran into severe turbulence, the aircraft inverted out of control, and they were both thrown out through the cockpit canopy into the sea and killed. They were brought home to Ipswich and buried side by side in Ipswich New Cemetery, together with other dead brother officers. Set in a quiet tree lined square, this last resting place bears several names of ex-Martlesham pilots, both pre-war and war-time, although the much larger War Graves Cemetery is in the Old Cemetery on the other side of the road.

Wing Commander PERCY CLARK SHERREN M.C. R.A.F.
   10th September, 1937. Aged 44 years.
Wing Commander EDWARD GOODWIN HILTON D.F.C. A.F.C.
   10th September, 1937. Aged 41 years.
Flight Lieutenant ERIC WOLFE SIMONDS.
   22nd July, 1937. Killed on flying duties.
Flying Officer PETER CHARLES VICKERY.
   28th May, 1937. Aged 28 years. No. 64 Squadron.
Flight Lieutenant NORMAN HUGH JENKINS O.B.E. D.F.C. D.S.M.
   who died at Tunis, North Africa, December 17th, 1929 in the
   execution of his duties. Aged 34 years. Erected by his brother
   officers at Martlesham Heath.

Scenes at the Funeral of Wing Commanders Sherren and Hilton. High ranking Officers march through the Camp. The cortege in Ipswich Cemetery.

To jump forward a few years, but still in this hallowed spot lies another who died during the early war years, killed at Martlesham in a Hawker Hurricane.

Pilot Officer PRINCE A. OBALENSKY Pilot R.A.F. A.A.F.
29th March, 1940. Aged 24 years.
His undaunted spirit and endearing qualities live for ever in the
hearts of all who knew him.

Another Officer of Martlesham fame to die was Flight Lieutenant H. N. Leech, aged 31, and he was buried in the churchyard of the nearby village of Eyke, near Woodbridge. Flight Lieutenant Leech was the "baby" of the victorious Schnieder Trophy Team of 1931, and married a local girl in October, 1937. He contracted a tropical fever whilst serving in an aircraft-carrier off the South Coast of China, and was taken ill in flight. He managed to fly back to his base but collapsed after making a successful landing. After being in the hospital at Wei-Hai-Wel for some time he was eventually brought home and invalided from the Service, but never fully regained his health and died in St Bartholomew's Hospital, London. The funeral was attended by Group Captain Groom, Squadron Leaders Hyde, Groom, Bonham-Carter and Isherwood, and Flight Lieutenants Menzies and Moir.

Not only was Martlesham to the forefront of the aeronautical world, but it assisted materially in the development of that great wonder of the modern age, Radar, or as it was known in its early days, "radio-location." Several later well-known scientists or "boffins" worked in the district, firstly at Orfordness and then at Bawdsey Manor, a large rambling country mansion built and owned by the late Sir Cuthbert Quilter. These scientists were led by Mr (later Sir) Robert Watson-Watt. Situated as it was, on a headland at the mouth of the River Deben, Bawdsey Manor was not many miles as the crow flies from Martlesham and it was logical that the aircraft to be used for their experimentation should be stationed at the A & A.E.E., although Orfordness was still used, in a small way, as a satellite flying base.

Large aerial towers reached skywards, constructed of both metal and wood, from the grounds of the Manor, visible for miles around and these caused all sorts of speculation and rumour. Stories were current at the time of "engine-stopping rays", even a vague type of death-ray. Local folk told stories of their car engines stopping whilst in the Bawdsey area, and R.A.F. personnel telling them that they would be able to proceed again at such and such a time. Reports also state that at this time considerable interest was shown in the landscape beauty of the district by "artists" who spent quite long periods "painting" the local scene. The mystery was deepened by the amount of aircraft which spent long periods flying up and down the coast at various distances and heights. The German airship Graf Zeppelin had flown over Martlesham very low previously, and having hovered over the 'drome, this also led to all manner of rumours of its intent.

The German airship "Graf Zeppelin" leaving Martlesham Heath after hovering over the airfield, watched by a group of off-duty airmen.

The first airborne set was installed in a Handley-Page Heyford bomber, a large twin-engined biplane, with the crude aerials mounted between the large undercarriage wheel spats under the lower wing. An Avro Anson also sported aerials which were far too large for its cabin and protruded upwards and outwards through the fuselage sides and roof. Nevertheless, these two aircraft played a tremendous role in the development of radio-location, and the experiments continued with gratifying results.

During 1937, more convincing results were obtained when the Avro Anson K.6260 carrying its airborne set and aerials, managed to locate the Home Fleet, through cloud, as it passed along the East Coast on its way to the north of Scotland. As this "fix" was "blind," it really proved that the new aid was becoming a real success. Henry Tizard was still actively engaged in this work, and from his previous sojourn at Martlesham Heath, and subsequent visits, was well conversant with the district, which no doubt aided him considerably in his work. In the A & A.E.E. Aircraft Availability Lists for 1938, a special section was listed and entitled "AIRCRAFT IN EXPERIMENTAL CO-OPERATION UNIT" and these were the machines engaged in the radio-location development work. It is interesting to note their varied types.

Avro Anson	K.8758	Fairey Battle 1	K.9230
Avro Anson	K.6260	Miles Magister (All-wooden)	L.8168
Fairey Battle 1	K.9207	De Havilland DH.60M Moth	K.1876
Fairey Battle 1	K.9208	Handley-Page Harrow	K.7021

The intensity of the work is shown by the fact that during the three months of 1938, shown in the list, the above aircraft logged 94 hours in the air. The work continued apace, and during 1938 other groups of aerials raised themselves skywards along the coastal belt not too far distant. The ones at Great Bromley near Clacton, Essex, were visible from Bawdsey, and in the other direction they were at

Darsham near Saxmundham and Kessingland, near Lowestoft. It was not until later years that the full story of these large towers was revealed and how much they helped during the Battle of Britain. At the end of the Martlesham era of radio-location research the Station was visited by Mr Winston Churchill, who landed at Martlesham en route for Bawdsey Manor in order to see for himself the progress being made. On his return to the A & A.E.E., the airborne side of the device was explained and demonstrated to him.

In order to appreciate the tremendous amount of research carried out by Henry Tizard, the reader is well advised to read Ronald W. Clarke's fine book *Tizard* published by Methuen, as this covers his activities in great detail both at Martlesham Heath and elsewhere.

Although night flying had always been undertaken at Martlesham on a limited scale, mainly during periods of moonlight, at this time it was stepped up considerably, the new fighters carrying out, during the summer months, a number of hours of night flying. The locals were intrigued by the new flashing beacons, mounted on trailers, which were stationed nightly at different sites around the 'drome. Many a lad including me, were reprimanded for being home late having spent the evening watching the beacons on the heath at Kesgrave or Brightwell.

Security on the Station was now much stricter and loiterers were gently but firmly moved along both the aerodrome roads and also the main road on the perimeter. The various paths around the edge of the aerodrome were closed up, and a little later, barbed wire made its first appearance. During the Munich Crisis, September, 1938, the airfield itself was covered with a mixture of soot and sand, as camouflage, but this did not prove very satisfactory, each take-off resulting in clouds of black swirling dust. The clean white concrete aprons in front of the hangars were also tarred, but this was also not too successful, especially in the summer sun. During this period, an American Lockheed 12 Super Electra airliner, G-AFGN, was on test at the A & A.E.E. for British Airways, and this was hastily despatched from Martlesham to London in order to convey Mr Neville Chamberlain to Munich and back. This aircraft featured in all the Press photographs of that gentleman descending the aircraft steps, with his umbrella raised promising, "Peace in our Time."

The more secret types of new aircraft spent far less time outside the hangars than previously, and one aircraft remembered specially was the twin-engined Westland Whirlwind fighter, which remained only momentarily outside "A" Flight hangar, long enough for an engine run, and then across the road for take-off. On its return, the procedure was much the same, with a quick withdrawal back into the hangar.

New and larger notices appeared warning the public of the dire consequences of photographing the aircraft or installations, but the roads remained open and

Westland Whirlwind prototype L.6844 which caused quite a stir when it appeared for testing during 1938. The four 20mm cannons can be seen protruding from the nose whilst the bead and ring sights are visible on the front fuselage and in the cockpit.   *Westland Aircraft Co.*

it was still possible, especially on a Saturday morning when the majority of the aircraft always appeared to be brought out of the hangars, to see what the aircraft strength consisted of. They were all usually back inside by 11.30 a.m. ready for the 12.00 finish and week-end break, and the only glimpses were through the hangar windows alongside the road.

During the summer of 1939, a Hawker Hurricane was taken from the A & A.E.E. at 4.00 a.m. in the morning by road to Christchurch Park, Ipswich, where it was assembled for display purposes on the occasion of the Ipswich Co-operative and Labour Fete. Great interest was shown by the general public and the airmen in attendance were busily engaged in answering questions about the aircraft.

During the 1930's the Royal Air Force Hendon Air Pageant was superseded by a more "Meet the R.A.F." campaign, and instead of thousands flocking to one R.A.F. Station near London, to see the air displays and static aircraft on show, many more thousands visited R.A.F. Stations up and down the country, in a much less formal atmosphere.

One of the by-products of this day was the reduction in the size of the "aircraft grave-yard", the spot on most aerodromes where crashed or derelict machines were dumped. These assisted materially in the activities of the day as the burning aircraft set-piece with its attendant red flame and clouds of black smoke followed by the dash of the Station Fire Brigade and their swift use of masses of white foam always had the crowds on their toes.

Interest never faded either in the various set-pieces which altered from year to year, but usually were acted around the theme of the desert outpost being attacked by hostile tribesmen, or their determined attack on an R.A.F. convoy in "foreign parts." The highlight was always when a mixed bag of A & A.E.E. aircraft arrived after a call for help, and the flight of the tribesmen from the attacking aircraft, which often included even machines of the Fleet Air Arm. Flying low and fast their imaginary bombs caused well-timed and "placed" explosions to render the position safe, but often also with the loss of the "canvas fort."

The last Empire Air Day to be held at Martlesham Heath will be remembered by many of the thousands who attended for included in the line-up that day was the Armstrong Whitworth Ensign airliner, the largest landplane seen by the public at the A & A.E.E., as well as the first sight at close hand of the then new Hawker Hurricane and Supermarine Spitfire fighters. The Spitfire caused a stir when it flew from Colchester, Essex, a distance of some 25 miles, to Martlesham at high speed, the pilot giving a running commentary over his radio telephone via the public address system, of his speedy progress. At this time the speed appeared phenomenal and when he eventually appeared over the western side of the 'drome, the Spitfire's Merlin engine leaving a thin trail of black exhaust, he flashed over the upturned faces of the crowds.

Empire Air Day 1939. General view showing the Armstrong-Whitworth Ensign G-ADSR.

The "crazy flying" episode by the "drunken spectator" never failed to "take-in" a fair proportion of the audience, causing consternation among the "less informed." Heyfords, Virginias, Bulldogs and Furies "dog-fighted" in deadly earnest, members of each side alternately dropping out of the fray belching vivid orange and red smoke to disappear behind the trees surrounding the airfield, ultimately creeping in for a surreptitious landing later.

Airmen of all ranks with unlimited answers were on duty to explain and demonstrate, but for the "noise-lovers" the aircraft at the firing-butts, and the engine test-beds were real value for money. The N.A.A.F.I., on this occasion had a real gala day, dispensing vast quantities of tea and cakes, ice-cream and soft drinks, many of the customers little thinking at the time, that before long they would be queuing in many such an institution for "char and wads."

During 1939, 20th May, a fine Saturday was "the" day at the A & A.E.E. and a quick run through the programme will give a good idea of the varied and interesting items to view. The Station opened to the public at 1.30 p.m., the flying commenced at 2.15 p.m. and the Station closed at 6.00 p.m.

In "C" hangar could be seen a very comprehensive display of instruments and engines together with armament, photographic, wireless and other equipment. Hangar "E" had on show aircraft representative of those being used in the Service at the present time, whilst in hangar "G" there was an R.A.F. Exhibit arranged by the local East Suffolk County Council with the object of showing the up-to-date A.R.P. equipment. An Information Bureau dealt with all answers to the exhibit and the public were invited to avail themselves of this feature, which covered all aspects of the scheme, including respirators, a model Cleansing Station, an "Anderson" Steel Shelter, examples of the technique of sand-bagging, Trade Vehicles adapted as Ambulances, and Fire-Fighting equipment.

As well as several of the technical buildings open for inspection were the Barrack Rooms, Dining Room and Kitchen and the Gymnasium.

Of great interest was the flying programme and the organisers had to wait until the last moment to detail this not knowing until that time which aircraft would be available for the day.

EVENT No. 1. TAXI PAST.

All the aircraft in the programme taxied past the enclosures in approximately the order in which they appeared in latter events.

EVENT No. 2. FLIGHT AEROBATICS.

A flight of three Gloster Gladiator aircraft from R.A.F. Hornchurch, Essex, carried out a series of aerobatics in close formation.

EVENT No. 3. FLYING INSTRUCTION.

This event consisted of a flying instructor trying to impart the rudiments of flying to a "difficult" pupil, with the inter-cockpit conversation relayed over the public address system. The aircraft was an Avro Tutor.

EVENT No. 4. SYNCHRONISED AEROBATICS.

Two Gloster Gladiator aircraft performed simultaneous aerobatics in facing directions calling for a very high degree of skill in the performance.

EVENT No. 5. HIGH SPEED EVENT.

The Supermarine Spitfire patrolling over Colchester, Essex, was called home at high speed, crossing the aerodrome low in a very fast passover, followed by fast circuits of the area, firing the aircraft guns at the same time.

EVENT No. 6. CAVALCADE OF THE AIR.

The majority of the aircraft stationed at the A & A.E.E. took part in this event, and showed the development over the previous two decades. First off was the Vickers Virginia and the latest machine to be shown was the Supermarine Spitfire.

EVENT No. 7. INDIVIDUAL AEROBATICS.

A Fairey Fantome single-seat interceptor demonstrated complicated manoeuvres built by combinations of the looping and rolling movements. This was extremely interesting as the aircraft was the only one of its type and was being evaluated at the A & A.E.E.

One of the best known and most loved of the Martlesham resident aircraft, the Vickers Virginia, All-metal Mark XJ7130, which flew off to Boscombe Down on 1st September, 1939.

EVENT No. 8.   DEMONSTRATION OF GUNNERY TRAINING.

Whilst a Hawker Demon towed a large target sleeve, it was fired on in simulated attacks by a Hawker Fury fighter giving a slow speed demonstration of the movements. This was followed by a Hawker Henley and a Hawker Hurricane repeating the same movements but at a much greater speed. It will be noted that all these aircraft were of Hawker manufacture with Rolls-Royce engines.

EVENT No. 9.   FLYING BOATS.

Interesting low fly-past of marine aircraft from the M.A.E.E. Felixstowe.

EVENT No. 10.   AMBUSHED IN THE DESERT.

The set-piece of the afternoon, with the R.A.F. Convoy passing close by a local chieftain's fortress. Led by an armoured car and escorted by a Westland Lysander aircraft, the trouble began when the armoured car was mined, blocking the path of the convoy, which was rapidly surrounded by fierce tribesmen. A lucky shot forces the Lysander down, but its gunner bravely continued to fire his gun at the "infidels." Help comes in the form of Blackburn Skua aircraft of the Fleet Air Arm, which drives off the attackers with machine-gun fire and light bombs, and then demolished the fort with heavy bombs. Plenty of noise and smoke, as a Bristol Bombay transport comes in to carry off the wounded and survivors.

EVENT No. 11.   HANDICAP RACE.

Many aircraft of varying ages and speeds took part in this popular event raced round a course as follows:— Martlesham Aerodrome — Ipswich Airport — Felixstowe — Martlesham — Ipswich Airport — Rushmere Water Tower — Martlesham. The limit aircraft completed the first leg of the course before the scratch machines took off, but the handicapping, carried out by Mr Fred Rowarth, one of the official handicappers for the King's Cup Air Race, resulted in a very close finish, the winning aircraft being the then very new American Lockheed Hudson patrol bomber in R.A.F. colours.

The Vickers Valentia K.3603, which ended its days at Boscombe Down in the early 1940s.

The Martlesham "hack" Vickers Valentia K.3603 taxies past the crowds before the Handicap Race.

During the afternoon, an urgent call to Martlesham from Felixstowe saw Air Commodore D. W. Bonham-Carter C.B., D.F.C., airborne in a Cierva C.30 autogiro bound for the Marine Aircraft Experimental Establishment at Felixstowe. On arrival over the base, the message he was about to drop, instead of going down, flicked upwards in the whirling rotor blades, causing some damage and had the effect of throwing them out of balance. After making a rapid descent near the rifle range at the back of the then Felixstowe hangars, he taxied the aircraft over the football pitch, along a road to the hangars, where, after some discussion, repairs were carried out and the aircraft returned to the A & A.E.E., amid all the other flying activities. The same gentleman, who was with "C" Flight, Performance Testing at the A & A.E.E. from 20th May 1936 until 24th July, 1939, also recalls an item on Daily Routine Orders.

VOLUNTARY CROSS-COUNTRY RUN.

All personnel will take part with the exception of the following airmen. (Here were named several airmen in the nursing orderly, telephone operator and cook category).

CHAPTER THREE

Thunder over the Heath. 1939—1943

THE arrival back from Munich of Mr Neville Chamberlain with his assurance of "peace in our time" did little to allay the fears of the forthcoming conflict, and almost feverish haste was made in order to make good the years of stagnation and hopeful dreams of disarmament. Security was further tightened, sightseers moved on more frequently, and on the 'drome, many of the aircraft were now dispersed around the airfield, instead of all being housed in the hangars. As many of the machines were now wearing the new camouflage finish they were fairly well concealed among the trees and bushes, but this procedure called for the mounting of guards around the perimeter, a not too popular decision with the lesser rank and file. The many civilians employed on the camp were hastily trained in the use of gas-masks and trenches were dug for use during air-raids, several dummy alerts making sure that all personnel knew their positions in the event of such an occurrence.

When the dreaded day arrived, a Sunday when the Station would normally have been in a "stand-down" state, the activity was without parallel. All the aircraft were wheeled out and placed as far as possible under the trees at the Dobb's Lane side of the 'drome. Several machines were still in trainer yellow, and these were rapidly toned down when airmen with buckets of water pulled up sods of grass and heather, and dipping them in the water, spread the muddy mix over the upper surfaces: others were disguised with large clumps of cut gorse and branches of trees. The surface of the airfield was once again covered with a mixture of soot and sand, the aprons tarred over, or at the least washed with a mixture of dark oil, and the hangars painted drab greens and browns. The transport changed from its smart polished sheen to one of matt colour, and all personnel carried gas-masks and gas-capes at all times, and for the first time, the guards instead of their usual truncheons carried rifles and tin-hats.

The roads through the Camp were of course, closed to the general public, and all civilian employees had to show passes in order to enter or leave the Station. Their jobs, in many cases, were also re-organized, as the gardeners and handy-men were no longer required as such, and took up fresh roles as waiters and mess-assistants in the various Messes. Station Headquarters was evacuated and empty houses in Deben Avenue, which runs down the western side of the 'drome, were requisitioned to accommodate this Section, although later in the year it moved to Playford Hall, a large country mansion nearer to Ipswich, whilst the Station Sick Quarters took up residence jointly at Kesgrave Hall and Westerfield House.

Little flying took place for these first few days, the majority of movements being visiting aircraft on their varied and apparently urgent duties. Bristol Blenheim bombers from R.A.F. Wattisham, on the other side of Ipswich were frequent visitors, and more so when a detachment of these aircraft were stationed at Ipswich Airport, from where they made the first offensive sortie of the War.

Owing to the proximity of the Establishment to the East Coast, and therefore the danger of enemy air attack, it was decided, as an urgent measure, to move the A & A.E.E. to a less dangerous site. Some preparations had already been undertaken, but now matters were of a more immediate nature and the plan to move swung into action. On 1st September, 1939, the A & A.E.E. "moved" itself to Boscombe Down, in Hampshire, not too far from where the Experimental Squadron had moved to Martlesham some twenty-two years earlier. The Martlesham test-pilots flew the more valuable prototypes to their new home, and then flying round to several training units in the district, picked up trained flying instructors, and ferried them back to Suffolk. On arrival at Martlesham, they were hastily briefed on their mounts, both prototypes and "hacks", and then, taking-off they formed up in loose formation and departed westwards, carrying as many of the "key" personnel as possible. Many Ipswich people looking upwards on that day to the sound of aircraft engines, must have felt regret at their departure, and at the same time, wondered what would now replace the familiar testing unit.

Thus ended the life of the A & A.E.E. at Martlesham Heath—twenty-two years of endeavour and progress—but it left behind the reputation of a Unit which had always been respected and liked by the local people. This is not so significant to those who do not know Suffolk people who are reported, and reputed, to be slow to "accept" strangers and time must elapse before one can really come to free-speaking terms with them.

The Daily Routine Order for 3rd September, 1939, issued by the Commanding Officer, Group Captain B. McEntegart stressed the situation:—

"The Commanding Officer, on the outbreak of war, wishes to call the attention of all personnel to the duty which is required of them. He fully realizes that there is no need for further instructions on this point as he knows full well that he can count on the loyal support of all personnel, service and civilian, on the Station.

The Commanding Officer, in appreciating all the hard work that has been done within the last few days, wishes all personnel the best of luck in the future."

64

After the departure of the A & A.E.E., and its personnel, only a "Holding-Party" remained and activity was down to a low ebb. The expected enemy attacks had so far not materialized and the Station was visited by the occasional fighter or bomber for reasons best known to themselves. Shortly afterwards, a Unit took up residence, "foreign" by nature to Martlesham, it being No. 4 Recruit Wing, but its stay was only short-lived, remaining only for a couple of months or so. The Heath vibrated to the roar of aircraft engines again during the late autumn of 1939, when squadrons on detachment arrived and departed for short or long stays, and notable among these were Nos. 17 (F), Hurricanes, No. 25 (F), Blenheim I's, No. 29 (F), Blenheim I's, and No. 56 (F) with its Hurricanes, all in No. 11 Group. A full list of the squadrons stationed at Martlesham Heath during the war period appears as Appendix IV.

The appearance of the airfield changed considerably during these first few months of the War, as gangs of men levelled out the more serious hollows, and removed and levelled the tree-topped tumuli in the north-west corner of the 'drome near the main road. The airfield area was also extended by the removal of many of the huge clumps of gorse around the perimeter. Work on the bomb-dump and ammunition store went on apace, whilst the smaller buildings like the Station Workshops were sand-bagged, and blast-protected, and black-out precautions were applied to the whole of the Station buildings. More thin tar was sprayed on the airfield and aprons to break up the image from the air, and the hangars now wore coats of brown and green camouflage.

Just before Christmas, 1939, personnel of No. 264 (F) Squadron arrived, and awaited the arrival of their Boulton-Paul Defiant two-seat fighter monoplanes. When they eventually appeared, working-up exercises began, but the aircraft ran into a spate of mechanical troubles and it was well into the spring of 1940 before the Squadron became operational. The prototypes, had of course, passed through the A & A.E.E. the previous year, but the troubles of an aircraft on squadron

Boulton-Paul Defiant 1 of No. 264 (F) Squadron being re-fuelled at Martlesham Heath. The four-gun turret can be clearly seen, and the aircraft's likeness to the Hawker Hurricane which deceived the enemy over Dunkirk.

duty are always multiplied in comparison to those of the prototype cared for and nursed in the experimental stages.

Early in the New Year, the aerodrome was equipped with Parachute and Cable Equipment (P.A.C.), a defence device consisting of a rocket which, when fired, carried aloft a parachute which was released at the maximum height of the rocket's climb. Attached to the parachute was a long length of thin piano-wire, which dangled down, the idea being to fire the rocket across the path of approaching aircraft, especially dive-bombers, and thus ensnare their airscrews in the hanging wire. As far as can be ascertained, this device was never fired "in anger" and the only time that it went into action was as the result of a false alarm, and on this occasion, the masses of thin steel wire, in their descent, "shorted out" many of the electric and telephone wires in the district.

Another interesting arrival in the district at this time was sited in a field on the Brightwell side of the 'drome, this being one of the R.A.F.'s three mobile radio-location units. Whilst on this site, it suffered a fire which partially destroyed the living accommodation van and some of the generating gear.

No. 56 (F) suffered one of its first casualties early in the New Year, when Pilot Officer F. C. Cooney flew into a house at nearby Playford, in his Hawker Hurricane 1, L.1984. The house was repaired, and to this day the new work can be seen on the house end, and although injured in the crash, the pilot recovered from this experience. On 26th April, another Hurricane landed on the Waldringfield Heath after suffering engine trouble and once again the pilot escaped serious injury, but Hurricane II, Z.2748, piloted by Pilot Officer W. R. Phillips of No. 3 Squadron was not so lucky when it crashed at Oakwood, Little Bealings, and caught fire; the pilot was killed.

The aerodrome was now fully alive again, pulsing with the beat of motors and aircraft which it had known as prototypes only a short while earlier. The Squadrons of No. 11 Group came and went, some only stopping for a day or two, whilst others took up semi-permanent residence, as opposed to those which used Martlesham as a "forward base" for operations. Other aircraft types appeared both as visitors, or forced-visitors, when for one reason or another they were glad to see Martlesham and to make a landing there.

During this period the development of radio-location continued at Bawdsey Manor which since 1938 had been working on the twin projects of ground detection of enemy aircraft and airborne equipment for the same purpose. When Sir Hugh Dowding visited Martlesham during June 1939, he had flown in an Aircraft Interception—equipped Fairey Battle to see for himself the progress which had been made.

Early Mark One A.I. sets were installed in the Bristol Blenheim Mk. I's of No. 25 (F) Squadron, which had moved to Perth, Scotland on the outbreak of hostilities; the Radar Flight of this Unit then returned south to St Athan in South Wales, and then on to Worthy Maltravers in Dorset. Eventually some of the members of this Flight filtered back to Martlesham during 1940, and operations were then carried on again from the Heath, by Blenheims of the Bawdsey Radar Flight, these being used to some extent to track down the nightly expeditions of German mine-laying aircraft operating off the East Coast. Other duties performed included calibrating the newly-erected radar stations in the district. Although at this stage only Blenheim I's were fitted with A.I. sets, during the Dunkirk period a Blenheim IV was also equipped with it. Eventually the Flight was made semi-operational and on one night sortie over the North Sea, a Blenheim I brought down a Heinkel III bomber, only to have to beat a hasty retreat back to Martlesham, when the gunner of the crashing German bomber hit the Blenheim, and started a fire, causing the bomber to crash-land back on the Heath. The pilot of the Blenheim was decorated for saving the lives of his gunner and operator in the ensuing crash.

Martlesham-based aircraft must have been amongst the first to make sorties against night-flying enemy aircraft, during the period following Dunkirk, and before the "Blitz" proper, East Anglia was frequently visited by small groups of raiders. During this period, a fairly heavy night raid developed in the Cambridge area, and the Blenheims of No. 25 Squadron took off from Martlesham to intercept. For this duty they carried additional armament in the form of a gun pack under the forward fuselage.

A Bristol Blenheim Mk.I fighter in all-black night fighter finish, similar to the aircraft operated by No. 25 (F) Squadron during early 1940. Note the early radio-location aerials above and below the port mainplane.   *British Aircraft Corporation*

By the late spring of 1940, Martlesham was for the first time in its life a fully operational airfield, with No. 264 (F) squadron operating its Defiants and it was over the beaches of Dunkirk that this Unit made its first sorties, destroying a large number of German aircraft without loss to themselves. Unfortunately, however, their success was short-lived, as in the same week, they suffered heavy losses, including the death of their Commanding Officer Squadron Leader P. A. Hunter D.S.O. and were withdrawn north for regrouping and rest.

No. 85 (F) Squadron, stationed at Martlesham during this period and at the beginning of the Battle, has an extremely interesting log-book to record their activity, and show up issues and facets of the Battle which are not so widely known as the main events.

July 1st, 1940.	Dornier Do.17Z destroyed by anti-aircraft fire near Harwich.
July 6th, 1940.	L.1750, the two-cannon Hawker Hurricane which had been in a hangar at Martlesham Heath for some time was taken over by No. 151 Squadron for further operational trials.
July 8th, 1940.	Flight Sergeant G. Allard brought down a Heinkel HE.111 H-2 before lunch whilst on patrol six miles off Felixstowe.
July 11th, 1940.	Squadron Leader Townsend badly damaged a Dornier Do.17Z whilst on convoy patrol off the Essex coast. Unfortunately he was hit by return fire from an enemy aircraft and suffered damage to his engine and coolant tank, resulting in his having to leave the aircraft off Felixstowe, but was subsequently picked up by a naval vessel. The enemy machine disappeared low over the sea flying in an unstable manner.
July 12th, 1940.	Convoys patrols off the Suffolk coast assisted by "A" Flight of No. 17 (F) Squadron. Enemy aircraft located and attacked a coastal convoy off Felixstowe and Flying Officer Count M. E. Czernin (No. 17) destroyed a Dornier Do.17Z, whilst another No. 17 pilot shot down another Dornier Do.17Z off Orfordness. (Pilot Officer Hanson). No. 151 Squadron from North Weald then joined the action and destroyed another Dornier Do.17Z near Orfordness. Pilot Officer Manger and Sergeant Griffiths of No. 17 jointly destroyed a Heinkel III H-2 whilst Sergeant Griffiths carried on to shoot down another Heinkel III H-2. Flying Officer Pitman and Sergeant Fopp also jointly destroyed another Heinkel III H-2. Pilot Officer Bickersdyke gained a victory over another Heinkel

III H-2, this being a No. 85 Squadron claim. R.A.F. losses in the action were:—

No. 85 Squadron   Sergeant Jowitt shot down by He.III off Felixstowe.

No. 151 Squadron   Flying Officer Allan shot down by enemy aircraft off Orfordness. Two aircraft suffered material damage.

No. 17 Squadron   Suffered no damage or losses.

July 25th, 1940.   Single enemy aircraft on reco destroyed by anti-aircraft fire off Harwich, and crashed into the sea. This aircraft was later identified as a Messerschmitt BF.110.

July 22nd, 1940.   In a night landing accident, the Hurricane of Pilot Officer Bickersdyke overturned and he was unfortunately killed.

July 26th, 1940.   Heinkel He III H-2's carrying torpedoes and heavy bombs attacked a coastal convoy whilst off the Suffolk coast near Aldeburgh, the escorting destroyer H.M.S. Wren being hit, severely damaged and eventually sunk.

July 29th, 1940.   A Dornier Do.17Z was badly damaged by Flying Officer P. Woods-Scaren of No. 85 Squadron, whilst it was attacking a coastal convoy. In this limited action, damage was sustained by one of No. 66's Spitfires which force-landed near Orford and a Hurricane of No. 151 Squadron made an emergency landing at Martlesham.

July 30th, 1940.   No. 85 Squadron claimed another joint victory when Flight Sergeant Allard and Flight Lieutenant Hamilton intercepted a Messerschmitt BF.110 near Orfordness and shot it down.

August 2nd, 1940.   Escorting a coastal convoy off the Suffolk coast between Orfordness and Felixstowe, the armed trawler H.M.S. Finisterre came under severe enemy aircraft attack, sustaining heavy damage and eventual loss.

August 6th, 1940.   Three members of No. 85 Squadron jointly claimed a victory of an enemy aircraft. Flight Sergeant Allard, now D.F.M., and Sergeants Cross and Ellis stalked and destroyed a Dornier Do.17Z off Harwich.

August 11th, 1940.   A north-bound convoy was attacked by a large formation of enemy aircraft, pressing home their attacks from all heights. These comprised Dornier Do.17Z's and Messerschmitt BF.110's. No. 17 Squadron attacked and Pilot Officer Stevens shot down a Messerschmitt BF.110 and No. 85 Squadron with its Hurricanes got three Dornier Do.17Z's, whilst commanded by Squadron

Leader Peter Townsend. Throughout the day defensive sorties were flown to combat attacking enemy aircraft which attacked this convoy during the day-light hours, and later in the day No. 85 Squadron claimed another Messerschmitt BF.110 damaged so badly that its chances of regaining base were slim. During the day, Pilot Officer Manger was unfortunately lost over the sea, whilst after suffering severe damage to his Hurricane, Pilot Officer Hanson managed to get it back to Martlesham. Sergeant Newton of No. 111 Squadron also suffered heavy damage but he managed to make it back to Martlesham. Airfield closed for two days.

August 15th, 1940. The morning saw standing and convoy patrols being flown, but during the afternoon Martlesham Heath was attacked by enemy aircraft. No. 17 Squadron in spite of the unheralded arrival of the raiders, managed to get three Hurricanes airborne. Flight Lieutenant Harper, Pilot Officer Pitman and Sergeant Griffiths attempted to intercept the outnumbering raiders, but were not successful, and the enemy made off without loss. No. 111 Squadron took-off from North Weald in order to intercept the enemy formation on its way home but did not sight them. Flight Lieutenant Harper from Martlesham was severely damaged and made a successful forced-landing near Felixstowe, whilst attempting to intercept the home-going enemy.

August 20th, 1940. Martlesham Heath again attacked by the Messerschmitt BF.110's of Erprobungagruppe 210, but little damage was caused, the majority of the bombs falling on the airfield and its precincts. Flight Sergeant Gillies in a Spitfire of No. 66 Squadron airborne from Coltishall managed to destroy a homeward bound Me.BF.110 off Aldeburgh.

August 21st, 1940. A lone enemy aircraft flying over Suffolk was shot down over Ipswich by a Hurricane of No. 56 Squadron flown by Flight Officer Brooker who was later unfortunately shot down by an enemy aircraft and badly burned in the ensuing crash-landing. The Dornier Do.17Z crashed on the S.W. Side of Ipswich, after the crew had baled-out and they were later captured and interned.

August 26th, 1940. No. 111 Squadron moved to Martlesham Heath as forward base, and during the day were scrambled to intercept a large formation of enemy aircraft attacking the R.A.F. Stations at Hornchurch and Debden in Essex. As a result of these sorties, 2 Heinkel III's were destroyed, and Flight Lieutenant Bruce and Sergeant Sellars of No. 111 Squadron, slightly wounded but landed safely. Whilst outward-bound No. 111 Squadron also destroyed a Dornier Do.17Z over the sea near Clacton and a Messerschmitt BF.110 near Chelmsford, Essex.

August 31st, 1940.   No. 257 Squadron moved to Martlesham Heath as forward base. Scrambled at mid-day to intercept an enemy formation of 50 plus Messerschmitt BF.110's approaching Essex near Clacton. In this action Pilot Officer Henderson was badly damaged and baled out to be picked up, whilst Pilot Officer Maffett was less fortunate in being lost over the sea. No. 66 Squadron airborne from Coltishall, Norfolk, joined in the battle claiming a Dornier Do.215 which crashed over the border in Suffolk. Later a Dornier Do.17Z-2 was destroyed off Felixstowe by Flight Lieutenant Giddings.

September 1st, 1940.   Blenheims of No. 25 Squadron at Martlesham Heath commanded by Squadron Leader W. W. Loxton. Whilst on detachment back to North Weald on 2.9.40 three aircraft of the Squadron scrambled from N.W. and were unfortunately attacked by the Hurricanes of No. 46 Squadron, who mistook them for Junkers JU.88's. As a result of this "action" the Blenheim of Pilot Officer Hogg was shot-down and he was killed, Pilot Officer Cassidy was badly damaged and made a successful forced-landing, whilst the leader, Squadron Leader Loxton made a safe return to Martlesham Heath. At Martlesham, No. 257 Squadron was airborne engaging enemy aircraft to the West of Colchester, Essex, in which action Flight Officer Hunt was set on fire, but he managed to bale-out and landed with burns. Pilot Officer Bon-Seignor also suffered severe damage which caused him to abandon his aircraft, and although he successfully baled-out he was killed on landing. Pilot Officer Grunday managed to get his very badly shot-up Hurricane back to Martlesham, whilst although not so badly damaged, Sergeant Nutter managed to do likewise.

September 4th, 1940.   Two Heinkel III's, a H-3 and a H-4 shot down over the

	sea by Blenheims of No. 25 Squadron whilst on patrol.
September 7th, 1940.	No. 257 airborne to intercept a large formation of enemy aircraft heading for London. In the following action Flight Lieutenant Bereford and Pilot Officer Mitchell were both lost to enemy fire, whilst Sergeant Hulbert although badly shot-up managed to successfully land his aircraft, as also did Sergeant Robinson.
September 14th, 1940.	No. 257 airborne to intercept enemy aircraft over Suffolk resulting in a Heinkel He III H-4 being brought down at Harkstead near Ipswich by Pilot Officer Mortimer.
September 19th, 1940.	No. 17 Squadron in action from Martlesham intercepting enemy aircraft and a Junkers Ju.88 A-1 was brought down near Aldeburgh by Flying Officer Count Czernin, and Sergeants Griffith and Barlett.
October 27th, 1940.	Small raid on Martlesham Heath by enemy aircraft. No. 17 airborne to intercept and a Dornier Do.17Z was shot down into the River Stour near Parkeston Quay by Flying Officer Count Czernin and Sergeant Hogg.
October 28th, 1940.	Flying Officer Count Czernin and Sergeant Griffiths destroyed a Dornier Do.17Z over the sea near Orfordness which was making a lone attack over Suffolk.

In passing it must be mentioned that Flight Sergeant Allard for his part over the beaches of Dunkirk and later in the Battle of Britain was awarded the Distinguished Flying Medal, and received during August 1940 a Bar to this award. At the end of August 1940 he was commissioned Pilot Officer, swiftly rising in rank within a few months to Flight Lieutenant when he was awarded the Distinguished Flying Cross. After the Battle, he was unfortunately killed in action, but nevertheless, must be regarded as one of the top fighter pilots to be based operationally at Martlesham Heath.

To return to the hot summer days of 1940, the nearby town of Ipswich was visited by bombers of the Luftwaffe during the night of 12th August, but on this occasion Martlesham escaped their attention. Several lone raiders flew over the district but without attacking, but the afternoon of 15th August, a lovely hot Sunday, proved to be different. At approximately 3.00 p.m., a force of Messerschmitt BF.110's and Messerschmitt 109's of the Luftwaffe Test Group 210 under the leadership of Hauptmann Walter Hubensdorffer hurtled in out of the sun. The Me.109's came in shallow dives, their bombs causing damage to various Station buildings, the airfield and the newly erected wireless station at the end of Dobb's Lane. Bombs from the BF.110's being of heavier calibre, made direct hits on further buildings, and one lucky hit struck a bombed-up visiting Fairey Battle bomber, which blew-up destroying the Watch Office and a part of the old A.R.S. hangar, together with various stores offices. The hangar with its boarded-up end remained in that condition until 1973.

As the then resident squadrons were either airborne, or at stand-down, the raiders were not intercepted in force, and virtually had the freedom of the skies, as only three Hurricanes managed to get off to chase them. Smaller bombs hit the Station Workshops and the Officers' Mess, whilst the Refrigeration Plant which had been one of the show-pieces in connection with engine-testing, was also badly damaged. Fortunately casualties were remarkably light, it being a Sunday afternoon, with many of the personnel not in the buildings which they normally occupied.

A smaller raid on the airfield occurred on 20th August, when a group of Messerschmitt 110's attacked, but the damage was mainly confined to the airfield itself and the surrounding heath.

During August, 1940, German Intelligence claimed that Martlesham Heath was one of eleven British airfields which had been destroyed, and the late "Lord Haw-Haw" mentioned it on several occasions, and if one were to believe these

German Target Map photograph taken during October 1942. The River Deben can be seen on the right with Martlesham Creek running into the centre, whilst the railway line from Ipswich to Lowestoft curves round into Woodbridge in the top right-hand corner. The runways have not yet been laid but the extension to the south is evident. *Christopher Elliott*

broadcasts, there should not have been much of the aerodrome left standing at this time.

The occasional German recco aircraft flew over the district at great height and this is evidenced by the fine photographs taken by them on these flights, and kindly loaned for inclusion here by Mr Christopher Elliot from his collection. It is interesting to note how the enemy Intelligence Service kept an eye on the site shown by the fact that some of the photographs show the aerodrome less runways (they were constructed during 1943) the runways under construction, and finally with the completed works and their extensions.

The bomber forces of the Luftwaffe visited nearby Ipswich again during the night of 14th September, 1940, and once again no heavy damage resulted, mainly as a result of large decoy fires being lit on the surrounding heaths which lured the raiders into dropping their bombs on the open spaces.

The main force of the Luftwaffe was now spent, and the huge formations of approaching enemy aircraft thinned out to small groups and single raiders, but before leaving the subject of the Battle of Britain, much has been written about the exploits of the R.A.F. pilots during this period, and although Martlesham Heath was only on the fringe of the main combat area, many of the more well-known names including Group Captain Bader, Group Captain Stanford Tuck, Group Captain Peter Townsend and Wing Commander Deere, to name a few, were at Martlesham at one period or another.

Wing Commander (later Group Captain) D. R. S. Bader, D.S.O., D.F.C., who served at Martlesham Heath with Nos. 222 (F) and 242 (F) Squadrons.

Group Captain Douglas Bader remembers his visits,

"I first visited Martlesham Heath during the war on May 28th, 1940, when I was a Flight Commander in No. 222 Squadron. On that day we flew from Martlesham to Dunkirk on a patrol, and then returned to Manston and subsequently to Hornchurch. On December 17th, 1940, No. 242 Squadron was posted to Martlesham where it remained until after I left on March 18th, 1941. It was not a lucky Station for 242 Squadron. Having lost only six pilots throughout the Battle of Britain, we lost five in a couple of months during our stay at Martlesham Heath through bad weather, trying to patrol convoys which did not need patrolling because there was no danger from the air, pilot error, icing conditions and one only through enemy action. Within a few days after my leaving the new Squadron Commander killed himself and two other pilots in a collision off Martlesham Heath. Strangely enough I landed at Martlesham last Summer (1968) in a small aeroplane and although it has changed quite a bit since I was there nearly 27 years ago there were still a few ghosts around."

The Martlesham days of Group Captain Stanford Tuck are very well described in the book *Fly for your Life* by Larry Forrester, and those of Group Captain Peter Townsend in *The Sky Suspended* by Drew Middleton, published by Secker and Warburg.

11th November, 1940, witnessed an action in the Martlesham area which was unique in that the combatants were the Royal Air Force and the Italian Air Force. Mr Christopher Elliot has carried out a great deal of research into this raid and the author is indebted to him for use of his notes on the subject.

Although the British Intelligence Service knew of the presence of Italian Air Units with the Luftwaffe in Europe during 1940, few details appeared in our Press until the Italians themselves released details.

In November 1940, one aeronautical magazine in particular published several interesting notes relating to the Expeditionary Force named "Corps Aerio Italiano" (Italian Air Corps) whose units were stationed along the Channel Coast, mostly in Belgium. Its strength was estimated to be equal to that of an Italian Air Fleet (between 300 and 400 planes) and the Corps consisted of fighter, fighter-reconnaissance-bomber, and bomber units. The Commander-in-Chief of the Corps was General Rino Corso Foulgier, who, as a commander of the Italian Air Legion, distinguished himself in the Spanish Civil War. Royal Air Force authorities were of the opinion that the squadron numbers of several Fiat C.R.42 Freccia biplane fighters which had been shot down, indicated that the Italian Air Corps with the Luftwaffe, consisted mainly of units belonging to the 1st Air Fleet (Headquarters Milan). The aircraft of the Corps, together with most of the ground personnel, were flown from their home bases to aerodromes formerly occupied by the German Air Force.

Up to 30th October, 1940, the Italian Press had reported nothing but victorious engagements for the Corps fighter squadrons over the Hurricanes and Spitfires of Fighter Command. The Fascist Press also proclaimed that Italian bombers collaborating with the Luftwaffe had "successfully bombed London". How dubious these claims must have been can be gauged from the fact that no Italian planes were brought down over this country until the following month. Indeed, had they actually joined their Allies in the bid to destroy London many of them would certainly have fallen victims. It is probably correct, however, that a few Italian airmen had merely "spied out the lie of the land" around Dover. Others may have participated in minor nuisance raids at night. General Guiseppe Santaro in his book *L'Aeronautica Italiana nella Seconda Guerra Mondiale*, Volume One, claims more raids and victories than were in actual fact.

It was not until the morning of 11th November, 1940, the anniversary of Armistice Day, after high-ranking Italian Air Force officers had inspected the cream of the Corps Aerio Italiano that 'planes of the Air Force, bearing cross-markings to indicate that they were operating under German orders, set out for their first and last raid in any strength against England.

It seems fairly certain now that the formation consisted of approximately ten Fiat B.R.20 twin-engined bombers (not Caproni's or Piaggo's) escorted by forty Fiat C.R.42 fighters. The bombers had as their objective the harbour installations at Harwich, Essex, only some twelve or so miles from Martlesham as the crow flies. During the following engagement, their formation was broken and all their bombs fell in the sea.

The R.A.F. Squadrons which took-off to intercept the Italians were No. 41 (F) Squadron, Hornchurch, No. 46 (F) Squadron, North Weald, No. 245 (F) Squadron, North Weald and No. 257 (F) Squadron, Martlesham Heath. The latter three squadrons made contact with the raiders and their score reads as follows:—

No. 46.   Two BR.20's and two CR.42's destroyed, two CR.42's probably destroyed.

No. 245.   One CR.42 probably destroyed.

No. 257.   Five BR.20's and two CR.42's destroyed. This squadron also claimed one BR.20 and three CR.42's damaged.

All the R.A.F. fighters returned safely.

Flight Lieutenant H. P. Blatchford who led No. 257 Squadron on that day as the Squadron Commander, Squadron Leader R. R. Stanford-Tuck was supposed to be off-duty, made rendezvous with No. 46 Squadron over the North Sea. At about 12,000 feet, the bombers were sighted in tight "Vic" formation, accompanied by numerous fighters. Not sure of their identity, the R.A.F. Squadrons flew over the formation and the R.A.F. pilots were surprised to discover that they were Italian. At about the same time, the bombers climbed for cloud cover at 20,000 feet, pursued by the eager Hurricane fighters. One Fiat B.R.20 looped-the-loop as its pilot, presumably shot, fell back pulling the control column with him. Despite intense opposition, the bombers that still remained flew steadily on in a westerly direction. Flight Lieutenant Blatchford, his ammunition exhausted, rammed the upper port wing of a Fiat C.R.42 with the propeller of his Hurricane, tearing a large piece off the wing. Despite the fact that the engine was vibrating badly, he made dummy attacks on other Fiats which turned and fled seawards. He stated afterwards, "It was the best party I have ever had in my life."

By this time the Italian formation was in complete confusion and many of the raiders were being chased pell-mell up the East Coast. Out of the autumn sky above Orford, Suffolk, a C.R.42 fighter spiralled down and made a forced-landing on the beach, a quarter of a mile north of the light-house. Apart from a broken propeller and minor engine trouble due mainly to its tipping on its nose when landing, the plane was intact. It exists to this day and is at the R.A.F. Museum at Hendon, after having flown with the R.A.F. for some time in an experimental role. Salvadori Pictio, aged twenty-three years, the pilot, was captured by R.A.F. personnel from the nearby R.A.F. Orfordness Station. Another C.R.42 piloted by Antoni Lazzari, also aged twenty-three years, landed in a ploughed field at Corton, near Lowestoft, Suffolk, where on touch-down the undercarriage collapsed and the aircraft suffered considerable damage. Several

Fiat C.R.42 fighter of the Corps Aerio Italiano which crashed at Hopton, near Lowestoft, on 11th November, 1940. The aircraft was damaged in the landing, but the Army seem very interested in their visitor.   *Ford Jenkins*

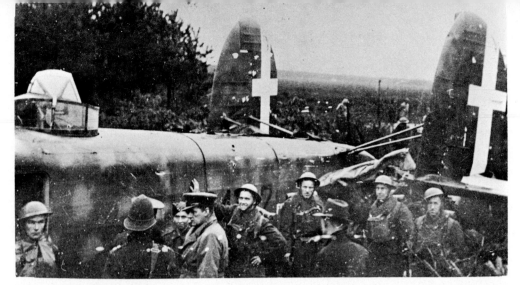

Crashed Fiat B.R.20 bomber on the edge of Tangham Forest, Bromeswell, near Woodbridge, on the 11th November, 1940. The mottled finish is interesting and the distinctive white crosses denoting that the aircraft was operating under Luftwaffe control. *Ministry of Defence*

splashes in the sea made by falling aircraft were noticed by people watching along the coast from Felixstowe to Lowestoft. An Italian plane, believed to have been a bomber, plunged into the sea off Aldeburgh, a little to the north of Orfordness. The local R.N.L.I. lifeboat was launched, but as the result of a long search, found only an open parachute bearing Italian markings. About this time, Squadron Leader Stanford-Tuck, who must have taken-off from Martlesham Heath after his squadron had departed for the fray, chased a Fiat B.R.20 bomber inland towards Woodbridge, Suffolk. The green and brown monoplane bomber, which shed a propeller near the town, had one gunner dead, and two members of the crew wounded. It finally came down, undercarriage retracted, to belly-land on the edge of Tangham Forest, Bromeswell, near the present R.A.F./U.S.A.F. Sutton Heath aerodrome, and partially buried itself in a plantation of young conifers. According to a police witness, a gang of foresters rounded up the three injured airmen, who, with the exception of the pilot, were wearing thin dungarees made of poor quality material. They were each equipped with a shrapnel helmet and a bayonet. The three crew members were Pietro Appaini (22) pilot, Elvine Corrosi (24) gunner and Mario Domonco Pensa (27) photographer. The prisoners, according to one authority "were the first Tuscan enemies to alight in this country since the Roman invaders left nearly 2,000 years ago." A pilot, believed to have been Squadron Leader Stanford-Tuck, had landed back at Martlesham, and hurriedly arrived on the scene by car, to carry out an inspection of the fallen machine, and found amongst its contents:—

    1 bottle of champagne.
    1 bottle of Chianti wine.
    1 5lb cheese (a cheese grater was found lying on one of the gunner's seats.)

Legend has it that the fare intended for an Italian toast upon the successful completion of the raid on Harwich was consumed in the Mess at Martlesham Heath that evening.

On 23rd November, 1940, the Italians tried again for the last time to establish themselves as successful airmen in the European theatre of operations. In attacking a North Sea convoy they lost seven more aircraft.

So ended the Italian Air Force's month's escapade against England. Why they left the comparative safety of Italy remains somewhat a puzzle to this day. Also, Italy's greater apparent need was for a strong Air Force in the Middle East. Was it simply a costly propaganda stunt? Did Mussolini in one of his more ambitious moods believe that his rather obsolete Air Force would accomplish what the hard-hitting Luftwaffe, with superior equipment and expert airmen had so utterly failed to do? The battle of 11th November certainly taught the confident Italian airmen, despite all their leaders had told them, that the R.A.F. was still as good a fighting force as it was at the start of Goering's offensive. Suffolk is proud to have had the honour of receiving the only Italian raiders ever to fall in England. In memory of the pilots of No. 257 Squadron, their individual scores read as under:—

F/Lt. H. P. Blatchford	Hurricane No. V.6962	1.B.R.20
		½.B.R.20 (Shared with P/O Davey)
		2.C.R.42's damaged
P/O G. North	Hurricane V.6864	½.B.R.20 (Shared with F/Lt Gaunce No. 46 Squadron)
		½.B.R.20 (Shared with F/O Mortimer)
F/O R. A. Mortimer	Hurricane P.2835	½.B.R.20 (Shared with P/O North)
P/O B. Davey	Hurricane V.7607	½.B.R.20 (Shared with F/Lt. Blatchford)
P/O K. Pniak	Hurricane V.7292	1.B.R.20
		½.B.R.20 (Shared with P/O Kay)
P/O J. K. Kay	Hurricane V.6680	½.B.R.20 (Shared with P/O Pniak)
		½.B.R.20 (Shared with P/O Andrews)
P/O S. E. Andrews	Hurricane —	½.B.R.20 (Shared with P/O Kay)
Sgt. L. D. Barnes	Hurricane V.6873	1.C.R.42
Sgt. S. E. Lucas	Hurricane R.4088	1.C.R.42
		1.C.R.42 damaged

The squadron claimed 8½ destroyed plus 3 damaged, and all the aircraft carried the squadron code-letters D T.

Of interest to many will be the logged day to day notes of the Engineering Officer of No. 257 Squadron whilst it was at Martlesham Heath, commanded by Squadron Leader Stanford-Tuck D.F.C. and 2 bars, D.S.O.,

November 7th, 1940.   Serviceability at 09.00 hours.   15 (flyable)

Worked hard on "Z" during loading of lorries, 15 took-off for Martlesham at about 09.00 hours. Pnick followed in "Z" (new mag) just before convoy left. I arrived at Martlesham 13.30 hours, convoy arrived 14.30 hours. Distributed lorries, sent men to dinner and commenced unpacking about 15.30 hours. Allotted large hangar. Men worked well, they like Martlesham. Phone O.K. Arranged for hangar boiler to be started. Had to clear out a lot of No. 25 Squadron rubbish, as usual. Dope store in particularly bad state.

Operational serviceable aircraft = 14. Left "C" at North Weald waiting for engine and undercarriage parts. Tackled stores re outstanding demands at North Weald. Sent party to Biggin Hill to replace engine of L.1659 (two bad internal glycol leaks). Forced landing ensued.

November 8th, 1940.   Serviceability at 09.00 hours.   12.

Bad day. Sergeant Page killed in V.6870, Category Three burnt out near Hawkinge. Believed enemy action. Fixed hydraulic system on "U" and oil leaks and trim tabs on "M". Flight Lieutenant Blatchford in "E" had elevators jam. Bad spin and wing skin started to buckle. Blacked out, fell 20,000 feet, got out and landed O.K. Started work on wings and actuating gear. Glycol pump went on "G". Supplied new one — Flight installing this themselves. Internal glycol leak on "U". Signalled for new cylinder head. Bad oil leak on "D". Flight corrected this themselves. Signal for H.Q.F.C. required numbers and reasons for 4 exchange aircraft required. Signalled this off. Two exchanges arrived from an Operational Training Unit. Sent them back, one was "L" series (V.H.F. cannot be fitted) and other was "P" in bad condition. Wing Commander Beamish at North Weald told me not to accept wrecks.

November 9th, 1940.   Serviceability at 09.00 hours.   12.

Sent men to flights to assist on "G". Still working on "E". Sent lorry to North Weald for outstanding spares. Asked for extra lorry for my flight, have only two for the Squadron. Signalled to Biggin Hill asking for full report on engine of L.1659 for 765C action. Git Seal went on "D", had just given our last spare to Howarth of No. 17 Squadron — took the chance and lost. Radiator temperature gauge went on "Z". Took instrument rep to flight with spare for replacement. Tail wheel broken off "N". Replaced in 2 hours.

November 10th, 1940.   Serviceability at 09.00 hours.   12.

Visit from Mr Goose (Rolls-Royce representative) re Merlins in general and cylinder block for "U" in particular. He is chasing these internal glycol leaks. "E" went U/S with punctured oil tank. Went to stores, got tank and started replacement in conjunction with 30 hour inspection. Tank off large file fits in hole. I am investigating. Took "R" in for 30 hour inspection in the afternoon. Delivered 12 new oxygen bottles in flights, also pitot covers. Disposal instructions for "Z" finished O.K. Demanded 6 paraffin stoves for hangar offices. Phoned North Weald and Debden for Git seals for "D". They hadn't one in stores at either place. Arranged to go to North Weald tomorrow.

Hawker Hurricane Mk.I L.1648 as used by No. 257 (F) Squadron and whose Engineering Officer tried so desperately to keep serviceable under very trying conditions.

Hawker Aircraft Co.

November 11th, 1940.   Serviceability at 09.00 hours.   10.

Snags on "E" and "R" ("E" oil gauge, "R" starter motor) "B" in with air system gone. Taking parts off "U" for "C" at North Weald. Arranged to go to North Weald with the parts required for "C". "C" got shot up in first fight with the Italians (N.2328). Signalled it off Category 2 (hydraulic reservoir, strut and elevator controls shot through). Got 8 Italians and 3 Germans during day. Collected parts and left for North Weald 4 p.m. Arrived 5.30 p.m. Handed parts over to Corporal in charge, arranged for him to let me know when "C" is serviceable. Visited Station Workshops, Stores, etc., enquiring re winter equipment and outstanding demands.

November 12th, 1940.   Serviceability at 09.00 hours.   10.

Having a lean time with serviceability. Returned from North Weald early in morning. "H" lost tail wheel. Sent replacement and men to fit same. "Z" port magneto dud. Took one off "U" and took it over to flight. Still unable to trace leak in air system of "B" — suspect cracked pipes. "M" in hangar having new tailplane fitted (shot in fight with Italians). Late in day Git Seals arrived (for "D"). Worked on after dark on "E" with Anglepoise lamps. Gales and rain, part of hangar roof glass fell in.

November 13th, 1940.   Serviceability at 09.00 hours.   9.

"B" air leak. "C" at North Weald. "D" Git Seal. "G" Category 2. "H" Tail wheel. "I" at Penshurst. "J" at Biggin Hill. "U" Glycol leak. "M" Tailplane. Organising lorry to take pilot to North Weald for "C" and bring back mechanics with tools. Booked call to Detling re "I" (civilians making too long a job on this repair). Inspector arrived from No. 54 Maintenance Unit — refuses to accept "C" as Category 2 (hydraulic pump, control cables and side strut) Made it Category 1. Received replacement V.7052. Called it "K". Cannot fix air leak in "B" yet. Chasing spares for the various aircraft. Signalled Detling asking about V.6741. Phoned Biggin Hill about L.1659 not ready yet.

November 14th, 1940.   Serviceability at 09.00 hours.   11.
    Git Seals arrived. Fixed "D". Fixed tail wheel on "H". Chasing spares. Phoned Wing Commander No. 56 Operational Training Unit. He is to send one of his pilots with exchange machine for N.2342. Talked to V.H.F. Head-Quarters Fighter Command Flight Sergeant. He will check the exchange aircraft when it arrives to see if it is suitable for V.H.F. before I accept. Afternoon fight. "L" shot up (Temporary repair and fly in to Henlow). "W" shot through sternpost. Category 1. "A" hydraulic pump. "N" compressor broke off.

It will be seen from the foregoing that during the Battle of Britain and indeed for a long time afterwards, the job of the Engineering Officers and the ground staff was one of make and mend and patch up wherever possible, with the non-availability of spares and components causing aircraft to be grounded when they were badly needed for combat operations.

If the reader is mystified by the use of letters, i.e. "A" in the reports above, these were used to denote a particular aircraft and followed the squadron letter painted on the fuselage sides, for example No. 17 Squadron was marked Y B (roundel) A etc.

While we are still with No. 17 Squadron at Martlesham Heath, reference must be made to one of its more illustrious pilots, Flying Officer Count Manfred Beckett Czernin D.S.O., M.C., D.F.C. Once again Mr Christopher Elliott has carried out a great deal of research into the activities of this pilot and the author is indebted to him for use of this research.

A fearless and indeed, ruthless fighter pilot, Count Czernin, of Austrian nationality, joined the peace-time Royal Air Force and therefore at the outbreak of hostilities was a fully-fledged fighter pilot, joining No. 17 Squadron from another well-known unit, No. 85 Squadron. On 11th September, 1940 he was awarded the Distinguished Flying Cross for destroying nine enemy aircraft, and as recorded in previous pages, he participated in many actions during the Battle of Britain, resulting in several victories over the enemy.

On 17th November, 1940, Flying Officer Count Czernin took off in his Hawker Hurricane I Serial No. V.7500, to intercept a large formation, some 40 aircraft, approaching the Suffolk coast. This formation which comprised the crack Luftwaffe units EG 210 and JG 26 were intercepted by No. 17 and No. 257 Squadrons and in the ensuing battles Count Czernin was badly damaged and forced to bale out, fortunately landing with only slight injuries, but his aircraft dived vertically downwards to crash into a field near Bredfield village church, not far from Woodbridge. It was learned some time later, from German sources, that Count Czernin had been shot down by no less an opponent than the top Luftwaffe fighter ace, Major Adolf Galland, leader of the JG 26 Gruppe. At the time of the crash, all the wreckage of the Hurricane above the ground was removed by an R.A.F. Salvage Unit, but during November 1969, Mr Ian McLachlan and Mr Stuart Evans assisted by many keen colleagues decided to probe this site, and as a result of their diggings, unearthed at some considerable depth the heavier items of the aircraft, engine, cockpit area, undercarriages and guns. Illustrations will show that the parts are very well preserved after their long sojourn beneath the earth.

The remains of Flying Officer Count Czernin's Hurricane V.7500 see the light after 29 years underground. Top left, the brake blocks and brake drum found some 2-3 feet down: top right, the control column grip with firing button still operative: bottom left, the Rolls-Royce Merlin III Motor No. 30527 found at the 15 foot level. *Ian McLachlan*

Two veterans in the air, Hurricane and Spitfire, and at the time of publication, still flying from Coltishall.   *E.A.D.T.*

During his career, Flying Officer Count Czernin was credited with 13 enemy aircraft destroyed, five shared, three probably destroyed and two damaged.

His Martlesham days over, he subsequently moved to Croydon and other R.A.F. posts, moving finally to work with Special Operations Executive in Italy. Here he carried out his dangerous missions with great skill and for this he was awarded the Military Cross and the Distinguished Service Order. He died during the early 1960's and one of his ex-colleagues has made the statement that he rated him "as the bravest man I ever met".

As a memorial to this gallant man, the Rolls-Royce Merlin engine from his aircraft has been lovingly cleaned and restored, and apart from minor damage caused by impact, looks at the present time every bit as good as the day it left the manufacturer's works.

As the enemy attacks diminished somewhat and the aircraft of Fighter Command were called less upon to defend their bases, the role of the squadrons gradually turned to the offensive, and during this second winter of the War, many units were based on the Heath, and it is interesting to note that, during the first year of hostilities, the aircraft based at Martlesham had been Hawker Hurricanes, but now, more and more Supermarine Spitfire squadrons took up residence, although latter marques of the Hurricane, Mk.2B's and Mk.2C's still persisted. During this period, the slower Hurricanes were engaged mainly on East Coast convoy patrols, whilst the Spitfires were "working-up" for their forthcoming offensive operations over the Continent. As the longer days of spring approached, the Spitfires increased their activities, flying offensive sweeps in large groups over France and the Low Countries, and also acting as bomber escorts to the daily increasing daylight sorties being mounted by the medium bombers of Bomber Command.

During April 1941, No. 71 (F) Squadron arrived at Martlesham, equipped with Hurricane I's, later converting to Spitfire VB's, and this Unit was notable in that many of the aircrew members were American nationals who had joined the R.A.F. as civilians, to fight, as at this time America was not involved in hostilities. These American pilots thus formed what was to be the first Eagle Squadron, and three of the pilots, Pilot Officers E. G. Tobin, V. C. Keough and A. B. Maimsdoff were the only Americans to fight in the Battle of Britain. On America's entry into the War, this Squadron became No. 334 Squadron, 4th Pursuit Group, United States Army Air Corps, still with their Spitfire VB's with American markings and R.A.F. squadron letters X R. The transition date was 29th September, 1942.

The Luftwaffe had not entirely finished with Martlesham Heath, as during the spring of 1941 a small formation of Junkers JU 88's flew inland just after dawn and bombed R.A.F. Wattisham, 12 miles to the west of Ipswich. On their return they flew low off the Heath and scored a direct hit on the road alongside "C" Flight Hangar and its adjacent hard-standings. The blast left the hangar roof-less and parts of the walls were demolished, the shell standing for a number of years, and only recently levelled. Several reports at the time stated that the aircraft involved were captured Bristol Blenheims, but Luftwaffe reports for the period mention only the JU.88's. The levelled site of this hangar still exists, and a dip in Portal Avenue refuses to stay level in spite of repeated levellings. This was the hangar in which the Parachute Section first saw the light of day and was the home of Flight Lieutenant Potter, Corporal East and Leading Aircraftsman "Brainy" Dobbs, who, by the way, has no connection with the local Dobb's Lane.

Through the summer of 1941, the tempo of offensive fighter activity increased, and most afternoons saw the Hurricane II's and Spitfires out on Fighter Sweeps, Fighter-Nights and "Rhubarbs"* as well as the occasional interception. Personnel of the squadrons varied, and many were the tongues, languages and dialects spoken now, Canadian, Rhodesian, Australian, New Zealand, Czechoslovak, Polish, French, Belgian and Norwegian. Another sight of the coming offensive was when No. 607 (F) Squadron arrived with its Hurricane IIb's and training began with the use of 250lb bombs carried under their wings. These became later known as the "Hurri-Bombers", and played a destructive role in subsequent actions.

In support of these operational squadrons at Martlesham, "un-sung" operations were carried out daily, and because of the close proximity of the 'drome to the North Sea, and its position beneath the daylight fighter and bomber flights, and the massive nightly formations of Bomber Command, the Air Sea Rescue squadron in residence was never short of customers. Not as glamorous as the offensive units, nor mentioned in daily bulletins, they nevertheless kept up a 24-hour watch and were ready at a moment's notice to go out in any weather to the aid of their fellow airmen down in the sea.

*Actions over enemy territory in adverse weather conditions.

Supermarine Walrus amphibian used so successfully during the Second World War for Air-Sea Rescue operations. These sturdy aircraft were capable of working in almost impossible flying conditions, and if forced down could make their way home taxiing on the water.

Flight No. 12920

Often flying semi-obsolete aircraft, not always armed, they ranged almost to the limit of their endurance whilst engaged in search and recovery, often returning to base only for sufficient time to re-fuel and pick up other supplies, before setting out again to resume, so often a fruitless search which was never given up until all hope of recovery had run out.

Flying the slow but extremely useful Supermarine Walrus, they flew out low over the Suffolk coastal ranges and the grey North Sea, escorted by a semi-retired Spitfire, or Defiant which could also search outwards from the Walrus and call it in when a dinghy was sighted. Lysanders also took part in these flights, carrying dinghy-packs and smoke-floats under their undercarriage stub-wings to assist in the operations. Occasionally the papers mentioned this work and one such report reads:— "Escorted by four gunboats, an Air Sea Rescue pilot who had saved a bomber crew from the North Sea, taxied his Walrus flying-boat through heavy seas for seven hours in an effort to reach the English coast.

Then, in darkness, his petrol ran out and the plane was taken in tow by one of the gun-boats. An hour later the Walrus had to be abandoned for the night and the rescued crew and the pilot were brought to Lowestoft by the gunboat.

The man who achieved this great feat of endurance was 26 year old Warrant-Officer Thomas Ormiston of Brighton, and today, it is announced that he has been awarded the D.F.C. for 'great courage, fortitude and resource in very trying circumstances'."

In July, Ormiston was sent out to pick up a bomber crew who were drifting in their dinghy 90 miles off Orfordness, Suffolk. He sighted the dinghy and though heavy seas were running, he skilfully brought his aircraft down on the sea and took the crew aboard. But a heavy swell was now running and he was unable to take-off again. He realized his position and the gun-boats were sent out to his aid.

At this time the fear of invasion was still present, and aerodrome defence was boosted by the installation of three hydraulic retractable machine-gun forts in the airfield itself. Each holding two men, in practise they were to raise themselves above the surface and discourage invading German paratroopers. At the time of writing they are still in position but are getting increasingly hard to find, as the vegetation encroaches above their steel tops.

Another major step in the aerodrome works was the conversion of the Station from the old D.C. electric supply, to the A.C. system with Ring Main and Airfield Lighting. Water, too was converted, the aerodrome installations being re-piped and pressures raised.

The official report of enemy damage to the airfield amounted to the following:—

August 15th, 1940.	Considerable damage to hangars and buildings. 30 - 40 High Explosive bombs.
October 27th, 1940.	30 odd bombs dropped (many did not explode). Considerable damage.
March 24th, 1941.	Two large bombs. Two hangars hit.
April 30th, 1941.	Slight damage by three bombs.
May 4th, 1941.	400 windows broken and sewer hit due to two bombs.
May 11th-12th, 1941.	Two bombs made direct hits on hangar and workshops.

The local public houses were home to many of the fighter pilots and ground crews of the R.A.F. and later the U.S.A.A.F., and no doubt the bars could tell remarkable tales of the nightly visits of "the lads". Languages very foreign to these parts were spoken, but in the main, the requirements could usually be made known and supplied. After the day's activities they journeyed, mostly on bicycles, "one, two or three up" to the *Bell* at Kesgrave, the *Red Lion* at Martlesham and to the hostelries at Ipswich and Woodbridge, for relaxation over a drink or two, when the beer was in, a chat and a song. It is recalled that certain orders had to be posted by the Station Commanders of the dangers of riding in large convoys, in the blackout, the leading and tail-end machines only carrying lights. Quite often as the drinks extended, so did the number of passengers a bicycle was never designed to carry, and at the same time, many cycles "changed hands" overnight, often without the previous owner's knowledge. With necessity being the mother of invention, no opportunity was missed to save having to invent!

The usual mobile canteens plied their wares around the "Flights" and Workshops, morning and afternoon, the N.A.A.F.I. and Salvation Army "Red Shield" vans being a welcome sight both winter and summer. Words of praise must be recorded to these wonderful people who, whatever the weather, whatever the conditions, made their rounds bringing whatever there was available for the pilots and men on duty on the far side of the 'drome.

As stated earlier many large houses in the district were requisitioned for Service use, but one that played a great part in the outside life of Martlesham, was the Military Camp Reception Station at Little Bealings Grove with its 72 beds, the home of Captain and Mrs Hervey. This beautiful, picturesque house standing about two miles north of the 'drome, was surrounded by stately parkland which had been visited in earlier days by Robert Louis Stevenson. Captain and Mrs Hervey, soon after the outbreak of war, had, entirely voluntarily, turned this lovely home into a Military Camp Reception Station and opened its doors at Christmas-time, 1939, remaining open until 6 weeks after "D" Day, during which period 7,000 bed patients and 15,000 day patients were cared for. The Grove's proximity to Martlesham Heath made it in many cases the nearest medical unit for the badly wounded. Originally staffed by seven Voluntary Aid Detachment ladies, under the leadership of Mrs Hervey, these were later replaced by a Sergeant and ten men of the Royal Army Medical Corps. Unfortunately the men had only been in the Service for about six weeks, so Mrs Hervey also had the task of training these men in their duties. Some of the first phosphorous burns of the war were treated at this hospital, the first patient arriving the day after Mrs Hervey had received an instruction on the treatment of such burns. Mrs Hervey had to rush into Woodbridge to get the necessary 1% copper solution necessary to treat this case which had arrived in a very bad condition. After treatment and careful nursing he was later discharged fit again. Later an American hospital was opened at Ely, Cambridgeshire, to which the seriously wounded were taken, but many were still treated at The Grove before going on to Ely, or back to duty.

When the American R.A.F. Eagle Squadrons were stationed at Martlesham, the pilots for one reason or another all passed through this little hospital. During the evenings, the comrades of the hospitalized "Eagles" would go over to The Grove to visit their mates, and Mrs Hervey recalls, "They would eat sausage sandwiches and try to cheer up their friends. They were a very gallant group of men".

Aircraft still ran into trouble in the vicinity of the 'drome and on 30th July, 1941, Hurricane Z.3256 of No. 258 Squadron crashed at Seckford Hall, Great Bealings, the pilot being killed. On 30th August, 1941, a Wellington bomber of No. 115 Squadron, coded KO-X, whilst attempting a landing, was intercepted by an enemy aircraft, and crashed near the western perimeter, only one member of the 6-man crew surviving. A Miles Magister landed heavily, but without injury to its crew on the Golf Links at Rushmere on 15th September, 1941, whilst a Hurricane was wrecked when it made a forced landing south of Beacon Hill, Martlesham. A Tiger Moth crashed with fatal results to the two crew at Purdis Farm on 21st October, 1941, on a flight from Hendon, and of course, at this time many of the aircraft setting out from Martlesham did not return and their fate remains unknown.

The death of a former Commanding Officer of the A & A.E.E. was reported on December 13th, 1942, and the obituary shows the esteem in which these men were held.

"The Royal Air Force and the British Aircraft Industry have learned with sincere regret of the death, on December 13th, of Air Vice Marshal A. C. Maund, C.B., C.B.E., D.S.O. It was as Commanding Officer of the Aeroplane and Armament Experimental Establishment, Martlesham Heath, Suffolk, (twice) that "Cissie" Maund, as he was inappropriately called, came in close contact with the Aircraft Industry, to test whose products Martlesham existed. He presided over the Establishment in 1921 and 1934, and was in the habit of pleading with aircraft constructors for better teamwork between themselves, the engine manufacturers, the research establishments and the test-pilots. At one of the Martlesham "Constructors' Dinners" he expressed the view that the 250 m.p.h. which we were then getting from our fighters was nothing like enough, and that we should aim for 300 m.p.h. at least.

Air Vice Marshal Maund combined with his great abilities a personal charm which won him innumerable friends in the Service and in the Industry.

He will be greatly missed."

Standing on the north side of the Ipswich-Woodbridge Road (A.12) almost on the boundary of the aerodrome, a pleasant stopping place for refreshment was built during 1936 for Miss F. E. Jermyn. The site had fine old beech trees to the east and across the main road to the south and these Miss Jermyn purchased to preserve the outlook. Flanking the site to the west was a plantation of dark pines. Although now almost surrounded by a new housing estate and a filling station, the building still stands crowned by the shining black tiles from which it derives its name. Travellers stop for tea and refreshment and doubtless very few know, probably most are unaware of the many famous airmen who had taken tea and rest in these rooms. The peaceful atmosphere of the place is further enhanced by the white doves which flutter down from the roof to pick up crumbs from the green lawns which encompass the wide-windowed tea-rooms.

After the outbreak of hostilities, the tourist trade naturally declined, but this was replaced by visitors from the adjoining airfield seeking something a little different from that which the Mess and the N.A.A.F.I. could provide. "Customers" of this period were pleasantly surprised, to find that, in spite of rationing, Miss Jermyn and her staff could provide such tempting and varied meals. Even at very short notice, such as a convoy of lorries arriving filled with hungry and thirsty troops, *Black Tiles* not only coped but did so unusually well.

About this time a Visitors' Book was started in a large ruled exercise book. Over the years this grew to considerable proportions, and eventually contained hundreds of signatures of airmen, soldiers, sailors, the Women's Services counterparts, and the auxiliary services.

When a new squadron arrived at the aerodrome, they would very soon make their way over to *Black Tiles*, and see "The Book", which is now considered to be one of the best collections of pilots' signatures in this country. The cosmopolitan nature of this collection is reflected in the names of serving personnel from all the four corners of the earth and it is the author's great pleasure to be able to reproduce some of these names on the following pages. The sheets were not limited to signatures alone, as Squadron Crests, cartoons, rhymes and general "chit-chat" also appeared. At the airfield, at one stage, the enthusiastic Security Officer of one of the squadrons decided that this book could be of use to the enemy and confiscated several pages of what he considered to be "offending material". These were later returned and the book is in the proud possession of Miss Jermyn who still lives in the district, enjoying a well-deserved retirement surrounded by a beautiful garden and house full of flowers.

Drawing of *Black Tiles.* 10th April, 1942. 71 Eagle Squadron.   *Leading Aircraftsman Smith*

The "Black Tiles".

L.A.C. LES. SMITH. 10.4.42.

Black Tiles is still very much the same as it was during those hectic days, and although the aerodrome is rapidly changing, it is still possible to sit out on the green lawns, look across the road, and in the memory hear the roar of Merlins running up, or the cough of a large radial engine bursting into life, or even the crackle of a throttled engine in a Spitfire or Hurricane coming into land across the road.

The following extracts are a few selected to give the reader an idea of the varied matter in the book. Pride of place is taken by this one:—

WHEN HIS MAJESTY KING GEORGE VI VISITED MARTLESHAM HEATH ON 3rd AUGUST, 1937, BLACK TILES SUPPLIED THE CAKES FOR TEA IN THE OFFICERS' MESS.

No. 132 Squadron.   CAVE LEOPARDUM.

> Two care-free Corporals here did dine,
> They craved not women, song nor wine,
> Each day a coffee they would order,
> And talk of days across the Border.
> All over Scotland they had dined,
> Many a book like this had signed.
> Their thirst had quenched in Orkney's Isles,
> But never as well as in Black Tiles.
> Although their stay here may be brief,
> Happy are they at Martlesham Heath.
> They hope that you've enjoyed it too
> As have the lads of one three two.
> Now that's our tale, we've told it well,
> From Corporals Stephenson and V. H. Bell.

An American Officer wrote:—

"When I think of England I shall think of tea, and all that it means, and when I think of tea, I'll think of Black Tiles. Someday I'll come back to England for tea at Black Tiles."

Its fame even reached the daily papers who commented:—

"A tea-house near one of the Eastern Counties aerodromes has become a cheerful place of call for airmen and airwomen. There is a big demand for coffee and some of the customers who are not natives of this country describe it as the best they have had since they came here. There are numbers of these modern young men, it appears, who honestly prefer soft drinks in the surroundings that the tea-rooms offer to the local beers and amenities that go with it. They write their names and home towns in the Visitors' Book and one bunch of them compiled a glossary of up-to-date airmen's slang which runs into pages."

To Black Tiles,   Jimmie Colvin, R.C.A.F.
   Thank you for everything,   Port Arthur, Canada.
     Eating is my favourite sport.

From the crews of three armoured cars who stopped here 10.4.42 and had the best cup of coffee since in England. One thing wrong, however, the convoy only partly got through with the sugar.

     Bon Chance,
       Members of the Belgian Armoured Car Squadron. England.

Crew of visiting Lockheed Hudson aircraft.

Charles L. Mood.	Pilot.	
Richard P. Spelling.	Observer.	
Steve Randell.	Air Gunner.	Sydney, Australia.
Frank Bradley.	Air Gunner.	Sydney, Australia.

No. 611 Squadron.

  Ten 611 boys drogue shooting fine,
    "Mac" hit the "Lizzie", then there were nine.
  Nine 611 boys all had a date,
    One with an Ipswich girl, then there were eight.
  Eight 611 boys, gazing up to Heaven,
    Black Tiles, white dove, then there were seven.
  Seven 611 boys all full of tricks,
    One went sailing, then there were six.
  Six 611 boys, C.O, said "I'll drive"
    Went in the Station Wagon, then there were five.
  Five 611 boys, all very poor,
    "Princey" cashed a cheque, then there were four.
  Four 611 boys out on a spree,
    River's deep at Woodbridge, then there were three.
  Three 611 boys, flying in the blue,
    Forgot the balloons at Harwich, then there were two.
  Two 611 boys each a 12-bore gun,
    One forgot the safety catch, then there was one.
  One 611 boy left to write this line,
    Had coffee at Black Tiles,
     AND JOINED THE OTHER NINE.

Among those who signed the book was John G. DuFour, an airline pilot, last heard of in California. He joined the Seaforth Highlanders, later appeared as a Pilot Officer with No. 71 (F) Eagle Squadron with whom he shot down a Nazi plane and claimed a probable. Later he transferred to the Old 8th U.S.A.A.F., and became Major DuFour A.M., three Oak Leaf Clusters, D.F.C., veteran of 115 missions over enemy territory.

High among the Royal Air Force pilots who signed were Air Commodore Donald E. Kingaby, D.S.O., D.F.M., and two bars of No. 122 (F) Bombay Squadron who once shot down four Messerschmitt 109's in one day and earned himself the title of "The 109 Specialist". Another junior officer to sign was "Pilot Officer Ian Smith", then serving with No. 65 (East India) Squadron, but now Prime Minister of Rhodesia.

Included are several pleasant odes to one Gwen, a waitress who resided in Woodbridge, and apparently often missed her bus home in order to provide refreshment for the pilots returning from late afternoon sweeps over France and the Low Countries.

Fate still visited the Heath and from time to time aircraft crashed with fatal results, one such being a Spitfire on 31.7.1942 at the Grange Farm near the perimeter of the 'drome. The machine belonged to the 1561 Met Flight of No. 416 Squadron, whilst on 19.9.1942, two Spitfire Vb's of No. 165 Squadron collided in mid-air over Home Farm, Martlesham and both the pilots were killed. A little later on 20.3.1943, a Mosquito Mk.IV, coded ES-A of No. 167 Squadron crashed in Foxburrow Wood, Brightwell, both the crew being killed, and a Hurricane based at Martlesham, and used for secret trials, crashed in the Orford Battle Area on 14.5.1943 and Group Captain Penderell was killed.

Martlesham Heath had now swung over to the offensive, with the squadrons based there ranging over the Continent in massed daylight sweeps. An unusual event for Martlesham occurred when a new fighter squadron, No. 182, was formed there. Equipped initially with Hawker Hurricanes as fighter-bombers, and then superseded by the new and more harder-hitting Hawker Typhoon fighter-bomber. This was the first of many squadrons to use Martlesham as a base for these operations, and many stayed there until the invasion of Europe, to take up residence once again on the Continent. Working in close co-operation with the fighter units was No. 1488 Fighter Gunnery Flight, its yellow and black diagonal striped Westland Lysanders towing sleeve and flag targets for fighter firing practice, whilst on the ground No. 2735 Squadron, Royal Air Force Regiment provided aerodrome defence.

Hawker Hurricane Mk.I. This version had 12 guns.   *Hawker Siddeley Aviation*

Hawker Typhoon Mk. 1A with early cockpit canopy.

Hawker Siddeley Aviation

The Air Sea Rescue Units mentioned previously still carried on their missions over the North Sea, when on the 22nd June, 1943, "A" Flight of No. 278 (A.S.R.) Squadron with their Walruses, in conjunction with units of the U.S.A.F., picked up 8 American and 7 R.A.F. aircrew from dinghies off the Suffolk coast.

Although one could not loiter near the 'drome during these troubled days, one enthusiastic spotter kept a remarkable diary, and a few extracts from it makes most interesting reading, showing several "rarer types" at the Heath.

January 3rd, 1942.	Douglas Havoc with searchlight in nose. Pancaked Avro Manchester with twin fins. Spitfire took-off with drogue which caught in trees on take-off. Aircraft returned to 'drome.
January 10th, 1942.	Junkers JU.88 A-1 flew low over 'drome without disturbance.
July 25th, 1942.	Boulton-Paul Defiant TT.1 DR.883 Target Tug with three drogue housings and inverted windmill.* Black and yellow diagonal stripes under wings and fuselage. Black tailplane, yellow elevators. Handley Page Hampden Mk.1 with yellow P in circle on fuselage. Lockheed Hudson coded C-OS. No guns. Avro Manchester without engines, leading edge hinged up. Handley-Page Halifax II G-ZA (No. 10 Squadron) under repair. Vickers Wellington Mk.1C Z.8754, R-SR being repaired. Spitfire Vb's dispersed around 'drome, D N (416 Squadron), Y O (401 Squadron), V Y (85 Squadron). Hawker Henley III drogue towing. Spitfire Vb XR-I (No. 71

*A windmill type winch said to be inverted when sails or flares placed in a position giving minimum resistance to the airstream and therefore not in operation.

	Squadron) on dispersal. Two Lysander II's target tugs lettered K and J. Two Walrus II's and five Hampdens on dispersal.
July 31st, 1942.	D.H. Tiger Moth II T.6105 flying circuits and bumps. 26 Spitfire Vb's (R M) arrived.
August 7th, 1942.	Spitfire IX's of No. 402 Squadron (A E) with 4-bladed airscrews. Walrus with squadron letters B A (No. 278 Squadron), Defiant II tug DR 915. Albemarle I landed.
September 8th, 1942.	Halifax II L D - W on dispersal. Manchester Z N - U with old type roundels in hangar. Wellington IC Q T - R being serviced.
September 9th, 1942.	Walrus crashed-landed in centre of 'drome. Starboard undercarriage leg broken-off and wing tip float missing. Boston III, Fortress IIA on dispersal as well as Mustang. Defiants, Spitfires, Magister, Tiger Moth and Lysanders and an Airspeed Oxford.
September 13th, 1942.	Unusual aircraft. Miles Magister complete with wheel spats.
September 27th, 1942.	Unusual Hurricane IIB with black and yellow bands on the top half of the fuselage aft of the cockpit. Lettered A X - P. Master III took-off. Boston III A - QM on dispersal. Henley III flying around with drogue and landed, A L - D. Typhoon IB U S - F (No. 56 Squadron) took-off and landed several times. New transparency aft

The Hawker Henley, although designed as a light bomber became a Target Tug and many served with the fighter squadrons on the Heath. *Hawker Siddeley Aviation*

of cockpit hood. Spitfire X R - X (No. 71 Squadron) with U.S. Markings.

October 2nd, 1942.	Four Handley-Page Harrows and 12 Spitfires landed. 32 Spitfires took-off, 9 Vb's D B (411 Squadron), 12 Vb's D W (610 Squadron), 11 Vb's O U (455 Squadron). Lockheed Lightning (RAF Atlanta) in hangar. Typhoon IB crashed in gun-pit, tailplane broken off. Halifax II BB 198 "N" in front of hangar.
October 11th, 1942.	Spitfire Vb F F - F (132 Squadron) took off with cannon barrels painted red, white and blue. Douglas DC.3 with all-green colouring and U.S.A.A.C. markings. Fairchild Argus landed and took-off.
October 25th, 1942.	Spitfire IX's of No. 306 Squadron, U Z with Polish crests on noses, complete bubble canopies, 12 exhausts, long thin cannon and much longer noses than usual. Some with long-range tanks. Typhoon IA R.8979 X M - D and R.7653 U S - U (No. 182 Squadron). Typhoon IB's X M - S EJ.952 and X M - P with 2 cannons, 6 machine guns and a bomb under each wing.
November 1st, 1942.	Manchester I E N - V on dispersal with motors missing. Blister hangars now erected on N.E. corner of 'drome with No. 182 painted on them. 14 American Spitfires on dispersal (No. 121 Squadron) A V - A. V.M.P.X.H.G.T. W.F.R.Z.J.G.
November 8th, 1942.	Typhoons now have their noses painted white and 8 black stripes under the wings. Lancaster B.I W.4126 K M - G on dispersal.
November 15th, 1942.	Hawker Henley III L.3374 with fabric covered main-planes on dispersal. Typhoon X M - L (182) lying upside down. Spitfires Vb's D N - W. R and U all smashed-up, W being the worst. No engine or rudder and only part of the wing. The fuselage lying sideways whilst 10 yards away the centre section with wheels attached lay. D N - R has starboard leading edge missing and its engine underneath. D N - U also had the motor missing. Spitfire Vb D N - P had red maple leaf crest on nose as well as name "City of Oshawa" — Blondie V.
November 22nd, 1942.	Avro C.30a autogiro landed. Typhoon IB X M - L R.7677 started up on its own internal batteries.
January 13th, 1943.	Halifax II with new rear fuselage wheeled out of hangar, W.1165 B - T L. Mitchell with R.A.F. Markings. Hornet Moth landed. Miles Martinet TT I HP.264 landed with

dinghy under one wing and 4 smoke floats under the other. All-silver Spitfire on trestle in hangar.

February 14th, 1943.	Four Hawker Henleys on dispersal L.3318, L.3358, L.3371 and L.3382 Thunderbolt of the U.S.A.A.C. No. 12607 near hangar.
February 27th, 1943.	Airspeed Oxford I V.3890 with night camouflage and gun in turret.
March 7th, 1943.	American Spitfire Vb Squadron in residence. M D No. 336 USAAC. Whitley I.K.7209 with radial engines near hangar. Stinson Reliant landed. American flag flying over one hut.
March 14th, 1943.	Three Martin Marauders circled 'drome with bomb-doors open. Tiger Moth II with U.S.A.A.C. markings circled and landed.
June 20th, 1943.	Typhoon T P - U (198 Squadron) raced across the airfield at about 50 ft going very fast. Over Bealings Station direction it banked steeply and spun in. A plume of black smoke went up, but on arrival the fire was out, and the aircraft completely scattered around the scene of impact, as well as many 20 mm cannon shells. Hampden P.1224 with yellow P in circle and cotton-reel tail wheel. Hornet Moth W.9384 G-AEZY in hangar.

It will be seen from the foregoing that Martlesham, placed in close proximity to the East Coast, was host to many visiting aircraft, in some cases it was the nearest place for crippled aircraft to make for after a nerve-racking homeward flight over the North Sea. After 1943 when the "crash 'drome" at Sutton Heath on the other side of the River Deben, was constructed, these crippled aircraft then made for the new extra-length runway which had been made for this purpose.

Although a fighter station during the Second World War, Martlesham had more than its share of bomber visitors like the Avro Lancaster shown. *Hawker Siddeley Aviation*

GB 10 145 bc (2. Ang.)

Nur für den Dienstgebrauch!

Bild Nr. 3141 Z 10

Aufnahme vom 31. 8. 43

Martlesham Heath
Flugplatz

Länge (ostw. Greenw.): 1° 16′ 30″   Nördl. Breite: 52° 03′ 30″
Zielhöhe über NN: 27 m

Lfl. Kdo. 3 November 1943

Karte 1 : 100 000

GB/E 25

Maßstab 1 : 17 500

1. 2 Startbahnen, je etwa 1600 m lang
2. Rollbahnen
3. Splitterschutzwälle für Flugzeuge
4. 6 Flugzeughallen   etwa   14 600 qm
5. 6 Flugzeugboxen   etwa   2 000 qm

6. 3 Fahrzeughallen   etwa   1 700 qm
7. Unterkünfte und Nebengebäude   etwa   9 000 qm
8. Munitionslager, 20 Füll- u. Munihäuser   etwa   900 qm

Bebaute Fläche   etwa   28 200 qm
Gleisanschluß nicht vorhanden

49 27 Funkstation mit Sonderanlage Jpswich

German Target Map photograph taken November 1943 which clearly shows the runways and perimeter tracks. The anti-aircraft gun (flak) sites are also positioned and noted for pilot's information.
Christopher Elliott

CHAPTER FOUR

Victory in Sight. 1943—1946

DURING the last quarter of 1943 Martlesham Heath became part of another Allied Air Force when units of the United States Army Air Force took up residence. These were wholly U.S.A.A.F. Units and are not to be confused with the Royal Air Force Eagle Squadrons previously stationed at Martlesham and later absorbed into the American Forces in Europe.

Just before their arrival bull-dozers, scrapers and tractors descended on the airfield in preparation for the construction of the runways. Before this, the surface of the aerodrome had been considered adequate for the aircraft using it, but when the Americans decided to come, runways were deemed necessary for the heavier aircraft involved.

During May 1941, a small experimental strip had been laid on the end of the marked-out grass runway, in order to test the possibility of such construction. Accordingly, after the evaluated trial period, it was decided to go-ahead with the laying-down of two runways. Writing on this subject the then Station Officer Section Engineer remarks:—

"The runways were a rather unofficial exercise by the Commanding Officer and myself. The main one over the sand-dunes towards the pre-war bomb dump was done by a Royal Engineers Mechanical Plant Training Company, as a training exercise, and at one time it was covered with pierced steel planking, but later when the Americans arrived, they laid bitumen sand mix, stabilized soil, with materials supplied by us, and machines by the Americans."

As the experimental strip had stood up well to the use by Fighter squadrons for two years, plus usage by heavy re-fuelling vehicles, a new specification was drawn up for completing the full works. No maintenance work had been carried out on the experimental strip and it was thought that its life would be preserved by tar-spraying every two years. The two runways were the major ones constructed on this principle and their construction is therefore unique.

Stripping.   Only the vegetation and top 1" to 2" of soil is stripped.

Foundation.   The next 3" to 4" of soil is then taken out for use on the foundation coat. This is mixed with 3% by weight of soil stabilizing oil and relaid on the foundation, which has been rolled to correct level. It

No. 2 Runway looking west toward Dobb's Lane from the Station Headquarters. The runway was 25 years old when photographed but shows the well preserved state at that time.

A. J. R. Frost

is important that the moisture content of this layer should be controlled and 10% to 14% moisture has been found to be best for the Martlesham soil. On one section imported clay was mixed with the soil in proportion of 5% and this was found to be an advantage.

Prime Coat. After rolling with a 2½ ton roller the foundation coat is sprayed with crude tar (from Ipswich Gas Works) at the rate of 6 to 7 square yards to the gallon.

Top Coat. This should consist of 1½" consolidated thickness of wet-sand mix using local sand from a burrow pit to the following formula:—

> 100 parts by weight moist sand.
> 2 parts by weight hydrated lime.
> 5 parts by weight Special Sand Oil.

Spray Coat. After one month the top coat should be sprayed with No. 1 tar at 5 to 7 square yards to the gallon, using coarse sand and ashes for binding.

The experimental work at Martlesham Heath was carried out under the advice of Mr W. L. Campbell, Research Engineer to the Asiatic Petroleum Company.

The aerodrome was not idle during the change-over period as even when the U.S.A.A.F. were in residence, the R.A.F. squadrons still operated from the aerodrome, mainly in the fighter-bomber role with heavy daylight strikes over France and the Low Countries in preparation for the coming invasion of Europe.

The three American squadrons which appeared were the 359th, 360th and 361st Fighter Squadrons, of the 356th Wing of the 8th Air Force, Europe, and they had arrived in England during the summer of 1943; their first residence in the U.K. was at Coxhill, in North Lincolnshire, where they equipped and received their aircraft. These were the large, heavily armed radial-engined P.47 Republic Aviation Thunderbolts, many of which had flown to England by the Northern Route, refuelling in Newfoundland, Greenland, Iceland and Scotland en route. After air exercises and familiarisation procedures, they moved south to Martlesham Heath on 5th October, 1943, as an operational unit and were firstly employed on long-range escort duties with the B.17's and B.24's on their almost daily daylight bombing raids on Germany and the Occupied Countries of Europe. These large fighter machines continued in this role until the spring of 1944, when the pattern changed somewhat and they mounted their own operations, bombing and strafing missions against U-Boat installations, airfields, radar sites, flak-towers, railways and communication systems. For the next few months they ranged over the Low Countries, roaring out of Martlesham to the thunder of their large Pratt and Whitney radial engines, bombs slung beneath their wings, to return some time later, often crippled and limping, smoke trailing, some to "belly-land" on the heather alongside the newly-constructed runways, or fortunately, only occasionally, to dissolve in a welter of tearing metal with the fateful cloud of oily-black smoke, tinged with blood-red flame.

Other visitors arrived, heralding the new signs of the times, and on 16th November, 1943, a Boeing Fortress, No. 230826 from the 385th Bombardment

Republic Aircraft P.47D Thunderbolt No. 276594 of the 361st Fighter Squadron at Martlesham Heath, late 1943. Named "Zombie" this aircraft had a locally designed and made cockpit canopy. Note the bombed hangar roof in the background.   *U.S.A.F.*

Group at Great Ashfield in Suffolk, force-landed, after being badly damaged in combat. Six of her crew-members had baled-out over Coddenham and Little Stonham in Suffolk, and the pilot remained alone to bring the large aircraft in at Martlesham, where he was not too badly injured in the eventful landing. Also during 1st December, 1943, another B.17F Fortress, No. 23562 of the 533rd Bombardment Group at Ridgewell in Essex, arrived badly shot-up over Martlesham, and after six of her crew had baled-out successfully, the pilot brought it in for a wheels-up landing.

The diarist also noted these changes and recorded them:—

October 10th, 1943.	The Americans appear to be taking over the 'drome completely, but a few R.A.F. personnel are still around. Work is going ahead on the runways. About 40 P.47D Thunderbolts are dispersed around together with the Hawker Typhoons of U S Squadron (No. 56) and American Spitfire IX's.
October 20th, 1943.	Boeing Fortress II fired 2 red lights when North of 'drome and then two more when South before landing. At 4-30 p.m. the A.S.R. Walrus took off and headed East followed by the 3 A.S.R. Spitfires. In batches of 4's and 3's about 60 Thunderbolts landed. A Consolidated Catalina with radio location aerials flew low across the 'drome, Fortress II outside hangar No. 230773 J - D P. Blue fin white triangle, blue A in centre of triangle.
December 30th, 1943.	45 P.47D Thunderbolts of OC, PI and QI Squadrons (359th, 360th and 361st) landed, the majority being gaily painted with colourful engine cowlings. Fortress B.17E landed, no turrets or guns, no squadron letters. U.S. Army under wings. No. 18030.
December 31st, 1943.	Cessna Bobcat landed CF 826. Marauder landed very fast using all the runway. Marauder then took-off using all the runway and only narrowly missed a lorry on the road. Walrus took-off and flew back and forth across the airfield touching the hull bottom on the grass.
February 6th, 1944.	Supermarine Sea Otter of A.S.R. landed. JM.745, fitted with radio location aerials. Lysander V.9545 (IIIA) B A - C, Hurricane I, L.1747, Spitfire II A.S.R. P.8179, R.H. Tiger Moth II DF.209, Hurricane I, Typhoon I, Typhoon IB EF.299, Oxford II AB.752 all on dispersal.
March 1st, 1944.	Two Typhoon IB's with long range tanks and new

	cockpit hoods. JX-O JP.685, JX-N JP.728. P.47D's with long range tanks. OC-N 28002, OC-F 22488. QI-W 267129, OC-Q 276416, OC-M 274689. Lockheed Hudson transport landed, American markings, glazed nose, no serials, R.A.F. No. AM.674.
March 19th, 1944.	Crashed Avro Lancaster II J I - A DS.820 (No. 514 Squadron) outside "C" Flight hangar. Pilot thought he was at Sutton Heath crashdrome and landed without flaps. Ran out of runway, pulled up too quickly and undercarriage collapsed. Engines all damaged and wooden propeller blades broken off. Hawker Tempest V JN 744 on 'drome. P.38J landed S E - 0 with large long range tanks. Famous B.24J named "PALLAS ATHENE" G.I. JANE (Goddess of Wisdom and Victory worn on U.S. W.A.C. uniforms) landed. Douglas Skytrain No. 2100749 landed and went to Watch Office.
March 26th, 1944.	Fairchild VC.61A Forwarder No. 14607 with damaged undercarriage near hangar. Fairchild Argus I brought in by young lady ferry-pilot. All-silver P.47D with black stripes. Three American Tiger Moths landed — one ran into fuel bowser and damaged wing-tips.
May 27th, 1944.	First modified P.47D's with bubble canopy. P I Squadron (360th FS).
May 28th, 1944.	50 P.47D's lined up on side of runway, each side, and then took-off in pairs and formed into fours when airborne. One of the first pairs crashed into the barbed wire. Another nearly collided with another aircraft, stalled, crashed into the wire, overturned and caught fire which was quickly put out. Pilot killed.
May 29th, 1944.	Lockheed 12A landed and went to dispersal, P.47D's took-off in sections of 4 and did steep climbing turns at the end of the runway leaving white vapour trails from each wingtip. Auster III landed with Polish insignia. Spitfire F.VIII JK 286 in desert colours of light and dark sand and azure blue underneath. Vokes air filter under nose.
June 6th, 1944.	A.S.R. Unit now equipped with 4 Avro Ansons with turrets, 2 clipped wing Spitfire Vb's, one ordinary Vb and 2 Walrus II's. Short Stirling circled 'drome with starboard undercarriage down. Walrus crashed on top of salvage dump after developing engine trouble. Lockheed FVB landed. P.47D crashed near Waldringfield.

From the foregoing it will be noted the tremendous activity which went on almost all the time during these hectic years, both on the offensive side of the business, and also the Air Sea Rescue side, as with more and more aircraft operating over the North Sea, their services were called upon almost daily. American aircraft worked in close co-operation with the R.A.F. Units, and the following incident illustrates this factor. On 29th June, 1944, a B.17 Fortress from the 390th Group at nearby Parham airfield ditched in the North Sea. After rescue by an Air Sea Rescue High-Speed Launch of the R.A.F., they were shot-up by a German fighter-bomber and the launch set on fire. Once again they took to their dinghies together with the survivors of the launch-crew, some of whom needed urgent medical aid. Two American doctors were flown from Martlesham Heath in a Walrus amphibian, which located the dinghies and the doctors attended to their immediate needs. Around this period the U.S.A.A.F. established A.S.R. Units in East Anglia, and together with the R.A.F. many gallant operations in the rescue field were carried out.

During November 1944, the three American squadrons at Martlesham re-equipped with the sleeker in-line engined North American P.51D Mustang long range fighter, and this aircraft somewhat changed the role of the Wing. In its early days, this machine had served with the R.A.F. in the Army-Co-operation role, not being quite up to the standard required of a first-line interceptor. Realizing its potentialities the R.A.F. had drawn up a re-design which was taken in hand by its American manufacturer including the substitution of the American Allison engine for a Rolls-Royce Merlin, built under licence in the U.S.A. by the Packard Motor Corporation, and thereafter known as the "Packard Merlin." This new design bore no resemblance to its predecessor, and was immediately ordered into quantity production in the U.S.A. Indeed to this very day, many of the smaller Air Forces around the world are still using this aircraft in one or the other of its many modified types.

Missions of greater range were now undertaken, Central Europe being reached for the extended bomber strikes, and as the bomber types had also been modified to carry more fuel for greater ranges, they were hitting new targets further from their bases. The need therefore arose for longer range fighter escorts, and it was in this role that the Mustangs from Martlesham found their daily work, providing protection for the B.17's and B.24's based in close proximity all over East Anglia.

At the end of hostilities in Europe, the Group returned to the United States where they were disbanded, later to be reformed as a reconnaissance unit during 1951 and then subsequently as a transport squadron within the U.S.A.F. Military Transport Group.

North American P.51D Mustang No. 472435 flown by the Squadron Commander, Colonel Philip E. Turkey Jnr., 360th Fighter Squadron. Colouring—red nose with blue diamonds, red rudder. In the middle foreground is the newly constructed perimeter track with flags indicating soft ground. *U.S.A.F.*

The diary recorded the new aircraft and some of their activities.

January, 1945.	Two runways with flares. Aircraft on dispersal.
	6 — Spitfire Vb's with clipped wings.
	6 — Supermarine Walrus II's.
	4 — Vickers Warwick A.S.R.'s.
	4 — Avro Anson A.S.R.'s.
	6 — Republic P.47D Thunderbolts.
	50 — North American P.51D Mustangs.
	1 — North American Texan.
	1 — Noordryn Norseman.
March 25th, 1945.	Fortress B.17G came straight in with both port motors stopped. Ambulance raced out alongside taxiing aircraft.
March 30th, 1945.	American Squadron markings and aircraft serial numbers. 360th coded P I. Red nose with blue diamonds. Red

rudder. P I - H 222780. P I - L 414754. P I - T 47235. P I - G 415114. Aircraft named:— "Dotty" "Starduster" "Lady Doris" "Raggedy Ann" "Margie Darling".

361st coded Q I. Plain all red nose. Blue rudder. Q I - C 463251 "Ava Honey" Q I - F 2 colour spinner. Q I - H "Look Jeff" Q I - T 415152 "Jersey Jerk" Q I - N "Jackie".

359th coded O C. O C - G 415183 "Never Happens". Red nose and decking and cockpit edge. Yellow spinner and rudder. O C - F "Swamp Fox" O C - E 415271.

Some of the known operations of the Group composed of:—

First bomber duties 23rd January, 1944. (P.47D's)

November 29th, 1943. Bomber escort towards Bremen led by Lieutenant Colonel Einar Malmstrom. From this mission 5 aircraft failed to return. (P.47D's)

January 16th, 1945. Severe weather conditions caused casualties among the Group aircraft, 2 P.51D's crashing on the airfield, one spun into a field on the perimeter and one was lost on the way home from the target.

May 22nd, 1944. Bridges strafed in the vicinity of Hassell, Belgium (P.47D's).

June 16th, 1944. The French railway system came under mass strafing attacks and the Group took a leading part in this operation. (P.47D's)

November 25th, 1944. Escorted some 50 P.47D's of other Groups on a large scale attack on the French airfields in the St. Omer district. (P.47D's)

August 15th, 1944. Mass strafing attacks in the vicinity of Laval, France, but doubtful navigation brought some of the aircraft a distance from their target and they unfortunately bombed friendly positions and one aircraft was shot down by our own anti-aircraft fire. (P.47D's)

September 17th, 1944. During the Arnhem Campaign they carried out extended bombing and strafing in order to neutralize enemy gun positions which were pinning down Allied troops in the Rhine Bridges sector. For these missions they received a "Distinguished Unit Citation".

March 14th, 1945. Low level strikes on the Biefeld district of North West Germany.

May 7th, 1945. The last mission, escorting B.17's on a propaganda leaflet dropping flight over Germany.

Returned and disbanded in the U.S.A. June 1945.

At the final reckoning the records show that the Wing destroyed 201 enemy aircraft, were credited with 23 probables and damaged a further 185. This Group sets a record which still exists as one of the best during the Second World War for the U.S.A.F., in that, after conversion to P.51D's, during their first mission, it destroyed 23 enemy aircraft in the air and 5 on the ground.

At the same time this Group is also known for being at the receiving end of plenty of bad luck as they headed the list of aircraft lost in proportion to enemy aircraft destroyed, and also the lowest total of enemy aircraft accounted for in the 8th Air Force Groups — 276½ aircraft.

The "ace" of the Group was Major Don Strait of the 361st Fighter Squadron, who in his mount "Jersey Jerk", P.51D Serial No. 44-13152, coded Q I - T was credited with 13½ enemy aircraft destroyed.

Shortly after "D Day," the little hospital at Little Bealings Grove, run by Mrs Hervey, closed and Mrs Hervey went along to work at Martlesham as Librarian and an extra Liaison Officer. She recalls sitting in her office one day and looked up to see a P.51 Mustang coming through the trees. It had developed engine trouble and was coming in for a crash landing. Leaving its wings in the trees, it skidded to a halt, the engine coming away from its mountings. The pilot, Colonel Philip E. Turkey Junior, Commanding Officer of the 356th Fighter Group, climbed out, staggered over to one side and collapsed in a heap. Released from hospital the next day, he was airborne in the afternoon.

After "V E Day" the aerodrome was thrown open to the public by the U.S.A.F., for them to see the aircraft, talk with the pilots and ground crews and generally see how the Station was run. Those who visited on the last Empire Air Day must have seen a tremendous change with the runways, the new Watch Office on the western side of the airfield and the blister hangars and blast-bays dotted around the perimeter. Thousands of people turned up for this open day and long queues stretched back from the two visiting B.17 Fortresses, people being eager to see inside one of the machines of which they had seen so many in the air. The hand-out read as follows:—

Open Day at Martlesham Heath, 1st August, 1945. Pilots show interested crowds over their aircraft, and at the same time pose for eager photographers.   *A. R. Fairweather*

As Commanding Officer of the 356th Fighter Group and of this Station, which the R.A.F. turned over to us in November, 1943, I am very happy at last to be able to invite you here, on Air Force Day, to see what we look like as an American Air Force Installation.

American Air Forces all around the world are today celebrating the thirty-eighth (38th) anniversary of the founding of the Air Force, and interesting information about our history is to be found attached to this leaflet.

The program we have arranged for you this afternoon provides that you shall be taken in our trucks from the gate around the airdrome so you can see, generally, what there is to be seen. This trip will finish at the 359th Squadron Hangar, near the center of the airdrome and the trucks and pilot-escorts will return to the gate to pick up another party of visitors.

Inside the hangar you will find displays of equipment and repair services, all of which will be explained to you by competent personnel in charge. There will also be several large panels showing operations history of this Fighter Wing.

Parked near the hangar will be several airplanes with platforms arranged for you to ascend for a close view.

In the area across the street are the propeller repair shop, and the machine shop which you are invited to visit. When you have finished the conducted tour, please feel free to wander around and visit what interests you. Members of the Military Police, all my Officers and soldiers will be glad to assist you. While the combat half of my command is the 356th Fighter Group, the 447th Air Service Group, under Lieutenant Colonel Austin L. Sands, my Station Executive, is the Unit which maintains and repairs the airplanes and equipment.

Headquarters.	Philip E. Turkey Jr.
A.A.F. Station. 369.	Colonel Air Corps.
A.P.O. 557.	Commanding.

Soon after the cessation of hostilities, Mrs Hervey's husband, Captain Eric Hervey, was instrumental in the erection of a memorial at the former saluting base at Martlesham dedicated to the memory of those pilots and aircrew who took off on their last mission from this base. It was entirely paid for by local subscription, people from the surrounding villages all giving their share, which was limited to a few pence each. This memorial, still standing, is unique in that it was the first memorial to be erected in Europe commemorating the American dead.

At the same time Captain Hervey was also producing a handsome, hand-written, leather bound book, produced by the Golden Cockerel Press in royal blue leather with gold tooling, in which he wrote all the names and addresses and

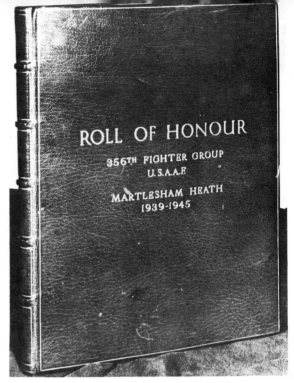

Left. The Martlesham U.S.A.F. Memorial, the first erected in Europe to commemorate the American dead. Seventy-two airmen are named on the plate as having lost their lives whilst flying from Martlesham. *A. J. R. Frost.*   Right. The Martlesham Heath Memorial Book made by Captain E. Harvey to record the names and circumstances of their loss of the pilots from Martlesham Heath. This now resides in the Library of Congress, Washington, D.C., U.S.A. *U.S.A.F.*

available data relating to each man missing from the base. The book, originally intended to rest in Martlesham Church, was presented to the Group and then later received by General Carl Spaatz, and now rests for all time in the Library of Congress, Washington, D.C., U.S.A. Captain Hervey, because of his close association with the 356th (the Herveys kept continual open house for the pilots throughout the war), maintained a record of the men lost in combat. To the parents, and loved ones in the United States, he sent a letter of condolence, and later, a photograph of the Martlesham memorial, upon which is engraved the names of the deceased. To each went an invitation which said in effect, our house is open to you if you should come to England and we would be pleased to show you the base at which your son served.

Since the War, a great many people have come to The Grove. "There would be a telephone call," Mrs Hervey remembers, "and some-one would say, 'We're at Woodbridge Station, but now what do we do?'" They would spend a week-end, going to Martlesham to view the memorial, to one of the big houses in the district in which the pilots were billeted and then go back to their homes in the United States. Mrs Hervey still receives mail from about 20 families in the U.S.A.

At a spot on the north side of the A.12 main road, about one mile towards Ipswich, a road-way leads down to a reed-surrounded small lake, locally known as "The Sinks", but nowadays a large rubbish disposal unit for Ipswich. Besides this lake stands a small pump-house built pre-war by the late Mr W. O. Jolly of Grange Farm as a source of water for his farm and greenhouses. During the American stay at Martlesham, an ex-commercial artist painted on the pump-house wall for Mrs L. Rope, the widow of Squadron Leader Rope, tragically killed in the R.101. airship disaster, a striking mural of Saint Francis of Assisi. Life-size, as the building was approached down a gentle slope, the illusion was complete, breath-taking, the brown habit of the Saint merging in with the waving reeds, and his outstretched hands calling the birds, which the artist had made to appear almost flying. Above, on the eaves, the inscription reads "PRAY FOR PEACE, 1945". Unfortunately now, the ravages of time have played their worst with this beautiful mural, and today it does not have the same wonderful feeling as it did in earlier years, mainly because the site has now become busy and lost its restful and quiet surroundings.

Mural of St Francis of Assisi painted on a pump-house wall at the "Sinks", Kesgrave, by an American artist during 1944. When viewed from a distance this painting is unique for its simplicity and quiet colouring and is extremely realistic, surrounded as it is by the waving rushes and birds on the roof.

Mrs Baker

CHAPTER FIVE

After the Hustle. 1945—1973

HISTORY often repeats itself and that of Martlesham Heath was no exception: after the immense activity of the War, which was the culmination of the pre-war "panic-buildup", for the second time in twenty-five years the pace rapidly slackened and the economies of post-war expenditure left little for new items. Exactly as before, large quantities of aircraft and equipment were readily available, even if they were not required, which as it happened, they were not, but this time the aircraft were of more substantial construction and their life expectancy was much longer, so with those "moth-balled" in the Maintenance Units were put away many of the hopes of new designs.

The A & A.E.E. had moved down to Boscombe Down at the beginning of the War, and were now firmly entrenched there, so the prospect of a return to Martlesham was very remote indeed. Equipment had been installed at their new home to deal with the rapidly improving new items of machinery, and coupled with the fact that the aircraft industry now had a new mode of propulsion, the jet engine, this in itself called for entirely new test procedures and the means to carry them out. The aircraft themselves had grown not so much in size, but in weight, and with the experimental type of runways which had been laid on the Heath, it was open to question as to whether or not they would be capable of accepting heavy jet-propelled aircraft. These new machines also called for extra air-space for landing and take-off, and this could have caused the purchase of additional land in order to make this possible.

With this prospect in view, the Station settled down for a while, resting as it were after the fray, to a period of very little activity apart from the odd visiting aircraft, or the squadron in residence for a short while.

September, 1945, saw a return to many active things when a Unit was formed at Martlesham, entitled the Blind Landing Experimental Unit, B.L.E.U., and this remained there until May, 1957, when it moved to the Royal Aircraft Establishment near Bedford.

Alongside this Unit was a companion named the Bomb Ballistic Unit, B.B.U., and these two worked together. It is interesting to note that the two units, although sharing a common site, differed in that one was composed of R.A.F.

personnel, whilst the other comprised Royal Aircraft Establishment scientists. Although they worked together in all respects as a team, they had separate administration, and in this way proved how well it was possible for civilian and Service personnel to work together.

The R.A.F. side of the Unit came under Maintenance Command, but was controlled by the Ministry of Supply and basically existed to provide aircraft facilities and aircrew to carry out the air-borne work for the R.A.E. During July, 1946, the two separate units became fully operational, but in May, 1950, the two Units merged and became the Armament and Instrument Experimental Unit, the flying side of the B.L.E.U. becoming the A.I.E.U. Instrument Flight.

The ballistics side of the business covered the Armament Section, and although operating and housing its aircraft at Martlesham, carried out its day to day work at Orfordness, the original home of the Armament Flight of the Central Flying School in pre-Martlesham days. The deserted and open marshland there made ideal rocket and bombing ranges for this function. The Unit was commanded at this time by Wing-Commander E. A. Johnson, O.B.E.

The aircraft used for these trials and calibration flights were unusual in themselves and consisted of four Avro Lincoln heavy bombers, ex-Bomber Command, one of which, Serial No. RA.716, was experimentally fitted with two Rolls-Royce Merlin piston engines in the inboard positions, and two Rolls-Royce Avon Mk.I turbo-jets in the outboard positions. This power combination gave the aircraft a tremendous rate of climb, which for high altitude work, saved a lot of time. Unfortunately the aircraft was not pressurized or heated, and therefore it was not possible to take it up to absolute ceiling. It is reported that on one occasion, carrying a very tough crew and a 10,000 lb bomb, it climbed to 43,000 feet. Also in this Flight was an English Electric Canberra Mk.2 bomber and one of the two Short Sperrin four-jet bombers. This very interesting aircraft, the first of the "new type bombers" to fly, was already outdated by the Vickers Valiant which followed close on its heels, the Sperrins being completed as an "insurance" just in case the Valiant did not come up to scratch. Only two Sperrins were built by Short Brothers at their Belfast Works, and the Martlesham one was Serial No. VX.161. Owing to its weight, in the main, it used the longer runway at Sutton Heath for loaded take-offs and landings. These aircraft were not wasted but carried out much valuable research work with secret electronic equipment, and also as a flying test-bed for the De Havilland Gyron Junior turbo-jet engine. Rocket trials were carried out with a Gloster Meteor FT.9 twin jet fighter and also a De Havilland Mosquito twin piston-engined fighter-bomber. Another unusual aircraft to be operated from Martlesham at this time, mainly in the transport role between this base and other stations, was the Avro Ashton, a four jet development of the ill-fated Avro Tudor airliners, some of which were lost over the Atlantic without trace.

Top. Short Sperrin four-jet long range high level bomber of which only two prototypes were built. One of these, VX.161 was used at Martlesham Heath for post-war experimental work.

Short Brothers & Harland

Bottom. Avro Ashton four-jet high speed transport developed from the ill-fated Avro Tudor airliner. One of these was used at Martlesham for fast transport between there and other experimental bases.

Hawker Siddeley Aviation

The bombers were stripped of all weight-consuming gear such as gun-turrets, etc., and normally flew with a crew of three, pilot, navigator-bomber and flight-engineer.

The day to day work consisted mainly of ballistic measurement and working in close co-operation with ground instrument crews at Orfordness. The piloting had necessarily to be of a very high standard to put the aircraft in the desired position, at the correct speed and height, in order to make the experiment a success. Although many years later, this work was in fact an extension of the research and development of ballistics started in the early days by Henry Tizard.

During 1952 the original Instrument Flight was divided into two sections, the All-Weather Flight and the Rapid Landing Flight. The All-Weather Flight was responsible for the development of the automatic approach equipment and worked in minimum conditions to try out the possibilities of an automatic landing system in conjunction with the Calvert Lighting System.

The Rapid Landing Flight was responsible for the investigation into landing aircraft at short intervals in bad visibility, a function long desired by Fighter Command.

Up to 1949, the equipment in use, although of an experimental nature, had enabled several hundred fully-automatic landings to be made using the runways at Martlesham Heath and the long runway at Sutton Heath. The aircraft involved in this work were a Vickers Viking, Avro Lancaster, De Havilland Devon, Vickers Varsity, English Electric Canberra, Douglas Dakota, Armstrong-Whitworth Albemarle, Gloster Meteor N.F.II's and an Avro 707A — the one third flying scale model of the Avro Vulcan bomber.

A De Havilland Devon carried out fog landing procedures during the winters of 1951/2 and 1952/3 using the Sutton Heath runway, the experiments being carried out later at London Airport. At this stage the Devon had been able to carry out a landing at London Airport with visibility down to 34/40 yards. Later equipment was installed in a Canberra WE.189 during 1953, but unfortunately this aircraft met with a tragic mishap whilst approaching Martlesham Heath. Both occupants were killed. The pilot, Flight Lieutenant Coe, and his civilian flight observer Mr J. Birkle, were both killed. After the success of the Devon trials, new gear was installed in a Varsity, a larger and heavier aircraft, which enabled further trials to be carried out. Although the object of the exercise was to enable aircraft to land in fog, the majority of the work was carried out in fine weather, various devices being used to simulate bad visibility. Opportunity was taken however, whenever possible, to carry out the work in real fog conditions. Reports show that when using the 1,700 yard runway at Martlesham Heath, with a visibility of 750/800 yards an aircraft could make a safe automatic landing without use of the runway lighting system.

The Rapid Landing Flight operated three Gloster Meteor N.F.II's, sometimes known as the Armstrong-Whitworth N.F.II's, and worked in close liaison with Fighter Command, who were, as previously stated, very interested in this system in order to get their aircraft down in bad conditions. It was also essential for the operation of all-weather fighter squadrons, a necessity in modern defence roles.

Much of the flying of this Unit had of necessity to be carried out in bad weather and in company with other aircraft, this was often a difficult and dangerous task. The coverage of flight tracks was by radar, and a feature of this Unit's work was that its aircraft had to be ready at any time to fly, as the weather dictated, and great tribute has to be paid to the ground crews responsible for their maintenance.

In summing-up the work of these Flights, the enormous amount of effort required to carry out the work, usually only with seventeen aircraft available, must be appreciated. Many were non-standard aircraft, ex-prototypes or just aircraft no longer required by operational squadrons. Most were continually being fitted with all manner of weird and wonderful gadgets, "black-boxes" and extra effort was exerted by the ground crews to keep this varied and motley assortment of aircraft in the peak of airworthiness.

From this early work, beset with trials and tribulations, has now stemmed the present proven system of full automatic blind landing being carried out so successfully by the aircraft of British Airways and other airlines.

These two Units started to pack up for their move to Bedford during the latter part of 1956 and it was about May 1957 when they completely moved from the Heath.

Before leaving them, two items of interest. On one occasion, when at the controls of an Avro Lincoln, on a night bombing trial over Orfordness, the Commanding Officer was forced to jettison his load of bombs near the village of Sudbourne, the only casualty being a cow which was killed. A modified Avro Lancaster of the "Dam-Buster" type was also on the strength and used to drop this special type of missile off Orfordness. Many "Grand Slam" ten-ton bombs were also dropped, suitably ballasted, in experiments with their flight characteristics.

One complication occurred at this period, as the Martlesham runways suffered considerable damage from the searing blast of the Canberra's Avon jets. Not being constructed with jet aircraft in view, the tar surface was ideal for conventional propeller machines, but with the use of jets, continual repairs were necessary, and concrete ends had to be laid-down to protect the runway from the jet-blast of braked aircraft running-up for take-off.

During 1958, a Unit moved into Martlesham Heath with a very familiar name but an unfamiliar role, it being No. 22 Squadron, operating as a Helicopter Search and Rescue Squadron, No. 22. It is ironical that a Squadron numbered twenty-two should return for service at Martlesham, as the reader will recall that it was No. 22 Squadron which was formed at the same place during 1924 and became the Experimental Unit of the A & A.E.E. The new 22 Squadron performed useful work whilst based at the Heath, and quotations from the local papers record its performance.

"Helicopter areas have been prepared at the local hospitals for emergency flights. The helicopters stationed at Martlesham R.A.F. Station for emergency rescue operations are being piloted over East Anglian hospitals to make sure there are suitable places for them to land.

This morning one machine was making a reconnoitre over the Heath Road Wing of the Ipswich and East Suffolk Hospital."

Another aspect of the work appears as follows:—

"Ipswich R.S.P.C.A. Inspector, 40-year old Mr Tony Hyde, flew for the first time in his life yesterday to save the lives of swans which were dying as they were trapped in ice-filled Suffolk estuaries.

Armed with a pick-axe and a lasso the Inspector hovered over the River Deben in a helicopter from R.A.F. Martlesham ready to be lowered in a bosun's chair to chip the birds from the ice.

Clad in an immersion suit, Inspector Hyde, said, 'I never had the courage to fly before but it is the only way to save these swans. If we don't get to them they will die from exhaustion.'

With him flew another 40-year old Inspector, Mr Frank Woods from Lowestoft. Earlier R.A.F. pilots had reported over 20 swans trapped in the ice along the Suffolk coast-line between Bawdsey and Southwold. The swans, forced close inland by the Arctic conditions, were unable to free themselves. There was no chance of reaching them from the land. After an hour's search yesterday only two swans had been sighted. The helicopter touched down in a field at Waldringfield and the panic-stricken swans managed to free themselves.

'The warm sun must have freed many of the birds,' said Inspector Hyde. 'If it freezes again many more will be trapped and we shall go flying to look for them again if possible.'

On the R.A.F. Station Martlesham Heath vans stood ready to pick up the swans as soon as radio messages came through."

A more formal occasion was the visit of the Prime Minister, Sir Anthony Eden to visit R.A.F. Units in East Anglia.

"The accent was on informality when the Prime Minister paid a series of visits yesterday to R.A.F. Units in East Anglia.

He had expressed the wish that it should be regarded as a normal working day.

Within four minutes of landing in his Devon aircraft, Sir Anthony was taken off again in a Westland Whirlwind helicopter of No. 22 Search and Rescue Squadron, Martlesham Heath, which was followed by three other helicopters containing high-ranking Royal Air Force Officers."

On a more sombre note, a report appeared:— Monday, 19th May, 1958.

"The winchman who was killed when an R.A.F. Air-Sea Rescue helicopter crashed into the sea at Felixstowe on Thursday afternoon was yesterday named as Sergeant D. W. Frampton of Manor Park, London.

The pilot who suffered a fractured leg and spine was Flight-Lieutenant K. Alderson of Felixstowe. The third member of the crew, the navigator, was unhurt."

During its stay at Martlesham Heath, this Unit performed valuable work in the rescue field, and the foregoing shows the varied nature of this work. Routine jobs included the patrolling, during the summer months, of the holiday beaches, when thousands of holiday-makers would see the Whirlwinds as they flew along the sea-shore, low over the water, their orange "Mae West" jacketed crews waving to the crowds.

Although Martlesham was now once again in one of its quiet phases, a Unit moved in which brought back many memories to the surrounding population, bringing with it a few Hawker Hurricanes and Supermarine Spitfires. These belonged to the Battle of Britain Flight of the R.A.F. and were based in the large "B" Flight hangar together with all their equipment. These aircraft were "officially" the last of the breeds to be flying with the R.A.F. and were used for Battle of Britain fly-pasts and restricted performances at air displays. The Hurricane usually used was a Mark IIC. No. LF 363 and the Spitfire, a Mark 19, No. PM.631.

The "Flight" warms up for its fly-past over the City of London, which unfortunately turned out to be the last of its kind. *E.A.D.T.*

The homecoming. Supermarine Spitfire SL.574 returns on a "Queen Mary" transport after its forced landing on a cricket-pitch at Bromley, Kent, 20th September, 1959. Note spare wings and fuselage against hangar well. Hawker Hurricane in foreground. *E.A.D.T.*

On 20th September, 1959, Hurricane LF 363 and Spitfire SL.574 took-off from Martlesham to make the usual Battle of Britain fly-past over the centre of London. The Spitfire, piloted by Air Vice Marshal H. J. Maquire, unfortunately developed engine trouble just after it had passed over the City, and made a forced landing in a cricket-pitch at Bromley, Kent. The pilot escaped injury, but the aircraft was badly damaged, but it was salvaged and returned to its hangar at Martlesham where it was carefully re-built to fly once again.

As a result of this accident, the Air Ministry deemed it too dangerous for these veteran aircraft to fly over London and so this was the last time that the people of that city saw the two aircraft paying their tribute to "the Few". Shortly after this the Flight moved to Coltishall, Norfolk, where it is still based, and we in this part of the world are indeed fortunate that during the summer months these wonderful aircraft are still to be seen in the East Anglian sky, still causing a stir in the hearts of young and old alike.

Activity on the airfield was now chiefly confined to the week-ends, when an Air Training Corps Gliding School operated from the old U.S.A.F. buildings and blister-hangars on the Western side of the 'drome. On fine week-ends, hosts of blue uniformed lads could be seen carrying out the various duties of gliding, running out the tow-rope, retrieving the aircraft and standing around in hopeful queues for their turn to get airborne. Administered by the Ipswich Air Training Corps, the gliding school set quite a record for the number of lads who gained their "Glider Wings."

The aircraft used were mainly the reliable 2-seat instructional Kirby Cadet, tough and designed for this type of work, easily maintained and, of greater importance, easily repaired to be ready for the next weekend's stint.

After the usual ground instruction and familiarisation with the controls and aerodrome procedure, the instructor and pupil would take their places, side by side in the glider, the tow-line would be attached, signals given when all safety measures had been taken, the winch-lorry gear engaged, and as the cable "ran-in", so the machine lifted and "kited" up to its maximum line height where it was released by the glider. If it had been a good "pull-up" and height attained, two circuits of the airfield were possible, during which time the pupil had a chance to get the feel of the aircraft, carry out several manoeuvres and finally come in to land.

Whilst the first aircraft was airborne, the ground-crews, working turn and turn about, retrieving the cable, would lay it out ready for the next launch, in this manner keeping up quite a steady number of launches in the course of a session.

When the instructor deemed the pupil ready for his first solo, this took place, the attainment of three solo flights in a row bringing to the pupil the coveted "Wings". With this behind him he could then set out for pastures new, and enter into the soaring field, climbing up on the thermals of a summer's day and enjoying longer and more exciting flights. Several of the "old boys" returned to the School as Instructors for their younger colleagues and so a real spirit of comradeship was evident.

It was interesting to stand on the main road when flying was in progress at the School, and to listen to the instructions from the instructor to his pupil as the glider passed overhead, quite often at some height. The gliders were housed during the week in the old A.R.S. Hangar near the Station Headquarters, and a small party of R.A.F. personnel maintained them.

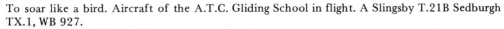

To soar like a bird. Aircraft of the A.T.C. Gliding School in flight. A Slingsby T.21B Sedburgh TX.1, WB 927.

The odd R.A.F. aircraft still arrived on some visit or other, but in the main, the Station was now very quiet, but still had one more card to play. During the spring of 1962, the Air Ministry was looking for a suitable aircraft for Transport Command, capable of operating from rough or even un-made airfields and small unprepared strips. The aircraft to be evaluated had narrowed down to two, the Avro 748 and the Handley-Page Dart Herald. Both these machines were powered by the same turbo-prop power unit, the Rolls-Royce Dart, but whereas the Avro 748 was a low-wing monoplane, the Herald was a high-wing, whilst both were twin-engined and had tricycle undercarriages.

A large stretch of the airfield on the western side was ploughed up and generally "roughened", small trees and bushes being removed, and the worst ditches and trenches levelled out before the aircraft arrived for test. Taxiing was carried out in the "rough" section and fast runs to test the aircraft's undercarriages and soft ground capabilities in front of a group of Service and civilian officials. After some time an announcement was made in the Press that the Avro 748 had been awarded a contract, and a new design was evolved around the 748, and eventually named the Andover. This machine incorporated loading doors under the rear fuselage, a dihedral tailplane, and a unique "kneeling undercarriage" which allowed the aircraft to sit lower to the ground surface in order to load large pieces of equipment.

This was the last aircraft to be tested in any way at Martlesham Heath, and although their stay was only a matter of a few days, the 'drome had once again, in a small way, helped the course of aviation.

Ploughing with an aircraft. The Avro 748 G-ARAY on rough ground trials during 1963. The surface had been specially prepared for this operation but the looseness of the soil will be observed.   *E.A.D.T.*

During 1963, two French-built Nord 1002's, Pingouin II, a version of the Messerschmitt BF 108B, manufactured at Les Mureaux after production of this type was transferred from Regensburg, Bavaria during 1942, were temporarily housed at Martlesham. Ex-French registration, F-BFYX and F-BGVU, they were painted up and used in the film "The Longest Day" masquerading as Me.109's, but were later sold to a buyer in the U.S.A. They made the journey by the Northern route, Scotland, Iceland, Greenland, and Labrador, but one was lost when it landed on the ice-cap and went through the surface before it could be salvaged.

The aerodrome buildings came under the eye of the neighbouring residents, blister hangars gradually becoming the homes of local farmers' field machinery, whilst the Control Tower which had been built for the U.S.A.F. became the headquarters of the local wild-fowling club. The runways were used at the week-ends by learner-drivers, whilst on the apron near the A.R.S. Hangar, a "skid-patch" was constructed and used by the Police and local Car Clubs for perfecting the art of skid control with motor vehicles. The Gliding School had moved away to Swanton Morley in Norfolk, but another kind of flying now took place, in model form, as the Heath was ideal for the Model Radio Club to try out their latest creations, diesel-engined aircraft of all shapes and sizes obeying the commands of their masters on the ground.

At this time the local papers carried long columns regarding the possibilities of Martlesham Heath becoming the airport for Ipswich, as the Nacton Road aerodrome serving this town was a grass surfaced one and therefore restricted to small and medium weight aircraft, a draw-back if regular commercial services were to be run. To many, Martlesham seemed the ideal solution to the problem, with its nearness to Ipswich, the ready-made runways, road and transport access and hangars ready for use. Alas, another problem existed, in that the twin bases of the ex-R.A.F. airfields at Sutton Heath and Bentwaters, only a few miles to the east, had been extensively modernised for use by units of the United States Air Force, with N.A.T.O. involvement, and these Units were usually at a high state of readiness. This meant that aircraft operated from these airfields at all hours of the night and day, and as the prevailing wind is South-Westerly, Martlesham Heath therefore lies almost directly in the path of aircraft taking-off and climbing out on this heading. Aircraft in the circuit at Martlesham Heath would then be directly involved in the path of these fighters, and in the latter days of flying from the Heath, so closely related with the approach and departure patterns of R.A.F. Woodbridge and R.A.F. Bentwaters that aircraft in the Martlesham circuit were frequently "held" for long periods to allow the U.S.A.F. machines to pass through the circuit.

Although hopes in some circles ran high at this time that Martlesham would replace Nacton as the municipal airport for Ipswich, these were short-lived and no further action took place.

Advertisements and announcements now appeared in the Press of space to let at Martlesham Heath for light industry and storage. Many local firms saw this as a "Heaven-sent opportunity" to expand into new premises and it seemed only over-night that the once busy Workshops vibrated again to the sounds of hammers and tools. "A" Flight hangar which had housed the cream of the fighters, often secret and lethal, now housed nothing more hostile than a plant for making concrete kerb stones, whilst "B" Flight Hangar, home of the bombers and large air-liners, offered shelter for many combine-harvesters, the products of a large agricultural engineering works in Ipswich. Almost swords to plough-shares! The barrack blocks no longer rang with the slang and song of the airmen but to the chatter of ladies making safety equipment, whilst the engine-test bays, proud of their tradition, were not disappointed, as they were now the home of a well-known racing car engine firm. The power of the former engines may not be there, but the noise certainly is! The only section truly still in its element is the old Transport Yard, which now housed the lorries of a large haulage contractor. The old A.R.S. Hangar became the works of a firm importing Danish agricultural and building machinery, and the proprietor, himself an aircraft owner, kept his machine in the hangar also.

Still in use. The Motor Transport yard, now used by a haulage contractor. The tower in the background was used by the Fire Section to hang their hoses from for drying-out purposes.

A. J. R. Frost

The old A.R.S. Hangar, at the time of the photograph, the home of Skandia Engineering, with the principal's private aeroplane in front.   *A. J. R. Frost*

The nature of the works now going on were reported in the local paper,

"Stanley Kay came to Martlesham 18 months ago to start his own welding and sheet metal working business. An ex-Navy Chief Artificer, he returned to Ipswich after 15 years in the Service to start up on his own. Early attempts to get going threatened to make him change his mind but after he had managed to get a site on the aerodrome he was established. His business is now flourishing, and his business expanded almost day by day."

Multiplied by 27, Stanley Kay's success story is the story of the Martlesham Industrial Estate. When the R.A.F. moved out in 1963, the industrialists moved in. Barrack blocks and hangars were quickly converted to house manufacturers equipment and there are now 27 firms operating from the site ranging from the "one-man" businesses to large industrial concerns employing 100 people for more. Early mornings at Martlesham find Portal Avenue thick with traffic as people make their way to work on the airfield.

Everyone concerned hated the term "disused airfield" which was immediately slapped on the 750 acre site when the R.A.F. "upped sticks". In fact the aeronautical connections have not been allowed to lapse as visiting executives find the site very convenient for their private aircraft when flying in for discussions. Included among the distinguished visitors who call by this means are racing driver Jack Brabham and fighter ace Douglas Bader.

Firms moving away from London, wanting to expand and find labour, discover that Martlesham has what they want. Over 130 local girls found work with Vacuum Reflex who rent two and a half converted barrack-blocks and

123

produce jackets, protective clothing, supply parachutes and radar reflectors for Government orders and export. Two years ago they decided to move from Tottenham, with lack of expansion and lack of labour as their two major problems. They solved them both at Martlesham.

The airfield site could be described as an "industrial kindergarten" with small firms blossoming quickly into prominence; such as Irvine Martin Plastics who during 1966 won the contract to make the Christmas street decorations for London's Regent and Oxford Streets. Potato merchants, contractors, lawn mower manufacturers, and racing car engine firms are all housed in the 60 unit complex of the airfield.

The development of this site has been guided by Mr Michael Cooke, the site agent, who was given the job of turning it into an industrial estate, and has been highly successful. In fact he has been put on record as stating that he has spent half his time turning away those who want accommodation on the estate.

Celebrations were the order of the day on 16th January, 1967, the 50th anniversary of the opening of the Station, and many gathered for this event. Misty weather marred the celebrations, and flyers from all over the country who were

Celebrating fifty years of Martlesham.

U.S.A.F. Officer Representative	R.A.F. Officer Representative	Air Commodore Bonham-Carter	Mr F. Fausing Host	Mr Stanley Ward C.F.I. Ipswich Flying Club	Mr Cook Aerodrome Site Manager

A post-war reunion and get-together of ex-Martlesham Heath men.

to have attended the informal get-together to mark the anniversary were prevented from arriving, although one aircraft did manage to get through the murk.

Dozens of distinguished flyers, civic dignitaries and representatives of the United States Air Force, came by road in response to an informal invitation by flying Suffolk businessman, Mr Freddie Fausing.

In a speech of welcome he said that since he was the last aviator at Martlesham he could not see the golden anniversary of flying at the airfield go by unnoticed.

Air Commodore D. W. Bonham-Carter C.B., D.F.C., a former base commander, in a speech of welcome gave some impressions of life at Martlesham during its heyday as the principal test centre for all military and civil aircraft in Britain.

Mr Stanley Ward, Chief Flying Instructor of the Ipswich Flying Club apologised for not flying in with a contingent, but he felt that the weather was too bad. Remembering his youth, Mr Ward said he was regularly chased away from Martlesham as he tried to spot new and rare aircraft being tested. Fortunately this had not diminished his undying interest in aviation.

A colour-guard of American servicemen then led the guests to the War Memorial on the old parade ground, where Colonel De Witt Searles, Commander of the 81st Tactical Wing at Bentwaters, and who had served at Martlesham during the 1939-1945 War, laid a wreath on the memorial.

During the proceedings the author had the pleasure of being interviewed by B.B.C. television and gave a brief history of the site for transmission the same evening.

After its long and varied aeronautical history one would not have expected the landing of an aircraft at Martlesham to make "paper news", but this was the case during 1969.

"A glider pilot from the Midlands made a forced-landing in Suffolk yesterday. The pilot felt unwell and made a landing at Martlesham Heath, but he found himself in a compound bounded by a nine-foot high barbed wire fence, and the gate was locked. He managed to climb over the wire all right and was rescued by a Police car, and the glider which had only missed the wire by inches was also not damaged, but had to be dismantled to be towed away.

The machine had flown from Coventry, and had touched down at Martlesham on land ear-marked for the G.P.O. for an experimental station."

Even greater consternation was caused by a later report of another event.

"Spectators gasped at Martlesham airfield on Saturday when they saw a Cessna 170 light aircraft land upside down after somersaulting.

The plane was caught by a strong cross-wind just before landing and turned over after a wing-tip hit gorse bushes at the side of the runway.

The pilot, Mr R. D. Dauberweiss, 23, and his two passengers, Rita Milward, 26, and Michael Pervis, 21, all from North London, escaped unhurt."

During 1968 it was announced by the Post Office that they were going to move their Research Department from Dollis Hill in North West London to a new

The 175 ft. radio tower, the six-storey laboratory block and the administration building.

Research Centre to be built at Martlesham Heath. The announcement gave details of a "pilot" scheme and an outline of the new buildings which were planned.

Since then, a large part of the building construction has been completed and travellers along the Woodbridge-Felixstowe road can now see the 175 ft radio tower to carry microwave dish aerials similar to those on the Post Office Tower in London, the six storey air-conditioned laboratory block and the administration building which also contains a restaurant, lecture theatre and library.

Even before construction of these buildings began, a group of single-storey buildings was erected to enable several hundred staff to move from the over-crowded laboratories at Dollis Hill. Even some of the old R.A.F. buildings were given a new lease of life — the N.A.A.F.I. became a precision mechanical work-shop whilst special waveguides were made in the old Station Headquarters.

One of the first projects on the site was concerned with experiments to evaluate the use of higher radio frequencies for telephone links. The Post Office is contemplating the use of frequencies which have been used only in laboratory measurements until the last few years. As Mr Bob Tattersall, who is working on this project, commented,

"At the high frequencies we are using, communication problems become really complex," he explained. "A shower of rain can cut off the radio link by absorbing the signal. Even the oxygen in the air absorbs the radio power. If we can use these high frequencies reliably, then we can open the way to hundreds of thousands more telephone circuits."

A by-product of Mr Tattersall's work could be short-range weather forecasts, as his equipment will show when the weather is about to change.

An alternative to radio links for carrying trunk telephone and television circuits is now being developed at Martlesham. Very high frequency radio signals can be persuaded to travel for miles along empty pipes called waveguides. These pipes do not have solid walls, but are made of a tight spiral of copper wire, held in place by a jacket of fibreglass. The first tests were carried out with the waveguide laid in a steel pipe buried in a trench along the boundary of the old airfield, but tests will soon begin with waveguide installed in a duct from Martlesham to nearby Wickham Market alongside the busy A.12 road.

The main runway of the old airfield provided a convenient place to test new equipment for laying submarine cables. Mr E. F. S. Clarke explained that the telephone cables between the UK and the Continent and to America must have amplifiers inserted in them every few miles to boost the signal, which gets weaker as it covers longer distances.

Modern cables carry many more channels than the old types, and they need amplifiers, technically called "repeaters", more frequently. This poses problems for the cable-laying ships, because every time a repeater is put in the cable the run must be stopped, the cable removed from the laying gear, and the repeater wired in. The new equipment makes it possible to feed the 10ft long solid steel cased repeaters over the stern of the ship without once stopping the laying operation. The equipment has overcome the problem of damage to the cables, and speeds up the whole operation.

The prototype machine or "cable engine" was tested under an "air house" on the runway but the final design has now been very successfully installed on several cable ships.

Laser communications have not been forgotten, and trials are to be held with light from miniature lasers passing along cables containing hair-thin glass fibre instead of copper wire. Scientists at Martlesham are now making some of the purest glass in the world, which is essential for the production of the glass fibres.

Even at this advanced stage of technology, the Commoners of Martlesham decided to pursue once more their claim for loss of grazing rights on the airfield.

From "time immemorial", the villagers of Martlesham had been able to graze animals, cut turf and gorse and gather bracken on 37 acres of the Heath, but as the estate developed, so this area became partly inaccessible.

During 1925 a sum of £5 had been agreed by the Air Ministry for compensation for the area on which buildings had been erected, and during May, 1927, and June 1936, additional payments of £4 and £5 respectively had been granted, making £14 a year in all. During November 1956, the Secretary of State for Air entered into agreement with the Parish Council for the suspension of rights over the remainder of the common, and in this agreement was an express provision for its termination by the Secretary of State by notice. Put into effect on 24th July, 1963, after the airfield was closed, the Secretary of State shortly afterwards surrendered the lease, which still had 959 years to run, to the present holders, the Bradford Property Trust Limited.

The new lease-holders were willing to continue the payment of £14 per annum but were not willing to entertain a new scheme and queried the validity of the rights of the Commoners.

The Parish Council, wishing to fight this suggestion, and not having the means to fight a long and costly legal action, took up the services of the newly appointed office of Ombudsman to fight their case, the petition being placed in the name of Mr I. R. Richards, Chairman of the Parish Council.

During the case it was revealed that as early as 1960, the Royal Air Force had decided that it had finished with Martlesham Heath, and during 1961, the Air Ministry had concluded that the only possible way to get back some of the investment at Martlesham, currently estimated at some £140,000, was to sell the lease, this being effected during December, 1962 and completed in July 1963, the purchase price being £72,500.

The Ombudsman, in his findings, pointed out that there appeared to be some maladministration in the Department of the Secretary of State's failure to follow up the meeting of March 1963, or to inform the Commoners of their proposal to assign the three agreements to the Trust. He also found that this had caused injustice to the Commoners because it deprived them of the opportunity of making representations so that when the R.A.F. no longer had need of the land, their interests should have been safe-guarded.

The Commoners unanimously agreed to accept the recommendations following the Ombudsman's finding that they be awarded £250 ex-gratia payment as compensation. They also agreed to accept a sum of £70 from the Bradford Property Trust for the five years loss of rights of the Commoners on the aerodrome. Thus that which began in a small way went all the way to the top, to prove that our birth-right is still very important.

A notice in the paper during 1972 would seem to sound the death-knell of the Heath when a Local Enquiry was called at the County Hall, Ipswich, under the Town and Country Planning Act of 1962, to consider a proposal for development of the site. This was in effect an application for permission to develop a "new village" on the Heath with provision for dwellings for some 3,000 people together with associated shops, schools, and facilities for employment and recreation.

Now at the beginning of 1975 a vast change has taken place on the Heath, and the ex-residents would find difficulty in orientating themselves on the ground they knew so well. The massive buildings of the G.P.O. Research Station are now visible for miles around, many of the familiar long standing Martlesham buildings disappearing to make way for these modern concrete and steel monsters.

At the north-west corner of the airfield, steel girders and concrete pillars are rising as the new Suffolk Police Headquarters takes shape. Covering some 30 acres, this complex will house many departments which are now scattered around Ipswich. The builders moved in during March 1974 and it is anticipated that the buildings will be completed during October 1976. They will comprise administration, traffic, training, planning and radio blocks, together with accommodation for personnel attending courses. Sports and recreational facilities will be fully catered for in the grounds surrounding the low profile structures.

In preparation for the "proposed village" in the centre of the airfield, new roads are in active preparation, a dual carriageway crossing the site from the A.12 near *Black Tiles*, over the airfield and joining the existing A.1093 just past the G.P.O. Research Station. As a result of this route large mounds of earth have appeared, being the spoil from a cutting which carries the road through the spot where the now demolished barrack blocks originally stood. The former "B" Flight Road or Portal Avenue from the A.12 to the A.1093 will, in its shortened form serve only as an access road for the Police Headquarters.

On the Ipswich side of the dual carriage way the proposed "new village" will be built, some 1000 residences with their own community centre, shops, service areas and recreational places, access to the estates being by way of two large round abouts on the new roads.

The industrial estate on the other side of the road continues to grow, many new and varied industries appearing and adding to the already busy atmosphere.

Not yet fully resolved, the Commoners are still negotiating the cause of "the common land", whilst the only aerial activity are the parachustists who drop on to what is left of the airfield when the wind and weather permit.

But now the bulldozers and their fellow machines have erased, for all time, the heather and sand where so many and "so Few" took-off and landed for the previous 55 years. A consolation, the name Martlesham Heath will not disappear since what the old airfield strived to achieve in the air, the new G.P.O. Martlesham will undoubtedly gain for itself in the realms of outer space and even beyond. The two will always be remembered in the memories of the old and the middle-aged men who knew aircraft as creatures of wood and fabric with engines and propellers, and the younger generation with visions of worlds beyond the planets, Jupiter and Mercury, names which the famous engines tested at the old Martlesham also bore.

CHAPTER SIX

For Better or Worse—Aircraft Testing. 1917—1939

Having dealt with the history of Martlesham Heath we can now take a closer look at the activities of the between-the-wars years, and the purposes for which this Station was established.

To recapitulate, the reader will recall that the Station was divided into two "squadrons" Nos. 15 and 22, and these respectively dealt with Armaments and Aircraft Performance, both under the control of Station Headquarters.

The Armament Testing Section, divided into three Flights, worked in close conjunction with the Performance Testing Section, and its duty was to try out and report on the military equipment of the aeroplane, machine-guns, bombs, bomb carrying gear, ammunition and bomb sighting equipment.

Its aircraft were housed in the three hangars alongside the Woodbridge-Felixstowe Road, whilst Armament Workshops and Gun Butts were on the other side of the road. The aircraft used by this Section were not always of the latest type as much of the bombing experimental work could be done by out-of-date machines. The majority of the practical work of this Section was carried out off Orfordness, where a special aerodrome and instruments for measuring results were installed.

The word "performance" as used by the Royal Air Force, is a very comprehensive term, and really includes almost every characteristic of the aircraft. It was the duty of the Performance Testing Section pilots to find out the exact speeds of the aircraft at all heights up to the "ceiling" (absolute attainable height), its rate of climb, the length of run required for getting off the ground and the length required after landing and also the general handling qualities of the aircraft in the air. While these were the main items of information required under the heading "performance", this Section also had to report on the engine and its behaviour under all conditions, the efficiency of the cooling system, the suitability of the airscrew, the instruments, the landing gear, and finally the construction and ease of maintenance. In fact, figures and reports had to be obtained about the behaviour of every part of the aeroplane and engine. It will be realised that the work of the test pilot is far removed from the popular conception of the "super" airman who dashes gallantly into the sky in a new aeroplane, throws its about the

Testing the strength of a tail-plane with the aid of sand-boxes. Weighed amounts of sand were added to the trays and when failure occurred, the imposed weight was the breaking point. 1918.
Wing Commander A. Boeree

A Hawker Fury on the scales. Another set of scales were placed under the wheels and then the complete weight of the machine could be arrived at.
A. Lee

skies, and after landing, reports that all is well and the aeroplane is suitable. Test flying involved hours of patient and careful work, often under conditions of extreme cold and discomfort, taking accurate figures and being able to check stop-watches and make accurate observations of instruments while the aeroplane was spinning or diving at high speeds. Perhaps the most spectacular of the test-pilot's work was these spinning and diving trials, always necessary to complete a full test. Naturally there were times when the test-pilot had to leave his aircraft and take to his parachute, but luckily these were the exception rather than the order of the day.

Over the years, the system was much the same for testing purposes, as detailed and well-thought out procedures had been established from the beginning, and an aircraft progressed from one stage of its evaluation and testing to the next by a well determined plan.

When the new aircraft arrived, either by air, or on its manufacturer's long lorry, draped in tarpaulins, it was usually for the Performance Testing Section. New military machines invariably had their armaments fitted at a later stage and the aircraft would be returned to Martlesham and the Armament Testing Section.

If the aircraft had been flown in, usually piloted by the firm's test-pilot, he would then give the service test-pilots any information necessary, the inventory which was carefully checked over, and the delivery papers for signature, as this helped to obtain payment for the machine if it had been a contract order.

Next came the draining of all tanks and checking of their capacities and the weighing of the empty airframe, sometimes an anxious ordeal, as any increase over the designed weight could affect the conditions of the contract, as well as reflect in the range and load carried.

Handbooks of instructions with illustrations and technical explanations and descriptions were handed over and discussed with the General Technical Office Staff whose duty it was to prepare a programme of tests. As stated previously, if the Armament Section was given priority it was because the airframe was usually a normal one, the testing of which presented little difficulty.

Usually, take-offs and landings by several pilots to judge the handling qualities came first. The cockpit layout was explained to them by the manufacturer's pilot, and how the various gadgets and controls should be used whilst the engine-maker's representative similarly dealt with the recommended handling of the throttle, altitude and boost controls and settings if the engine was a new type.

A Ground Engineer from the Works was usually provided to assist the R.A.F. personnel in getting to know the type, how to handle it, and the various maintenance points. In passing it must be mentioned that the majority of the Company test-pilots were ex-R.A.F. officers, in many cases ex-Martlesham pilots, and nearly all with engineering experience with the Service. Many of these pilots became household names such as Flying Officer P. G. E. Sayer (later at Hawkers and the first British jet pilot), Flying Officer "Bill" Pegg, (later of Bristols and the pilot of the giant Brabazon and Britannia airliners), Flying Officer "Mutt" Summers, who went to Armstrong-Vickers and took a great many of their new aircraft into the air for the first time, as well as Flight Lieutenants Boothman and Webster, both of Schneider Trophy fame, to mention but a very few.

Tests continued in all aspects of performance, and all items of equipment were included in the programme, the theme being that the aircraft was only as good as its support equipment, and its ability to be serviced and maintained. On completion of the programme, the aircraft, if it were a military type, would or would not be recommended for Service use, whilst civil types were granted or were not awarded their Certificate of Airworthiness.

The methods of testing became effective and better equipment was used as the experience of the years helped to show the needs. The efficiency of the pilots, and other staff, coupled with their helpful attitude to technicians, designers and engineers who visited them served to develop aircraft submitted to them for acceptance trials of a quality which subsequently proved superior to those of the enemy in the 1939-1945 war. Many of the technicians of between-wars Martlesham were promoted to do highly responsible work in other fields of aviation.

One unusual arrangement at Martlesham was that the post of Chief Technical Officer was held by a civilian, which sometimes lead to small difficulties, as explained by Mr H. L. Stevens, C.B.E.,

"I was the Chief Technical Officer for the five years, 1927-1931, and Wing Commander Blackburn was the Commandant when I arrived. He was a very likeable Yorkshireman, and was succeeded by Wing Commander Rees V.C., who was rather dour and suspicious of us civilians, but I must add that when he got to know and trust us, he did so completely.

My predecessor was Mr R. S. Capon, who had been promoted to Superintendant of the Scientific Research at the Royal Aircraft Establishment, Farnborough, from where he subsequently emigrated to Australia. Our combined period at the A & A.E.E. saw the birth of what Capon called "The Research Method of Testing" and which we developed into a routine which consisted in the beginning of doing sets of short climbs for about two minutes each — called "partial climbs" — at a series of speeds from below best climbing speed to level speed at a series of heights up to near the ceiling. In this we quickly got the optimum climbing speed and also the level speed at each height. Given a table of climbing speeds a pilot was able to fly the aeroplane in order to achieve the quickest possible climb.

We had a little difficulty sometimes with irascible senior officers of the R.A.F. — such as one affectionately known as "Bum and Eye-glass", who was apt to say, 'Don't mess about with all this science: all I want you people to do is just to climb up as quickly as you can to beat the ceiling and tell me how long it takes to get there and how fast the b----y thing goes.' To an enquiry as to how accurately he wanted the answer we got an indignant grunt. At the same time we had to be pretty accurate as during my period we had several competitions between aeroplanes built by different firms, to the same specification, and the differences in performance were not always large, nor were they swamped by other considerations such as ease of handling, convenience of armament layout, etc, etc.

I think that my most enjoyable and memorable recollections are of the delightful relations between the Service personnel and my Civilian Staff, and between us both and the Contractors' Test Pilots and Technical representatives. Of the latter, two names which stand out in my memory are Bennett-Baggs of Armstrongs and Bill Lappin of Rolls-Royce; but there are many, many more which I have not been able to recall."

This mutual enjoyment of each other's company used to come to its climax at the 'Contractors' Guest Night' held annually at which much fun and games of the rougher sort were enjoyed by all. 'High-cock-a-lorum' and the 'Performing Elephant' were two favourites. I believe some of the more sober members retired to some other room and played bridge — I never found them out."

On occasions, civil aircraft from some of the smaller makers arrived in red priming dope only, often devoid of registration markings, and only carrying the maker's identification code on their fuselage i.e. R - 6, P - 7 etc. etc.

A Private Venture aircraft (built at maker's expense) showing class and maker's letters, Blackburn B-6. *Hawker Siddeley Aviation*

Crashed Westland Wagtail on Sports Field. The airman appears more interested in the photographer than the salvage of the aircraft.

Many of the aircraft, that ended their usefulness as a result of an unfortunate crash or a bad forced landing, or because no longer needed, finished up as carcasses on the "grave-yard" which was located between the Rugger Field and "B" Flight Road. The large collection of wings and fuselages, covered and uncovered, stripped of engines and instruments and all other salvageable items, gradually grew in size and variety and many a famous prototype could be seen on the top of the pile. During the middle 30's the once proud winner of the Mildenhall-Melbourne Air Race, the De Havilland D.H.88 Comet, G-ACSS, sat on the pile as R.A.F. Serial No. K.5084, after a "wheels-up" landing, until recovered and restored once again to racing capabilities. If this heap were in existence today it would certainly be a collector's item!

Other components were found for use not strictly within their design specification, such as wheels, usually of the wire-spoked variety, which became the undercarriage for a series of carts and trolleys used around the aerodrome, but surely the lowest state was reached by mainplanes and tailplanes, denuded of their once taut silver-doped fabric, and brave roundels, which formed the boundary fences of the local coal-merchant's garden and yard at Kesgrave. Up until recent years the fuselage of a Hawker Hind and Bristol Blenheim lay concealed under a tangled mass of brambles on the outskirts of Ipswich, whilst a Westland Lysander's fuselage reposed in a yard near Ipswich Docks.

To return to the actual testing over the years, this is best told in the pilot's own words, and I am extremely happy to have been able to record so many of these wonderful accounts, from gentlemen who tested aircraft at Martlesham nearly fifty-five years ago.

Wing-Commander A. R. Boeree, recalls his days at Martlesham:—

"About May 1918, I had a straight-forward job to do in taking a Martinsyde

F.4 Scout with a 300 h.p. Hispano-Suiza engine on an altitude test with full load of guns and ammunition. Ceiling, climb and speed test with pilot's weight made up to 180 lbs. At 31,000 feet, on aneroid (27,000 feet corrected to standard atmosphere) the water-cooled engine froze solid so I had to glide down. The curve of the climb would have continued to a genuine 31,000 feet if the coolant had functioned. I could see the Wash over one shoulder and dirty London with the misty Thames over the other, and if I had dropped a stone, I could not say if it would have fallen on Ipswich, Stowmarket or Felixstowe. Open cockpit, three pairs of gloves, the inner silk ones electrically heated as was the waistcoat and boot feet. The speed was calibrated, 120 m.p.h. at 20,000 feet and 153½ m.p.h. at ground level.

Although our Hispano-Suiza engines were lubricated with castor-oil, at one time, there was a shortage of mineral oils, so the Air Board decided to try mixtures. We had various mixes of castor-oil with thick and thin mineral oil, tried out in various engines. Pilots took turns for some hours in the air, flying up and down the coast, reading books to while the time away, and recording oil pressures. The sequel to this exercise was the establishing of certain standards for lubricating oils."

During 1918 I crashed a Martinsyde F.4, later called the Buzzard, with a 300 h.p. Hispano Suiza water-cooled motor. As with many crashes, I must confess it was due to carelessness. I was hareing across the aerodrome, 'full-out' — 'grass-cutting', preparing to do some stunts. My speed was between 125 m.p.h. — 130 m.p.h. The one almost fatal mistake was that I forgot that there was a gentle cross-slope in the airfield surface. One of my wheels touched the ground and I catapulted over and over several times, wrapping the wings round the fuselage. I quickly grasped the guns to steady myself. My nose went through the small windscreen and I got two beautiful black eyes and was slightly concussed, but was able to crawl out and walk away. Quite a few accidents happened in those days by what today would be called foolishness — in the interests of progress."

The Martinsyde F.4 Scout which Wing Commander A. R. Boeree flew to a height of 27,000 feet during May, 1918. *Wing Commander A. R. Boeree*

Lieutenant Muspratt was killed about this time, with his observer, when the B.H.P.-engined De Havilland 9 he was flying, suffered structural failure near the aerodrome and crashed with fatal results.

Another Martlesham officer, Wing-Commander C. Hole remembers another personal incident:

"Speed and manoeuvrability were important parts of research but the ability to climb to maximum height in the shortest possible time was an ever-demanding requirement. To get above the enemy, this is, and always has been, fundamental to victory. After each modification we were directed to take the aircraft to their upper limits and the results were registered on sealed instruments which were examined after each test flight. This naturally went on day after day and was somewhat boring. I must explain that there is a point at which the air becomes so thin, that the engine and propeller are incapable of lifting the machine another inch, and this is referred to as the 'absolute ceiling'. Our instruments would indicate this point had arrived, the slowing upward creeping indicator would become stationary and then we knew that the top had been reached. Forward would go the controls, down would go the nose and in a few minutes we would be out of the intense cold and rarefied air, and then back on the ground presently to thaw out and a welcome hot drink in the Mess.

The only method of braking an aircraft at this time was the tail-skid which dug into the ground and acted as a stopper when landing. It was on one such climb as previously mentioned, that the following incident occurred. It was a normal climb to the top, the aircraft being one of the latest two-seat fighters, the rear cockpit having a tubular ring to which a machine-gun could be attached under combat conditions. On this flight, however, the rear cockpit contained me, a number of recording instruments and a writing pad on which messages were exchanged with the pilot.

After about one and a half hours, we reached our maximum height which was 23,000 feet. The pilot, as usual, indicated by hand signs that we were now going down and I could relax. A few moments later, however, I was handed a message which read "the trimming controls have jammed — I cannot get the tail down." To land with the tail up is courting disaster and would be like being in a car without brakes, going down-hill with a brick wall at the bottom. I claim no glory for what happened during the next fifteen minutes, but after a pause, the following plan of campaign was passed to me in the second note. The pilot was going to cut the engine power, and we would in consequence fall to earth by our own weight. We would not go down like a stone, but like a leaf in autumn falling from a tree in a series of spirals. This evolution was known to experienced pilots and providing the engine was used at the correct moment, coupled with the other controls, the spin could be corrected to normal forward flight in a short time.

This plan was alright but it did not get over the landing problem. We still had our tail up and this had to come down. This is where I came into the picture. We were to spin down to 1,000 feet and at this point the pilot would flatten out. I was then directed to get out of the rear cockpit and work my way along the top of the fuselage to the tailplane until I could go no further. Everything went according to plan and we flattened out at 1,000 feet, and now came my part of the performance, as the engine responded to the throttle with a roar. We were now flying straight and level. Keeping as low as I could to avoid the engine slipstream, I wriggled out of my cockpit, feet first and inched backwards until I felt the vertical fin touch my bottom. I wrapped my arms and legs around the thin part of the rear fuselage, closed my eyes and waited. My 200 lbs. of weight had done the trick. The tailplane came down, there was eventually the reassuring crunch, crunch of the tail-skid as it bit into the earth. It was all over and probably the first time that an aircraft had ever landed with someone sitting astride its tail.

Our experience was well worthwhile, as we had discovered a defect in design which after all was what were employed to do. In passing it might also be added that this was before the time of parachutes!"

It was from this position that Wing Commander Hole had to crawl back in order to use his weight to balance the aircraft for landing.
Mrs M. Martin

Test flying from Martlesham Heath during the First World War was not without its other hazards as the local paper recalled;

"The Military Cross has been awarded to a Courageous Officer after he had engaged seventeen enemy aircraft, three miles over the sea, whilst on a trial flight.

The heroism and daring of our flying men during 'recent hostile air raids' is recorded in the King's approval of the award of the Military Cross to Captain John Palethorpe of the Royal Flying Corps."

Captain Palethorpe and First-Class Air Mechanic J. O. Jessop, R.F.C., as gunner, were engaged in an endurance trial from a testing squadron. When about three miles from the coast, a squadron of 17 enemy aircraft were sighted. Captain Palethorpe at once attacked with great courage and determination under very heavy fire until his gunner was killed. He then landed, and having procured another gunner, endeavoured to renew the attack.

For his gallant and distinguished services First-Class Air-Mechanic James O. Jessop (No. 25501 – Killed in Action) has been "Mentioned in Despatches."

The natural hazards of test-flying also took their toll, and Vickers were unlucky to lose two consecutive aircraft when their second prototype Vimy B.9953, stalled on take-off due to engine failure and was completely wrecked, followed shortly afterwards by the third prototype, B.9954, which was destroyed when it crashed just after take-off with a full bomb load, which had been inadvertently fused and blew up when the bomber struck the ground near Spratt's Plantation.

A Vickers Vimy prototype which crashed. Second prototype B.9953 2 Sunbeam Maori engines. Stalled on take-off.   *Stuart Leslie*

A Vickers Vimy prototype with 2 Fiat A.12 engines which crashed with full load. *Stuart Leslie*

Shortly after this, Blackburn's torpedo bomber on test at Martlesham, the Blackburd N.113, also came to grief, but not with such disastrous results.

Another item dated January, 1919 gives a clue to the growing technical importance of the Station, when the World's Altitude Record was regained for Great Britain. "Only ten years ago a prize was offered for the first airmen to fly to an altitude of 30 metres. On 2nd January, Captain Lang, R.A.F. and Lieutenant A. W. Blowes, R.A.F. climbed to a height of 30,500 feet — over 5¾ miles high. It may be recalled that the previous world's record was 28,900 feet made on September 18th, 1918, by Captain R. W. Schroeder of the U.S.A. Air Service. Captain Lang and Lieutenant Blowes in the observer's seat of the De Havilland 9 biplane, with a 450 h.p. Napier Lion engine with which the attempt was made, started from the Martlesham experimental aerodrome near Ipswich at 11.30 a.m. A gale of wind was blowing and for the first 8,000 feet the machine was tossed about considerably, but afterwards calmer conditions prevailed. The first 10,000 feet was climbed in 6 minutes, 18 seconds whilst the 20,000 feet mark was attained in 19 minutes, 40 seconds. The machine climbed in big sweeping circles and was taken considerably off her course by the wind, so that when she finished climbing, she was about 25 miles out to sea off Yarmouth. The sun was shining brightly and through the haze Captain Lang said he could occasionally catch a glimpse of the Thames. Observations were taken at every 1,000 feet of the atmospheric temperature, speed of the machine, engine revolutions, water temperature, oil temperature, petrol pressure and petrol consumption. At 20,000 feet there were two mishaps, the cable in the revolution counter breaking, whilst the vibration fractured one of the pipes to the oxygen supply. Consequent

The De Havilland D.H.9A biplane C.6078 in which Captain Lang and Lieutenant Blowes gained the World Altitude Record, 30,500 feet. January 1919. *Stuart Leslie*

upon the latter, Lieutenant Blowes collapsed when he was trying to pass a message explaining the state of affairs to the pilot. Unaware of his companion's condition, Captain Lang carried on until at 28,000 feet he noticed a lack of oxygen. He then became aware of the situation, but went on to a height of 30,500 feet when the engine stopped owing to the pump failing to maintain sufficient pressure in the petrol tank. At 27,000 feet, the machine ran into very bumpy conditions and was so tossed about that it became uncontrollable. The first 10,000 feet of the descent occupied 25 minutes and the observer regained consciousness at 20,000 feet. Both of the occupants of the machine suffered frozen hands and toes, frostbite on the face, hand and toes."

It is reported that Captain Lang was placed under "open arrest" for divulging details of his climb.

Another result of the work at Martlesham was the fact that Wing Commander Boeree was sent to the United States of America during late 1918, together with Captain Hoffert, in an advisory capacity to demonstrate the methods used at Martlesham for performance testing to be used as a standard by the U.S. Air Service.

The unknown came to the forefront a great deal in these early days and Mr H. L. Stevens, a Martlesham C.T.O, as previously mentioned had one such experience:

"Whilst flying a semi-obsolete type, a Sopwith Pup, I inverted the machine by mistake and to my horror slid out through the retaining belt round my waist, this being before the standard Sutton Harness was fitted to aircraft, and finished up clinging to the trailing edge of the centre section of the upper mainplane. This unexpected movement came about partly due to my trying out an experiment with this aircraft. I had been going through a series of loops and rolls, finishing off with some spins and then the idea came to me that I would see if the machine would fly "hands-off", having the previous knowledge that the machine was not totally stable. Consequently I throttled back and removed my feet from the rudder bar and let go my hold on the control column. For a short space of time all was well and then the nose gradually came up and up, until unexpectedly it quickly dropped and the aircraft reared round into a spin. This did not unduly bother me as I knew the procedure for recovery but then the aircraft flicked into an inverted dive, a totally different matter, the forces of which squeezed me through the belt and outwards to the upper wing where fortunately I grasped the centre-section struts and hung on. With my toes I could just manage to reach the control column and exert some pressure on it in order to centralize the controls and put the aircraft in a semi-stable condition. This I did and dropped back into the seat, but lost contact with the control column, and up and over she went again, but I was able to hold on this time praying all the while that the fixing would hold. Very gently I managed to get the aircraft into a more or less normal condition, but was horrified on looking astern to see that the fin was badly bent and the rudder was not acting in that capacity any more. Having arrived home slowly but safely, I reported this mis-adventure to the appropriate people who put out a report that I had carried out this dangerous trial in order to test a known weakness in the aircraft which had led to a number of unexplained mishaps with this type."

On the 12th February, 1919, the Department of Civil Aviation was formed within the Air Ministry, followed on the 30th April by the issue of British Air Navigation Regulations and Conditions, whilst Civil Flying was authorised on 1st May, 1919. A tremendous step forward followed on 14th-15th June, 1919, when Captain John Alcock and Lieutenant Arthur Whitten-Brown crossed the North Atlantic, BY AIR NON-STOP, for the first time, in the Vickers Vimy with an elapsed time of 15 hours 57 minutes, and at an average speed of 118½ m.p.h. assisted by the prevailing Westerly Atlantic wind.

In those early post First World War days, the brave, or the foolish, according to opinion, travelled in crude and not very reliable or efficient conversions of the bombers which had only recently been employed "on other work" in Western Europe. In order to rectify this matter, early in 1920, the Air Ministry announced that it was sponsoring a contest, to be known as the "Air Ministry Civil Aeroplane Competition" which was to be held later on that year at the Aeroplane Experimental Establishment at Martlesham Heath, Suffolk. Prize money for the various classes amounted to £64,000, a very considerable sum at that time.

As in most Government circles, much talking was carried out in London, but finally the specifications were drawn up and released, the object being to determine the best designs of civil passenger-carrying aircraft which it was hoped, would ply the new routes in a once more peaceful world. It was extremely desirable that the "conversions" were replaced as rapidly as possible, as although the bombers were efficient in their previous roles, they had been designed to carry a heavy load in a confined space, i.e. bombs in a bomb-bay, and did not have the flexibility to carry lighter loads spread over a larger area, which in turn involved a difficult centre of gravity problem when loading the machine.

The aircraft for the Competition were to be divided into three classes, large aeroplanes, small aeroplanes and amphibians, the first two categories to be evaluated at Martlesham Heath and the latter at both Martlesham and the Marine Aircraft Experimental Establishment at Felixstowe. Main considerations in the Competition were the safety and comfort of the passengers to be carried and the specifications for all three classes covered speed, range, and take-off and landing performance.

During April 1920, owing to representations made by the British aircraft makers, the Air Ministry decided to alter the date of the commencement of the small type aeroplane competition until the 1st June, 1920. The dates which had been announced in connection with the other two classes remained the same.

As new designs, at this period, could generally speaking be constructed in a few months, or even weeks, it was disappointing that no new designs, as such, were entered for the contest. The entrants were mostly variants of existing designs with modifications to meet the specification of their class.

The final entrants were as follows:—

LARGE AIRCRAFT

Type	Registration	Capacity	Crew
Handley-Page W.8	G - E A P J	12 Passengers	Major H. G. Brackley
Vickers Vimy Commercial	G - E A U L	10 Passengers	Captain Cockerall

SMALL AIRCRAFT

Type	Registration	Capacity	Crew
Austin Kestrel	G - E A T R	2 Passengers and Pilot	M. D. Nares
Beardmore WB.10	G - E A Q I	1 Passenger and Pilot	G. Powell
Bristol Seeley	G - E A U E	2 Passengers and Pilot	C. Unwins
Sopwith Antelope	G - E A S S	2 Passengers and Pilot	Harry Hawker
Westland Limousine III	G - E A R V	5 Passengers and Pilot	Captain A. S. Keep
Avro Triplane 547A	G - E A U J	4 Passengers and Pilot	H. A. Hammersley
Central Centaur IIA	G - E A P C	6 Passengers and Pilot	—

AMPHIBIANS

Type	Registration	Capacity	Crew
Vickers Viking III	G - E A U K	2 Passengers and Pilot	Captain Cockerall
Supermarine Sea Eagle I	G - E A V E	2 Passengers and Pilot	Captain J. Hoare
Fairey III	G - E A L Q	2 Passengers and Pilot	Lieutenant Colonel V. Nicholl, D.S.C.

Messrs Saunders of Cowes, Isle of Wight, built the Kittiwake for this last class but it was wrecked on a trial flight when it ran onto rocks at Cowes, and was not repaired or proceeded further with.

Before the Competition proper got under way, several incidents occurred which may in some way have influenced the final results. Whilst on his way to Martlesham to fly the Avro Triplane, the Avro test-pilot, Captain D. C. Westgarth-Haslem crashed at Bentley, near Ipswich, on the 4th August, whilst flying the Avro Baby Type 534B, G - E A U G. Fuel trouble caused him to make a hurried forced landing and he was severely injured in the resultant landing in a rough field near Bentley Church. This eliminated his participation in the event and his place was taken at the last moment by Mr H. A. Hammersley. This crash is recorded in the locality, as a Court case ensued when a local resident removed a brass gauge from the wreckage and was summoned for doing so.

The Supermarine Sea Eagle amphibian suffered an undercarriage collapse on the 'drome but was repaired in time for the flying trials, whilst several contenders made swift engine and propeller changes as pre-contest trials conducted by themselves demanded changes to their satisfaction. Major H. G. Brackley flew the Handley-Page W.8 in the capacity of Company Chief Test Pilot, having only recently joined the Company on his return from Newfoundland where he had been waiting to fly the Handley-Page V.1500 bomber across the Atlantic for the *Daily Mail* £10,000 prize. As the Vickers Vimy with Alcock and Brown had "beaten him to it" he came home after demonstrating the bomber at several bases in the U.S.A.

In lighter vein, Captain Keep of Westlands, whilst on a demonstration flight, confirmed the safety of his Company's product by perturbing his passengers somewhat. In full flight and at some 80 m.p.h., he left his open cockpit aft of the passenger cabin and joining them, lit a cigarette and conversed whilst the Limousine III cruised leisurely along. Incidentally this aircraft carried its fuel in tanks under the mainplanes so that no fuel was carried in the fuselage, and therefore smoking was quite in order. On another day, to demonstrate the new approach to commercial flying Captain Keep took aloft a Company executive and his secretary, who typed letters for him whilst airborne.

In preparation for the event, the Chief Technical Officer at Martlesham Heath, Major Barlow, assisted by Captain Nightingale and Flight Sergeant Holles, surveyed the area and established the positions of, and the accuracy of the camera-obscura for use in the tests. Other officials taking part were Technicians Woodward-Nutt, Jennings, Scott-Hall, Rowe and Barren.

Towards the end of August, 1920, the evaluation of the twelve aircraft which had finally made the venue commenced and these were all put through the tests allotted. An example of the tension among the pilots in their efforts to do the best for their employers is shown in a tussle in the small aeroplane class.

After changing leading places several times, the Westland Limousine III and the Sopwith Antelope flown by Captain Keep and Mr Harry Hawker respectively, emerged as the leaders in this class. With one test to complete, the two machines were at level points, the final test deciding the winner. This all-important final test was the emergency landing, in which the pilots were required to make a steep approach, flare-out, land and stop as near as possible to the poles, supporting the balloon obstacles. This hazard consisted of two poles with a line from their tops stretched across the landing-path, the line carrying small balloons so that the approaching pilots could sight it.

This manoeuvre was to be carried out three times, the average of the three runs to be the final figure for the test. The rules also stated that should an aircraft become damaged whilst carrying out this test, automatic elimination would result. As the means of stopping an aircraft at this time was to dig the tail-skid into the ground and then throttle-back the engine, these two aircraft were revolutionary in that they were both fitted with wheel brakes and also small wheels carried on outriggers forward of the main undercarriage to prevent the machine "nosing-over" as the result of a too-heavily braked landing.

As both Keep and Hawker felt that they could soon be "home and dry" they were extremely anxious to make the most of their test, with good approaches and short landing runs. Being the sportsmen they were, as well as keen rivals, they tossed a coin to decide who should make the first run, Keep winning the toss, and putting Harry Hawker into the air first. His first attempt was, as expected from an airman of his calibre, very steep with the ensuing short, heavily braked landing run. This was followed by another in the same class which no doubt gave Hawker a feeling of confidence and lulled him into a state of self-satisfaction. His third approach over the obstacle was rather too steep and fast, resulting in a very fast and heavy landing, which when he braked resulted in his already over-taxed undercarriage not being able to take the strain and it collapsed. Captain Keep had only to make three safe approaches and landings to secure the top prize which he successfully achieved.

The final results were announced during the last week in October, 1920, the judges announcing their disappointment that the aircraft had not shown more advance in design and therefore they were not awarding the full prize money. In the large aeroplane class they withheld the first prize and awarded the second prize of £8,000 to the Handley-Page W.8 and the third prize of £4,000 to the only other aircraft in the class, the Vickers Vimy Commercial.

In the small aeroplane class, the first prize of £7,500 was given to the Westland Limousine III, the second of £3,000 to the Sopwith Antelope and the third of £1,500 to the Austin Kestrel.

The Vickers Viking III gained the first prize in the amphibian class, the Supermarine Sea Eagle I taking the second. No prize was awarded to the third contender in this class, the Fairey III, as it had failed to take-off the water at Felixstowe after the 24 hour mooring-out test.

Winner in the small aeroplane class: the Westland Limousine III.   *J. F. Brown*

Second in the small aeroplane class: the Sopwith Antelope.   *J. F. Brown*

Third in the small aeroplane class: the Austin Kestrel.   *J. F. Brown*

There was no winner in the large aeroplane class: but second place went to the Handley-Page W.8. *J. F. Brown*

Interior of the Handley-Page W.8. Note the ornate finish of the walls and the fire extinguisher on the wall. *J. F. Brown*

Third in the large aeroplane class the Vickers Vimy Commercial.   *J. F. Brown*

The more austere cabin of the Vickers Vimy Commercial.

First in the amphibian class: the Vickers Viking III.   *J. F. Brown*

Second in the amphibian class: the Supermarine Eagle I.   *J. F. Brown*

The only aircraft to see any service on the air-routes after the Competition were the Handley-Page W.8, the Vickers Vimy Commercial and the two amphibians, whose makers shortly afterwards amalgamated and they continued as one product.

After the contest the Handley-Page W.8 started on the London-Paris run during October 1921, for Handley-Page Transport Limited. Taken over by Imperial Airways during 1924, the W.8 finally crashed in that year. Her final demise was due to lack of gauges to indicate the fuel state in the tanks. These were situated in the upper mainplanes and were not interconnected and therefore when a leak developed in the port tank with the resultant loss of fuel, the port motor stopped when the tank emptied. The Captain quickly selected a suitable landing spot and put the aircraft down but whilst still running fast with the tail up, G - E A P J dropped into a sunken road, turned over and broke her back, the crew escaping with bruises and a shaking. The design continued through many more similar planes both civil and military until the early 1930's and beyond.

The Vickers Vimy Commercial went into service on the London-Paris run with Instone Air Lines, and then Imperial Airways, carrying its daily load of passengers without incident until it was relegated to freight duties which it still carried out without trouble until scrapped during 1925. This design also carried on through many more Vickers aircraft and the design outline can be clearly seen in the Vernon, Vanguard, Victoria and finally the Valentia, one of which, K.3603, flew from Martlesham Heath when the A & A.E.E. left for Boscombe Down during the summer of 1939.

The joint design of the two winning amphibians developed through the years and through various aircraft in this category finally to give us the well-loved Supermarine Walrus, which in later years operated from Martlesham and was the most welcome sight many a shot down, dinghy-borne aircrew had ever seen.

In the small aeroplane class, none carried on in the airways role, Westlands proceeding with other designs, Sopwiths became mainly devoted to military types, Austin and Beardmore left the aircraft industry for a while, whilst Bristols carried on the Seeley design through other types and Avros produced a few 547A's for service in Australia where they did not meet with great success. The Central Aircraft concern packed up after their aircraft, the Centaur crashed on its way back to London after the trials.

Fate made another of its periodical calls at the Heath during 1921, and the local paper recorded the incident, when the Bristol Braemar II C.4297 passenger triplane crashed into a hangar. Piloted by Captain O. M. Sutton, M.C. and crewed by three airmen, the massive four-engined triplane, started its take-off run across the 'drome, but when the pilot realized that he had insufficient room he

The wreckage of the Bristol Braemar Mk. II, C4297 after crashing into the hangar, with the remains of Airco DH9 H.3629, in front. *Stuart Leslie*

tried to stop but was unsuccessful and crashed into a hangar. It was reported in the style of the day: "Mr Walter Brooks, Coroner for the Liberty of Saint Etheldreda, resumed this Friday afternoon the Inquiry into the cause of the deaths of Captain O. Manners Sutton, M.C. and Air Mechanic Charles Sheridan who were killed in the aeroplane accident at Martlesham on Tuesday.

Corporal Cecil Ellison, a Mechanic said that on Tuesday he was one of the four who were in the triplane which met with the accident. It was a Bristol Braemar triplane and Captain Sutton was the pilot. The usual inspection was made and in witness's opinion everything was correct. On Tuesday, after starting the machine bumped off the ground, but came down again and witness felt her swing to port. Witness could not see outside the machine because he was directly behind the pilot, looking after the engines. At the time the machine swung all four engines were throttled down by Captain Sutton, and were all running smoothly. Witness said that in his theory, Captain Sutton, finding he had not sufficient room to clear the Squadron Offices, turned to port with the idea of making another start but had not enough room and crashed into the hangar. When the crash came, witness slid out of the machine.

Robert Charles Chipps, a rigger, said he thoroughly examined the rigging of the machine on August 11th, prior to the flight on the following day. The flight did not take place, and the machine was not touched until it was taken out for the flight on Tuesday.

The Coroner returned a verdict of 'Death from injuries received through an aeroplane colliding with a hangar.' "

Another witness writing many years later:

"I was posted to Martlesham Heath during January 1920 after returning from overseas service and at the time the Bristol Braemar stood in "B" Flight hangar having not flown a great deal since 1919. Early in 1920, a complete overhaul was ordered to prepare the aircraft for full tests. Right from the start there seemed to be a hoodoo on that triplane, as nothing went right and the whole Squadron was steeped in gloom when one of the 400 h.p. Liberty engines fell from its trestle and killed the "B" Flight sergeant-fitter who had the misfortune to be inspecting the engine from beneath at the time. The work was eventually completed and flight tests started, but either the third or forth flight proved to be the Braemar's last. The pilot did not attain sufficient altitude to clear "A" Flight hangar, ploughing through the hangar wall. Both the pilot and an airman who was sitting in the co-pilot's seat were killed. Perhaps the most surprising thing about the accident was the lack of fire, as all four petrol tanks were full."

Captain Oliver Manners Sutton M.C., was the inventor of the Sutton Harness, used exclusively on all R.A.F. aircraft until the advent of the ejector seat.

With the First World War now in the background, things began to move once again, with new types appearing at Martlesham Heath for evaluation and testing and two test pilots of that period who still live in the locality, Air Vice Marshal John Gray and Air Commodore Fred Battle, show very interesting notes in their log-books. The latter's log shows "The English Electric Wren which I flew at Martlesham was number J.6973, and took me up to 2500 feet (uncorrected) in one hour. Not bad for 3½ h.p.

Also test flown was the Raynham monoplane, Serial No. J.7518.

The Siddeley Siskin V had a good performance and I quite like it as an aeroplane, but its pilot's view for fighting was poor.

German Dornier Komet tested was a high wing monoplane with the undercarriage attached underneath to a small auxiliary plane.

The following 2 seat light planes were flown and tested:—
Hawker Cygnet I & II. British Anzani — Very Good. A.B.C. Scorpion — Not so good. Parnall Pixie III both as biplane and monoplane. Bristol Cherub. G - E B J G. Bristol Brownie. Bristol Cherub motor. G - E B J L. De Havilland 54 Humming Bird with J.A.P. motor. Single seater. Later accepted. Beardmore Wee-Bee I. G - E B J J.

I flew the Hawker Hedgehog on a number of occasions between 16th and 24th October, 1924. A nice well-behaved machine with no apparent vices, designed and built as a Private Venture by Hawkers to meet any possible requirement for a General Purpose Bomber in the Middle East or for use by the Navy. Not designed for any specific role it fell short of them all. Whilst at M.H. it bore no registration marks and had a very ordinary performance (stalling speed 47 m.p.h.). The Admiralty, of course, chose the Avro Bison because of its lovely cabin for the Admiral — although a very bad aeroplane with the gliding angle of a brick!

Flying Officer Charles Horrox was an expert on multi-engined aircraft and he was in "B" Flight under Flight Lieutenant E. Hilton. At one R.A.F. Hendon Display he was pilot in charge of the Armstrong Awana, a huge twin engined troop carrier. The Duke of York visited the Experimental Aircraft Park chanced to approach the Awana, in the cockpit of which Horrox happened to be sitting. The passenger door suddenly opened and a fitter popped his head in and shouted, 'Mr Orrox, the Dook to see yur'.

The C.L.A. 2 was a side by side two seater, grossly underpowered for its weight. Could only just get off the ground — perhaps the heather at M.H. was too much for it. I understand that they put a more powerful engine in later and that it performed more reasonably.

The De Havilland 42 with Jupiter engine proved better than its sister mounting an Armstrong Siddeley Jaguar. Both were called Dormouse. Rather heavy on controls but good visibility for both pilot and air gunner. Flight Lieutenant "Bob" Usher was doing aerobatics in it at Northolt a week after I had flown it at M.H. when the centre-section failed.

The Breguet 19, used by the French Air Force, and tested at M.H. was not much liked. The throttle worked the wrong way, i.e. to open it up it had to be pulled back, and this proved its undoing at M.H. When about to leave the hangar on a test, its pilot was called to the telephone. He therefore gave up his seat to a mechanic, who, finding the aeroplane moving forward, promptly pulled the throttle back. Result — much damage to hangar and write-off of aeroplane.

An exciting incident occurred when the Handley-Page Monoplane was being tested as a deck-fighter for the United States Navy at M.H. A single-seat monoplane, it was powered by a Bentley B.R.2 rotary engine. We in the R.A.F. were not allowed to fly the aircraft and all tests were carried out by a special pilot, Mr F. P. Raynham, engaged by Messrs Handley-Page. After some preliminary flights, Raynham took the aircraft on the speed course to ascertain necessary speed corrections to the A.S.I. This was done by flying at certain steady speeds low down along the measured timed distance. He had just completed about two runs and was half way along another at a fairly high speed when the aircraft shot up vertically, flattened out, throttled down, then proceeded to fly twice round the aerodrome in a very unsteady undulating manner. It then came in to land, the pilot apparently "pump-handling" like mad. Luckily he finally hit the ground at the bottom of a swoop and managed to switch off. The aircraft went over on its back and was badly smashed, Raynham sustaining a broken arm.

He later explained to us that the duralumin ball joint connecting the bottom of his control-column with a fore and aft rod actuating the elevators suddenly broke.

Luckily he spotted this in time and was able to grab the push and pull rod lying under his seat and between his legs, by one hand and could just reach the throttle and fine adjustment controls for the engine with the other. But in doing so, he could not see out of the cockpit, so he had to keep popping up and down. His was a magnificent effort!

We had a lot of trouble with the De Havilland 9A petrol system owing to the rubber hose connections. Maintenance standards were low until the introduction of regular inspection schedules, well under way by 1926."

Squadron Leader Orlebar, whilst testing a Westland Weasel, J.6577, had a narrow escape when the machine caught fire and he side-slipped it neatly down and jumped out quickly by which time the aircraft was burning well.

The 1927 model Vickers Virginia broke its back shortly after take-off and crashed, fortunately without fire, at the western end of the aerodrome. Corporal Gray the rear gunner escaped with a severe shaking, but Aircraftsman Minns in the front cockpit, was less fortunate, as having jumped out at the moment of impact, he was struck by one of the Napier Lion engines which had broken loose, and crushed to death. This accident is remembered by many who have related it, as the Station Medical Officer on arriving at the scene of the crash, entered the darkness of the wreckage, and in the fastness of the fuselage, heard a loud moaning. Feeling in the gloom he located a human posterior and administered a pain-killing injection with his syringe. Unfortunately the moaning still continued, but a would-be rescuer, already in the wreckage, slept for some time!

Blackburn's Turcock fighter arrived at Martlesham Heath for testing in a civilian guise, as this beautifully streamlined biplane had not met with success in getting a place in the R.A.F. However, its makers, not wishing to abandon this design, looked for a foreign buyer and received some encouragement from Turkey. As the previous design had been named Lincock, it followed that this machine became the Turcock. Whilst carrying out speed trials on 13th February, 1928, Flying Officer Dauncy passed over the measured mile in one direction, followed at a greater speed in the opposite way, and then followed by a much faster run from the eastern end of the course. Hitting a tree at the western end, the Turcock cartwheeled along the ground, the pilot being killed instantly.

Vickers' contender for the single-seat interceptor role, the low-wing monoplane Jockey, J.9122, failed to recover from a flat spin, and crashed near the aerodrome although the pilot managed to escape by parachute.

The Vickers Jockey Interceptor J.9122. *British Aircraft Corporation*

Squadron Leader Noakes was posted to Martlesham Heath during 1927, after being the Chief Flying Instructor at the Central Flying School and recalls two of his "Martlesham Incidents."

"We had at the time several aircraft for testing, one of which was the Parnall Pippit, a single-seater fighter undergoing acceptance trials. It was reported to me that the aircraft had a distinct turning tendency to the right. So on a certain morning before breakfast I took off to see what the trouble was. I found that the report was correct and on returning to the aerodrome, when pulling out of a slight dive the leading edge of the tailplane broke away downwards. I released my safety harness ready for jumping but then found that I could keep the aircraft on a safety speed glide and made to land down the straight extension of the aerodrome, but could not flatten out for the landing. The result was that the aircraft struck the ground throwing me out when turning over on its back — result, a broken neck. I was deposited some distance from the aircraft in fairly tall bracken and one of the first to find me was Flight Lieutenant "Poppy" Pope. He was later sent down from Martlesham Heath to test the second Pippit at the Works aerodrome. He took off and when at 2,000 feet, flew into cloud, turned right, the rudder broke off and the aircraft turned on to its back dropping "Poppy" out and he hit the ground just after his parachute opened. This was the end of the Parnall effort!

After being in Ipswich Hospital for some time, my final departure from Martlesham Heath was on a stretcher inside a Vickers Vernon ambulance aircraft and flown to an R.A.F. Hospital. I have always been known throughout the Service as "OOGY".

Previous to this a notable event with more pleasant results took place. The Beardmore Inflexible was, until the advent of the Bristol Brabazon, the largest landplane ever constructed in the United Kingdom. Designed by Doctor Rohrbach at the request of the Air Ministry, who were at the time interested in the construction and performance of large all-metal monoplanes and built in Scotland by the well-known engineering firm of William Beardmore and Company, the aircraft was shipped to Ipswich Docks in large pieces, and in the words of one of the men responsible for its transit, "we had one hell of a job getting it up from the Docks and through the streets, the pieces only missing the corners of buildings by inches."

At the time of its construction it was the largest aircraft in the world, and its size caused many headaches in the design offices of the makers and the design team led by Mr W. S. Shackleton were further confronted with difficulties when Doctor Rohrbach withdrew half-way through the construction and Beardmores were left to finish the design. Tests at Farnborough of a model in the wind tunnel showed up various defects in control design, necessitating servo assistance and vibration dampers for the very large rudder. Aerodynamic balances were also fitted to the ailerons and elevators. The design was, in fact, on the drawing-board some 5 years before the first flight. It was the most rectangular flying machine ever seen, all angles except the angle of incidence being right-angles. The fuselage was of square-section, the plan view of the wings and tail, rectangular, as were also the fin and balancing horns. Powered by three 650 h.p. Rolls-Royce Condor engines with two bladed wooden propellors, the engines were controlled by three separate throttles. An interesting feature of this enormous plane with so many unusual features were the 8 foot diameter landing wheels made by the Dunlop Company, fitted with independent hydraulic brakes, one of the first machines to be so fitted. Another feature was a system whereas when the weight of the aircraft was taken on the tail-wheel, the main wheel brakes were automatically actuated.

The first flight was made on 5th March, 1928, by Squadron Leader Jack Noakes, the only other person aboard being a representative of the makers. It

Largest aircraft erected and flown at Martlesham, the Beardmore Inflexible. Note the 8 foot diameter wheels and the cable from wingtip to wingtip to maintain the dihedral angle. 1928.

was thought at the time of erection that the take-off area available would not be large enough for the machine, so extensions were carried out on the aerodrome side of "B" Flight Road in order to increase the length of run. Temporary gates were erected in order to control the traffic, and the first take-off was delayed for several days in order to make certain that the wind was in the correct position for the operation.

As it turned out, all this was unnecessary as the giant aircraft was airborne before she had reached the main runway area proper! The aircraft handled well, was very stable and without vices, although with a loaded weight of 37,000 lbs. was somewhat underpowered. Its top speed was around 100 m.p.h., and although passing its tests, it had served its purpose and its last test was one of loading to destruction to ascertain the ultimate strength of all the component parts. During 1931, the wings which had a large diameter cable running from wing-tip to wing-tip via the fuselage bottom, were removed and the pieces were left to weather alongside "B" Flight hangar, testing out anti-corrosion coatings for metal.

During its life at Martlesham, which was its only home, Squadron Leader Noakes flew the Inflexible to the Hendon Air Display where it was demonstrated to the crowds and on its return home to Martlesham the aircraft's lower surfaces were covered with scores of signatures and names and addresses of people who had written on the metal skin of the fuselage.

In passing, the Inflexible had a wing span of 157 feet 6 inches, and a length of 75 feet 7 inches, stood 21 feet tall and had a wing area of 1,967.25 square feet, truly a giant for her time.

This was still a time of "financial cramp" and many designs had to make do with existing components. Mr Gaunt recalls presenting one such aircraft for evaluation at the A & A.E.E.

"One of my longest visits to the A & A.E.E. was on the occasion of the Acceptance Trials of the Westland Wapiti, a general-purpose biplane. There was a competition to determine the most suitable type built to a specification which was based on long experience with the De Havilland 9a's in the Middle East. Westlands had built many D.H.9a's and realized the improvements needed in this type which was of course not of their design — they built them as sub-contractors. One stipulation of the design was that it must use D.H.9a type mainplanes, and so Westlands kept virtually the same standard wings, in either wood or metal, but mounted on a new metal framed, fabric covered fuselage with a Bristol air-cooled radial engine and a more modern undercarriage. The need to meet desert conditions and to carry a large variety of spares such as a tail skid, jack, engine tool-kits, screw pickets, engine covers, locking devices for the controls etc., etc., led to great ingenuity in the disposal and securing thereof. Glosters, Faireys, Vickers and Bristols were our main competitors and there was keen rivalry between the firms' representatives. As the "sticks" and "unsticks" tests were followed by the "pitch and toss" and "partial climb" and "climb to ceiling" with oxygen, the figures were secretly discussed and first one and then the other became favourite. Time needed to change a wheel, propeller or engine (or any other main component) were all taken into account, so that it was not the fastest aircraft which won but the best "all-rounder". Gunnery and bombing trials were followed by Squadron Trials, and I recall visiting Eastchurch and Worthy Down to obtain the views of Flight Lieutenant A. W. Tedder (later Air Marshal) who was a "bright and coming" gunnery and bombing expert, and he flew and approved the Wapiti.

We had incidents from time to time and I recall two involving Westland aircraft. The first was when Flight Lieutenant Webster was piloting the Wessex, a small three-engined air-liner with myself and Scott-Hall as passengers, on a fuel

Flying view of the Westland Wessex, indicating (1) where the undercarriage pin sheared and (2) the direction in which the assembly swung down and up again.   *Westland Aircraft Co.*

consumption test. We were fully laden, passengers being represented by lead weights and shot-bags. On take-off we passed over some of Martlesham's many hollows when a heavy "bonk" sheared a pin securing the oleo strut of one undercarriage to its outboard engine mounting, thus allowing it to swing down and under the fuselage, where it hung suspended by its radius rod. Ground staff held up wheels to show us that there was a failure — in fact, we thought that we had lost a wheel, the absence of which was observed from the cabin windows. Not relishing the idea of a one-wheel landing with full load, we began to lighten ship by dumping ballast via the side door, Scott-Hall holding it open whilst I dumped each time "Webby" flew over a suitable part of the Heath. Next, after debating the comparative safety of land or sea, "Webby" decided to fly around to reduce fuel, and then brought her in with a nice side-slip and gentle contact on the sound wheel. This caused the hanging wheel to hinge up again into the engine mounting and we heeled over with the wing-tip scraping, but without injury to the components. The most alarming effect on touch-down was caused by Scott-Hall ripping open the fabric escape panel over the cabin which seemed to cause more noise than the crash itself. The fault proved to be a tube above the oleo leg not bedding fully into its socket so that the taper pins securing the same against gravity were sheared and allowed the half undercarriage to fall free.

The second incident was more serious and involved the Westland P.V.7 high wing general purpose monoplane piloted by Harald Penrose (our Westland test pilot) who was putting it through its paces in the vicinity of Martlesham, but out of sight of the aerodrome. His failure to return at the due time was followed by a telephone message that he had landed by parachute some miles away and that the aircraft was a complete "write-off". As we neared the scene, with relief for his safety, we were amused to see him holding his trousers, as, in being dragged along the ground by his parachute, all his trouser buttons had sheared off. A careful piecing together of all the recovered pieces of the aircraft by McKenna and his staff led to the sequence of failure being found — an outrigger strut failed "in compression" under a severe down load. "Hal" Penrose's escape, the first from an enclosed cabin aircraft, certainly proved the working of the emergency escape hinge pins on the doors. The ironical thing about this incident was that after the aircraft had taken-off for this test, a telegram was received at Martlesham Heath from the Westland design office at Yeovil asking for the test not to be carried out as they were not too certain of the strength limitations of the components.

The nature of the countryside at Martlesham led to some trouble with partridges and I recall one of our test-pilots, Flight Lieutenant Louis Paget, running into a covey on take-off and having a pitot-tube and interplane strut damaged thereby. Must have been one of the earliest bird-strikes. The aerodrome surface tried out the prototypes and their undercarriages and many aircraft became bogged-down and had to be helped in. When tail wheels came into use there were many cases of "shimmying" (wobbling from side to side) which the grass-covered testing grounds of the makers had not induced."

Stuart Culley, mentioned previously as the victor over the Zeppelin L.53, returned to Martlesham Heath as Adjutant and test-pilot and remembers:

"I commanded "C" Flight during 1929, the two-seater flight. This flight fully or partially tested many aircraft during my stay and in particular I remember the Hawker Naval Hart. I personally did most of the testing of this navalised Hart, with folding wings for carrier work. The final tests in those days were spinning and also newly put into operation was one called "T.V." or Terminal Velocity.

It so happened that the spinning trials coincided within a few days with the Schneider Trophy Race at Calshot, in August and September. Naturally the original Hart had been spun and I did not think much about any difficulty, but even so the drill was always to start spinning tests to the right or left according to the propeller rotation, so that in the event of any difficulty one could put on engine and come out.

Thus I started my first spin, and after the required eight to ten turns I tried to come out and could not. I blamed myself and went back to the standard 10,000 feet and went in again. Same result. I then became very interested indeed, and although feeling not too well, I went back a third time and the same thing occurred again. By this time, I came to the conclusion that something was wrong and feeling very ill indeed, came down and landed and made my report. This was the Friday and the next day I went to Calshot on board the motor yacht of Fred Bennett of Hawker Aircraft who had built the aircraft. There was also present P. W. B. Bulman, the famous "Georgie" Bulman, Chief Test Pilot of Hawkers, who later in the evening asked how the Hart tests were going and although I tried to ride him off, he finally demanded to know what was wrong and when I asked him if he had spun the Hart before delivery, he thought a long time, and then said that he had not done so. I can assure you things moved very quickly then and he got on the telephone!!! On the Monday, we had a meeting with Mr "Tom" Sopwith present at the Felix Hotel, Felixstowe, and they agreed, after further reports, that the aircraft must be modified.

Later the same week, the also famous test-pilot "Gerry" Sayer, flew down to Martlesham in the Hart, and arrived over the Officers' Mess at 10,000 feet and then spun the aircraft down to 1,000 feet before attempting to come out, then coming in for a perfect landing, with the job well done.

I also did the Terminal Velocity Dive which meant putting the aircraft into a straight dive from 16,000 feet for a dive of 10,000 feet duration and obtaining the highest possible speed. This had first been done by Flight Lieutenant N. H. Jenkins, who was commander of "C" Flight before I took over, and who was unfortunately killed in North Africa in the long-range attempt to the Cape.

His T.V. speed came out at 325 m.p.h., and I managed to push it up to 330 m.p.h. Now I manage to travel horizontally to London in perfect comfort in a Trident at double my speed in that T.V. dive."

When the Westland Westbury C.O.W. Gun-fighter was being "run-up", the wheel chocks slid forward on the concrete-apron, thus allowing the aircraft to over-run the Hucks Starter which had just started it up, causing considerable damage to the aircraft and the Starter. At the Court of Inquiry carried out under the Station Commander, Group Captain Rees, V.C., evidence proved that chocks would hold aircraft "running-up" on tarmac but not on concrete. It must be appreciated that this was, of course, before the general use of brakes on aircraft.

"Bill" Pegg of Bristols recalls his Martlesham days, but as a junior R.A.F. officer, and whose early experience was of having to "bale-out" of an Avro Cadet when the wings parted company with the fuselage during a T.V. dive near the aerodrome. When such an incident occurred, all the pieces that could be recovered were brought back to the Station, and plotted on a large-scale map. Afterwards they were assembled on a large hangar floor and by this means the cause of the accident could usually be found. In the case of the Avro Cadet, it was discovered that the wings had been subjected to overloads caused by aileron flutter.

On another occasion, he had to climb up to 20,000 feet in an Armstrong-Whitworth Siskin fighter, above cloud, in order to try out experimental cockpit heating equipment. The flight was timed for one and a half hours duration and as no oxygen was carried, a state of muddlement came over him. After about two hours, the engine stopped owing to lack of fuel and the long glide down started through the clouds finally coming out into the clear over the coast. A suitable landing site was located, a field large enough for this purpose, and a successful landing carried out. This was followed by a search for a telephone. After quite a long walk, a main road was located and an approaching bus stopped to convey the walker to the nearest town. The passengers eyed the new "arrival" with more than usual interest, fully dressed in flying gear, and to the pilot's consternation, it appeared that the bus's destination was BRIGHTON. Upon arrival at a suitable garage, 10 gallons of petrol was purchased and conveyed to the aircraft, which was now partially refuelled, and a take-off made and flight to Tangmere, where arrival was successful with nothing in the tank and a somewhat evasive explanation for the visit. After refuelling, an equally swift take-off was made and a hasty retreat beat back to Martlesham.

The Percival Mew Gull, a very small civil racing monoplane had been brought to the A & A.E.E. by Mr Edgar Percival, the designer and builder, and as the aircraft had been entered for the King's Cup Air Race by a member of the Royal Family, it needed a Certificate of Airworthiness in order to enter. It arrived on a Sunday morning and Percival expected to take it home to Luton that evening.

On inspection, it was discovered that there was no way of turning off the petrol from the cockpit and this operation had to be carried out from the outside. This was dangerous from the fire point of view and was pointed out to the designer, who, sportingly perhaps, being an Australian, argued a little, and then flew it back to Luton to have it fitted in the cockpit. He returned some three hours later, and Flight Lieutenant John Boothman, later Air Marshal Sir John Boothman, and of Schneider Trophy fame, and myself did the test flying alternatively during the rest of the day until the evening and completed all the tests necessary for a C. of A. to be issued. Flying this aircraft was rather un-nerving as the wheels were very small and its high landing speed, and the rough surface of the aerodrome, made landing and take-off "touchy". This must have surely been the quickest an aircraft have ever gained a C. of A. Certificate, as nowadays, these tests take anything up to a year to complete.

During my time at Martlesham there arrived the first aircraft which we had seen with a retractable undercarriage. This was the Airspeed Courier, a civil low wing monoplane by a relatively new maker. There were some earlier experimental aircraft fitted with this drag-reducing device, but I believe this was the first to be designed into an ordinary machine intended for regular commercial operation. We were extremely sceptical about the whole apparatus. What happened, we wondered if, after raising the undercarriage on take-off, it got stuck and would not or could not be lowered for landing. The makers of the aeroplane had wisely anticipated this scepticism and shortly after the arrival of the aircraft for its first flight tests, a large lorry appeared. On this lorry was mounted a full-scale working model of the undercarriage together with a smooth-talking gentleman. We pilots were given a 'pep' talk on its operation with particular emphasis on the various safety devices which made it 'absolutely fool-proof.'

We were all encouraged to get on the lorry and operate the mechanism for ourselves and altogether the demonstration was making very good progress. None of us had caught him out with any awkward questions, and as he explained 'any pilot with the most limited intelligence could not possibly make a mistake and we have pilots here of considerable intelligence, etc etc.'

Just about this time I was looking out over the aerodrome and to my horror saw the Courier approaching to land with its undercarriage still neatly tucked up in the wing. I just had time to yell out to bring the other fellows into the picture before there was a splintering crash and a cloud of dust. One of our experienced pilots had apparently performed the impossible and landed without the advantage of an undercarriage to cushion his arrival. He had been carrying out altitude tests with various throttle settings and had disconnected the warning hooter as it annoyed him. This hooter sounded a loud warning that the undercarriage was still retracted when the throttle was brought back to the setting that they would require for landing.

Another "design incident" occurred during 1931, when the Hawker Super Fury was being piloted by Flight Lieutenant Ward on a high speed trial. The pilot's attention was attracted by the Hawker representative, Mr Thompson, waving a large handkerchief, and the aircraft was carefully brought down on the edge of the 'drome. The undercarriage design had doubtless been well covered for landing-loads, but the loading in high speed flight had some more work to be done on it, the pilot being most surprised when one of the landing wheels with its struts appeared through the cockpit floor.

Wing Commander Mumford recalls that whilst on a night flying exercise in an Armstrong Whitworth Atlas 2-seater, carried out on a very dark night, a landing was attempted. As this resulted in an "over-shoot", another "run-in" was made, but the under-wing landing flares failed to ignite. Climbing round again, and now without the assistance of a flare-path to guide them, they gained height in order to orientate themselves, and then decided to fly towards the sea in order to pick up a land-mark on the coast. Having reached the sea near Felixstowe, they flew along the coast in an easterly direction until they picked up the mouth of the River Deben at Bawdsey. Following the river upstream they arrived at Waldringfield, east of Martlesham, and turning again on this point, they then proceeded westerly, gradually losing height and eventually picked out the newly installed electric lighting of the billiard-room of the Sergeants' Mess, which had been switched on by some unknown, but in this instance, very helpful person. Using these lights as a direction and height indicator, a safe landing was effected after a somewhat unorthodox navigational experience.

The M.1/30, Blackburn's bid for a torpedo bomber specification crashed into the trees almost opposite where *Black Tiles* Restaurant now stands after engine failure just after take-off, but the crew got away with a shaking and bruises. In happier circumstances, a Gloster Grebe, returning from firing practice at Orfordness, ran out of petrol and landed in Powling's Field at the back of the farm near the 'drome. The field in question had just been lined out with heaps of pig manure, all of which the pilot just managed to miss, finishing up almost in a recently completed pig-sty. The aircraft had to be dismantled in order to get it back to the Station.

Another fatal crash occurred on Friday afternoon, the 19th May, 1933, but this was of a different nature as it did not involve test flying. Three Bristol Bulldog single-seat fighters were practising formation aerobatics with smoke ready for the forthcoming R.A.F. Hendon Pageant. The three aircraft, watched by the author who was standing on the apron near "C" Flight hangar, left the aerodrome and climbed to altitude piloted by Flying Officer Pegg, Flight Lieutenant Moir and Flight Lieutenant Campbell. At this stage it is desirable to mention that these practices were carried out in the pilot's own time and that was the reason for the lateness in the day when the crash occurred.

Whilst on the top of a formation loop, over the southern perimeter of the 'drome, two of the inverted aircraft touched, those of Flight Lieutenant Moir and Flight Lieutenant Campbell. One dived down to explode in a cloud of smoke and flame, whilst the other spun down to crash near the burning aircraft. Flight Lieutenant Campbell who was carrying out this exercise for the first time, taking the place of a sick colleague, was killed, whilst Flight Lieutenant Moir parachuted to safety after struggling from the spinning tangled wreckage. Flying Officer Pegg made a circuit and landed safely. As the incident took place after working hours the crash was witnessed by the pilots' wives and many of the aerodrome personnel.

Also during 1933, on 21st October, 1933, as it approached to land after its third test flight, the Boulton and Paul Mail Carrier, G - A B Y K, a civil high speed biplane, flown by Flight Lieutenant Richmond, stalled and crashed on the perimeter near Dobb's Lane Corner. The pilot was thrown out, sustaining multiple injuries but fortunately the machine did not burn.

A Bristol Bulldog fighter, three of which were involved in the tragic formation crash of 19th May, 1933.   *C. H. Barnes*

A civil casualty that came to grief whilst approaching from the Dobb's Lane end—the Boulton and Paul Mail Carrier G-ABYK.
Boulton-Paul Aircraft

Aircraft testing, both military and civil continued through the 30's, many interesting and often unorthodox examples of the aircraft designer's art appeared for flight certification and evaluation. Allied to these machines, of course, were the newly developed engines, as at this time the leaders of the race for efficiency changed hands many times between the airframe and the engine. The new engines, both radial and in-line, air-cooled and liquid-cooled, not forgetting the steam cooled examples with their many and varied radiators placed around the aircraft, were presented for testing, sometimes in new aircraft, married to a new airframe for the first time, but more often than not, in an established design picked for its known reliability. It was for this reason that at Martlesham one could usually see many of the elderly types of aircraft performing this useful unglamorous duty for aerodynamic testing of components, engines or armaments. Up to the outbreak of hostilities in 1939, Vickers Virginia and Valentia, Hawker Harts and their many variants, Bristol Bulldogs and Vickers Vincents could be seen going about their daily duties around Martlesham.

As the engines became larger and more complex, the inertia starter and the gas-starters became more widely used, and thus a vehicle so often seen running around the 'drome was less and less required until it finally disappeared. This was the Hucks Starter Vehicle, designed by Captain Hucks, and usually comprised a Ford Model T chassis, with a superstructure above and behind the driver's seat carrying a long rod forward with a "dog-claw" or clutch on the other end. Driven by an unguarded chain over sprockets straight from the engine, this rod revolved when the engine gear was engaged to drive it. The starter was driven up to the front of the aircraft, or back if it were a pusher, and positioned so that the dog-claw engaged with another similar unit on the propeller hub. The marrying of these two units was carried out by an airman standing on the front of the Starter. On instructions from the aircraft's cockpit, relayed via another airman on the wing-tip, the Starter's engine was revved-up, the gear thrown-in, and the propeller and engine turned-over. Smart work in the cock pit would result in a roar and a stab of flame and cloud of exhaust smoke as the engine burst into life, but laxity in the "office" would only cause this operation to be carried out again and perhaps yet again.

After several false starts, the engine would become flooded with petrol, and the ground crew would then have to turn the airscrew, by hand, in the opposite direction to its normal rotation, in order to clear the cylinders of the neat petrol which had accumulated in them, giving a "wet" engine.

Coupled with the new and more powerful engines, the need arose for new airscrews capable of absorbing the power, and it was about this time that the

Hucks Aircraft Engine Starter Vehicle, locally manufactured by Ransomes, Sims and Jefferies Ltd., Ipswich.   *Ransomes, Sims and Jefferies Ltd.*

large wooden laminated propellers gave way, at first to the fixed-pitch metal propellers and then to the variable-pitch unit. The number of blades per airscrew also changed, as up to this time, the standard had usually been two or four blades, and now three became the standard. Some time later, however, the four bladed variety appeared again, then for the first time, five, followed by the contra-rotating examples, with three or four blades, combining six or eight blades on one airscrew.

As with the engines, the airframes also changed, through the all-wooden, to the composite, and finally the all metal structure, now the standard. Fabric covering lived on for a long time, as although airframes became all-metal, apart from engine cowlings and panels, fabric remained king of the covering materials. It was comparatively cheap, easy to handle, and easy to repair, but high speed finally ousted it out of the airframe, except for control surfaces. Ailerons, elevators, and rudders retained their fabric covering where lightness was an advantage for control purposes. The frontal panels gradually worked their way aft until they eventually covered the whole fuselage over tubular steel structures. These panels were gradually replaced by the stressed-skin covering, or "monocque" construction where the skin carried all the loads.

Undoubtedly the greatest change was the advent of the cantilever monoplane over the multi-strutted biplane. In all fairness, it must be stated that the development of the biplane reached a stage of almost perfection, advancing from its many strutted and rigged forebears, to the cleaner, drag-reduced types at the end of its career. In many cases, designers had substituted flying and landing wires, the crossed rigging wires between the planes of a biplane or triplane, with streamlined tubular struts and many graceful and efficient designs ensued. Examples of these were the Fairey Fantome and the many and varied Hawker designs. In the civil field, a variety of large and reliable aircraft appeared, such as the Handley-Page H.P.42, surely the safest aircraft ever flown on commercial routes.

The elegant streamlined biplane which almost reached perfection, the Fairey Fantome of 1938.
Westland Aircraft Co.

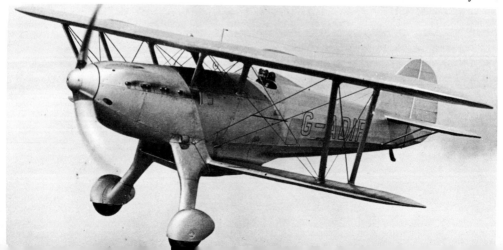

The beautiful streamlined all-wooden four-engined airliner, the De Havilland DH 91 Albatross
"Frobisher" G-AEDL. *B.O.A.C.*

The inspections needed daily to keep the biplane at the peak of efficiency faded to a more conservative form with the cantilever monoplane, and experimentation had shown only too well the rich gains to be obtained from streamlining, resulting in designers striving to give their aircraft the cleanest passage through the air. Frontal facing radiators for liquid-cooled motors had first of all turned to their sides, and then disappeared into fairings and troughs, finally disappearing within the leading-edges of the wing itself. Undercarriages at first reduced their number of struts, and those which remained incorporated ingenious methods of internal springing within the wheel itself to carry the landing loads after the tyres had taken the initial impact. Naturally, wing loadings increased, but with the stiffer structures now employed, greater internal loads such as fuel, armament and stores could be accommodated without increasing drag.

Aircrews were not forgotten in this new thinking as cockpits became enclosed, glazed with Perspex panels, gun turrets appeared affording protection to the gunner from the new-increasing slipstream, also assisting the aiming of the guns.

The more homely cockpits brought about a change in flying apparel of the crews, no longer were they subjected to the battering effect of the slipstream, so lighter and less cumbersome kit was the order of the day.

The over-all appearance of the aircraft also changed, as after the cessation of hostilities in 1919, fighter machines reverted to their all-silver finish, with the red, white and blue roundels on the upper and lower surfaces of the mainplanes, and the vertical stripes on the rudder, first of all with red forward and then after 15th August, 1930, the reverse. After 1st August, 1934, the size of the roundels decreased so as not to cover control surfaces, and the rudder stripes disappeared altogether.

The Expansion Schemes brought with them the green and brown wavy camouflage, wing and fuselage roundels with a yellow border, and small vertical stripes on the fin or fins. Bombers went all-black underneath, whilst fighters ranged from pale-blue to grey, black and white and, in some cases, silver. Trainers, hitherto all yellow, went green and brown on topsides and "Alert Yellow" beneath with wide yellow bands round the fuselage and wings.

Both Firsts, but the last and the first. The all-metal finished prototype Bristol Blenheim K.7033 and the camouflaged prototype Handley-Page Harrow K.6933.

C. H. Barnes and Handley-Page Ltd.

More incidents occurred in the later 1930's, when the prototype Bristol Bombay troop carrier crashed on the North-West perimeter of the aerodrome, killing all the crew as it burned in the garden of a house, and only a short distance from where a Fairey Gordon had dived into the ground a few months previously.

One of the later well-known types made an unfortunate start, this was the Armstrong-Vickers Wellington, the "Wimpy": as a graceful all-silver prototype, the B.9/32, serial number K.4049, she crashed on an early test flight. Of all metal geodetic framed construction, fabric covered and powered by two Bristol Pegasus radial engines, it was on an evening test flight during April 1937 with Flight Lieutenant Hare at the controls and Leading Aircraftsman Smirthwaite as flight observer, carrying out diving trials. Whilst passing over the aerodrome in a southerly direction, the mass-balance in the elevators became detached, causing violent flutter and final collapse of the rear fuselage. The pilot was thrown out through the cockpit roof but luckily parachuted to safety, the observer being less fortunate as his parachute was stowed aft in the fuselage, adjacent to the portion which had failed and he was carried down with the main wreckage to crash on the Brightwell side of the 'drome. During the next few days, numbers of airmen from the A & A.E.E. carried out an extensive search in the final flight path area of the crashed aircraft looking for pieces of evidence to help ascertain the cause of the mishap. It is to their credit that the mass balance, consisting of a strip of lead, was finally found and proved to be the trouble.

The Vickers-Armstrong prototype B.9/32 Bomber K.4049 lost at Martlesham whilst carrying out diving trials.   *Vickers Ltd.*

A short while afterwards, a Fairey Battle from the A & A.E.E. "force-landed" on the shingle beach near Orfordness. Owing to the extremely heavy weight of this aircraft, and the loose nature of the surface where it rested, the salvaging of this machine was extremely difficult. Having lifted it off the beach, it had to be jacked and packed-up, high enough on the support trolley to clear the parapets of the numerous small bridges to be negotiated on its journey across the marshland from the beach to firmer ground.

Several of the latter well-known aircraft suffered set-backs of one kind or another whilst on trials at Martlesham Heath, and these included the Spitfire and the Hurricane, whilst the Gloster F.9/37 twin-engined fighter was unfortunate, in that as the result of a landing mishap at Martlesham during trials, it was not rebuilt in time for production and lost its place to the Bristol Beaufighter which was in the same category. The aircraft purchased by the British Purchasing Commission in the United States arrived late in the A & A.E.E. period and were tested, and whilst carrying out these trials one of the first North American Harvard 1's crashed at Eyke near Woodbridge with fatal results.

Squadron Leader Collins was awarded the Air Force Cross for bringing safely back to the Station the second prototype Westland Lysander after it had lost the majority of the upper surface wing fabric covering during recovery from a test-dive. The pilot of a Miles Magister, carrying out spinning tests just off the coast at Felixstowe was not so fortunate, as he was drowned when the aircraft failed to recover from the spin and crashed into the sea.

It was thus that when the A & A.E.E. was at its busiest period, just pre-war, that it was forced to move due to the outbreak of war to Boscombe Down, where it still resides continuing the work started at Martlesham Heath. In the annals of aviation history, Martlesham Heath has carved itself a niche that cannot ever be erased as its work had the effect of making British and indeed international aircraft better in every way for their visit there. In the same class, a Martlesham pilot was the supreme craftsman in his art, and the mention of almost any well-known pre-war name would automatically couple the name with that of Martlesham Heath.

Strangers in the Camp. North American Aircraft Harvard 1 N.7003 at Martlesham for production trials. 1939. *Flight 16449*

CHAPTER SEVEN

The Other Firm—Armament Testing. 1917—1939

WITH the word "Armament" in the Unit's title a few words must be said on this subject which was always shrouded in mystery and was never as obvious as the aircraft side of the business.

Lord Trenchard once made the statement that, "The Royal Air Force exists for armament" and although early thinking was that the purpose of this Service was defence of the British Isles and its cities and industries, this turned more and more to the other swing of the pendulum with the emphasis coming down on the offensive role of both fighters and bombers. In order to achieve this object, constant review was kept of the latest methods and ideas and worked mainly along the following lines: continuous research to broaden the radius of offensive and continuous research into the betterment of delivery methods and the effects of the weapon/s when delivered.

The guns installed in the aircraft of the First World War period were basically only lightened and hastily adopted versions of existing ground weapons used by the Army and Navy, and in all cases used Army ammunition. The Vickers, usually used as the fixed forward armament of fighters, had the cooling water jacket removed, for lightness as the slipstream in flight provided the cooling medium. Flexible guns for the observer or wing mounted guns for fighters were the Lewis gun, offered to the British by its American inventor, Colonel Lewis, firstly taken up by the Belgian Government and finally accepted by the British Government with large fees payable to the Belgians. Also in the case of this gun for airborne operations, the cooling jacket was discarded allowing the airflow to deal with cooling duties.

In the observer's position, this gun was normally mounted on a ring mounting known as the Scarff Ring Mounting, named after its R.N.A.S. inventor, Warrant Officer F. W. Scarff, and this saw many years service until the coming of turrets.

Sighting of guns both fixed and moveable had created problems over the years and a great deal of research in this field was carried out by Professor Melville-Jones. Fixed guns were usually sighted by means of an open ring-sight with four crossed spokes at the breech-end, whilst at the fore-end the normal fitting was a single

Midships gun position on Vickers Vimy showing drum-fed Lewis gun. Note how the biplane tailplane obstructed the field of fire from this position. *Wing Commander A. Boeree*

Cockpit of captured German Fokker D.VII *Wing Commander A. Boeree*

bead-sight. In some cases an Aldis telescopic sight was fitted to fixed guns and proved to be an advantage provided the pilot had time to be able to sight it. The other great advantage of this device was that it could be illuminated at night.

At this time the flexible guns also sported another refinement, the Warren Vane Sight, fitted to the fore end of the barrel and this allowed for wind movement on the gun and the resultant sighting.

In the case of the twin Vickers fixed guns on fighters, these were of .303 calibre and were fed by twin belts, usually comprising tracer, solid or armour piercing bullets. Often incendiary bullets, known as "Brocks" after the makers, were included in the regulation requirement, but more often than not to the individual pilot's fancy. Aiming was assisted by the tracer bullets and in many cases materially assisted in setting fire to the enemy aircraft.

The guns could be fired together or singly by pressing the two thumb buttons on the control column. The guns had first to be loaded before firing and this was carried out by the Hyland Loading Lever. Jambs were usually cleared by the simple but effective method of striking the breech of the gun with a small hammer carried in the cockpit for this very purpose. As the breeches of the guns extended in most cases into the cockpit over the instrument panel, they presented a real hazard in the event of a "nose-over" or a crash landing. Also the rubber eye-piece of the afore-mentioned Aldis telescopic sight posed the same problem as it also protruded through the wind-screen.

The guns were fed from a magazine by a continuous belt of cartridges, linked by light metal clips which swung apart on entering the breech. They ejected with the spent cartridge cases down a chute and thence overboard.

The fired bullets passed through the airscrew aided by the Kauper mechanical or the Constantinesco oil pressure operated interrupter gear. These devices only allowed the guns to fire when the airscrew blades were clear of the gun muzzles. Before the advent of these gears, the guns were fired through the airscrew haphazardly with only steel plates to protect the blades and nothing to protect the pilot from the bullets which bounced off at all angles after striking the revolving blades. The absence of any interrupter gear also influenced the design of the aircraft and led to the large numbers of pusher types with the airscrew behind the cockpit and the guns.

Whilst engaged in mortal combat the pilot had a full-time job, with his left-hand usually placed so as to adjust the rotary engine throttle and fuel fine adjustment control on the left-hand side of the cockpit, whilst the other hand was then left to perform all the other duties, control column for flying control, gun loading, hitting the cocking levers to release jambs, pumping petrol through to the engine from the petrol tank, map holding and turning and anything else

Royal Aircraft Factory F.E.2.D pusher aircraft. These were developed in order to obviate the use of interrupter gear, as the airscrew was at the rear of the gunner.   *Stuart Leslie*

required. All this whilst at the same time engaging the enemy aircraft and lining his own machine up in order to obtain a sight for firing.

Bomber aircraft usually carried one or more drum-fed Lewis guns, Scarff ring mounted, in the open gunner's cockpits, situated forward of the cockpit, amidships on the top decking aft of the mainplanes, with in some cases a hatch in the belly for a gun-position, and in later days, a position aft of the tailplane. In some installations, twin guns were fitted, mostly Lewis's, on double-yoked mountings to increase fire-power. As the majority of bomber aircraft of this period had biplane tailunits, the firing of the midships gun must have been a hazardous task. The Lewis gun cartridge drum held a mere 47 rounds of .303 calibre bullets but the double drum, introduced later, was capable of holding 97 rounds.

Experimentation was carried out at Martlesham Heath into the effects of cordite burning in machine gun barrels, and also the fouling of the rifling by a composition of carbon and metal from the cartridge rim. Extensive air firing trials aimed at dispensing this fouling matter were carried out by Flight Lieutenant (later Air Vice Marshal) Harry Broadhurst, who received the Air Force Cross for his work on this subject.

The Army ammunition as used by the R.A.F. was standard issue and found to be inaccurate owing to the airflow slowing up the flight of the fired bullet, so research dictated a bullet of slimmer form and this was designed for R.A.F. guns.

Cordite was still used as it had been found to be the best propellant and stored well, and although it had other disadvantages, it had to be used, as when R.A.F. ammunition was "time-expired" (too old to be used for air-firing guns) it was handed over to the Army for rifle use. Therefore, as the Army rifles had been designed to use rimmed-cartridges, the R.A.F. was still restricted to its use for machine-guns as the ones adopted had of necessity to use rimmed ammunition.

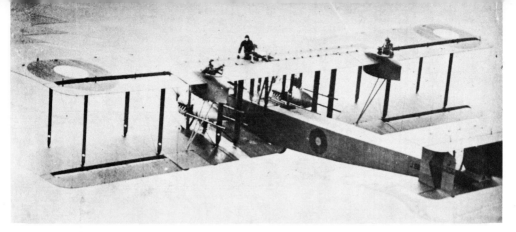

Another go at the problem of upper and stern defence. Vickers modified Vimy J.6856 with fighting tops on upper wing as an experiment.

In order to save the weight of the interrupter gear and give a faster rate of fire, experimental installations were made of machine-guns under the wings of aircraft, operated at first by Bowden cables, but found to be not fast or reliable enough, so new systems were needed. Pneumatic control appeared to be the answer, so the Dunlop Rubber Company of Birmingham was approached and asked to design a suitable system. Squadron Leader A. C. Wright was instrumental in the design of the system which was tested at Martlesham by, once again, Flight Lieutenant Harry Broadhurst, and after testing and improvement, this was the system used so effectively in the Hurricane and Spitfire.

Oddly enough, Britain's two standard machine guns were both American designed, the Lewis by Colonel Lewis and the Vickers by Hiram Maxim. Over the years, Vickers had gradually improved their product up to the Mark V model and this was just about as far as this design could be stretched. The urgent necessity was a gun for use in open cockpits or the new turrets then coming along, and Vickers produced a new model named the Central-Action Gun. Although new in concept, this gun still retained several of the old faults and failed to gain any production status.

Undaunted, Vickers then took up the patent of a foreign-made weapon, the Berthier Machine Gun, and after ironing out production problems, offered it as the Vickers "K" Gun, but unfortunately this gun still retained the drum-feed and therefore was still only suitable for free-mounting and as a Lewis replacement.

The Dhame Gun was of French design, belt fed and gas operated, a powerful well-made weapon manufactured by Fabrications Dhame. Extensive trials were carried out on this weapon, but once again it failed to meet all the requirements of the specification in order to put this country ahead of the rest.

A Czechoslovakian gun tried out at this time was the Kiraleji, and although a wonderful design it was far too intricate for mass-production.

Gloster SS.19 K.9125 experimentally fitted with 2 Vickers guns firing through troughs in the fuselage sides and four Lewis guns mounted under the upper and lower mainplanes.

Hawker Siddeley Aviation

During 1933, Flight Lieutenant C. W. McKinley-Thompson was engaged in carrying out prolonged trials at Martlesham Heath to examine the effect of machine-gun fire on aircraft. These trials were carried out at Orfordness using a large banner target to record the hits. From this collected data, comparisons were made and a pattern established as to the best rates of fire and types of ammunition. The Martlesham tests proved without a doubt that the then orthodox armament of two fixed forward-firing machine guns were in no way capable of doing the job asked of them and in order to be able to do this task the engaging aircraft would have to close to an impossible range.

Later during 1934, further trials were conducted after a conference on armaments had been held at the Air Ministry during July 1934. A committee was formed to deal with this work and the solutions involved. The Senior Technical Officer (Ballistics) Captain F. W. Hill, B.Sc., A.M.I.Mech.E., explained to the Committee the results of the tests. Fields of fire and rates of penetration were shown on charts and also photographs of targets after firing. He explained, that in his view, a new fighter must of necessity carry at least 8 guns to give a rate of fire of not less than 1,000 rounds per minute. His findings were accepted and put into practice. Several more types of machine-guns were obtained and evaluated at Martlesham Heath and these included the Vickers, Dhame, Kiraleji, Madson and the Colt. The last named was the most promising and the Air Ministry negotiated with the makers, The Colt Automatic Weapon Corporation, Hartford, Connecticut, U.S.A. The weapon was then re-named the Browning, and a licence was obtained for it to be manufactured in Great Britain. Re-drawing of the plans was necessitated by the need for the gun to be of 0.303 calibre instead of the American 0.300. It had also to be capable of accepting the standard British rimmed cartridge ammunition instead of the American rim-less. Birmingham Small Arms Limited of Birmingham were entrusted with the manufacture of the 0.303 Browning machine-gun.

The Browning had also to be left or right hand feed or convertible from right to left hand or left to right hand. A Hendy Heck low-wing monoplane was purchased by the Air Ministry and used at Martlesham Heath for trial installations and carried every refinement thought possible, also several other systems for trials use. This aircraft was virtually a flying workshop for gun installations and even at one time carried a battery of coloured lights in the cockpit to give the pilot indications of the various system's performances. For the interested this machine was K.8853, manufactured by Westlands, and known originally as the Hendy Heck, later Parnall Heck.

Over the years the 37mm shell-firing gun produced by the Coventry Ordnance Works and known as the C.O.W. Gun had caused rising and waning interest to the Powers That Be, and several aircraft had been designed round this weapon. From the early post-war days to the middle 30's, specifications were issued for aircraft with this armament either in single or double installations, and these ranged from the large Westland Westbury with two of these guns, to the smaller Westland and Vickers designs. The last pusher aircraft designed as an operational fighter, the Vickers C.O.W. Gun Fighter, J.9566, employed this layout in order to install the gun in the front of the fuselage. The Westland machine to the same specification, J.9565 was on more conventional lines, but both aircraft were peculiar in that the specification called for the gun to be installed at a firing angle of 55° upwards from the centre line of the aircraft. Once again, although extensively tested at Martlesham Heath, neither went into Service. The earlier Westbury, J.7766, with two such weapons experienced trouble with the blast from these guns and never progressed past the experimental stage. The centre section cladding had to be replaced with rubber mounted panels to absorb the blast from the gun muzzles when they were fitted.

The Vickers 161-2 C.O.W. Gun Fighter J.9566, the last pusher aircraft built for the R.A.F.

The Westland F.29/27 C.O.W. Gun Fighter J.9565. It will be noted the angle of the gun and the difficulty which must have been experienced in loading and sighting it.

Westland Aircraft Co.

Whilst on the subject of this gun, a story is told, and although I am not prepared to vouch for the authenticity of it, it is worth recounting. Whilst this weapon was making one of its periodical visits to Martlesham, it resided in the Armament Performance Testing Hangar which was situated alongside the Woodbridge-Felixstowe Road. At the same time a delegation from a "foreign power" arrived to look over the "wares"; these folk belonged to an Eastern nation who decided later to do battle with us. When the evening festivities were being enjoyed in the Officers' Mess, it was noticed that two of the visitors appeared to be missing, and a search hastily mounted failed to find them. The Orderly Officer thereupon took up the search and after some time espied the two gentlemen trying to see through the windows of the aerodrome side of the hangar in question. On being asked, much to their embarrassment, if there was anything they wished to see, the guard which was mounted on the doors was asked to unfasten the door and show the visitors the contents of that part of the hangar — a finely marked-out badminton court! The lethal weapon in question had been removed before the arrival of the visitors and for the duration of their stay resided uner a tarpaulin in the "Works and Bricks" Yard.

Mr Bishop of Woodbridge, who was connected with this gun had another story relating to it.

"The C.O W. Gun was a 1½ pounder, recoil cannon, and on firing the barrel recoiled and ejected the empty shell-case and a couple of hefty coil springs broke the shock of recoil and took over and pushed the barrel forward. In the forward movement another round was fed into the breech from a clip which held five rounds, and the gun could fire single or repeat. With the breech of the gun more or less at the pilot's side and firing upwards and forwards at approximately 55° to the line of flight, it was difficult for the pilot to fire and reload.

This now leads to the occasion in the Armament Workshops when we were dismantling a C.O.W. Gun. The weapon was mounted on a large heavy wooden frame and several men having passed a rope over the end of the recoil springs, hauled back and compressed them. Another man was then able to remove the retaining nut and the spring was eased forward and so removed. At one end of the Workshop was an adjoining room which was the Stores, with a half-door, acting as a counter and also preventing unauthorised entry, dividing the two rooms. The barrel of the gun pointed in that direction.

A certain Flight Sergeant had had a motor cycle accident and when he returned to us on "light duties" was given the task of running the Stores. His vision was impaired, and when he wanted to study anything closely he had to put a hand over one eye, to cut out the double-vision, and look with the other. He also had a large nose, which had also suffered, and he spoke "through it" when holding conversation.

We were preparing to strip the gun and were hauling on the rope. Being a team of young airmen as you can well imagine, the task was not being carried out in silence. To the cries of "Heave! Heave!" and "Hurry up and get that ------ nut off" full strain was on the rope, when it parted and the springs leapt forward. Just as the rope broke, the man working on the nut had loosened it and removed it, so with a tremendous "clang" the springs with nothing to retain them, sprang off the barrel, shot through the air straight through the top-half of the open door into the Stores and crashed against the wall on the far side. As it went past the open door so "Beaky's" face (our name for him) appeared in it, one hand over one eye and asked "What's goon on out there"?

The timing was perfect, how the springs missed him we'll never know for when they went through the door and his face came out, only a fraction of a second elapsed and he missed death by a hair's breadth."

In the middle 1930's various shell-firing guns or cannons were tried out, again the most interesting being the one installed in the Hispano-Suiza motor of the Belgian-built Fairey Fantome or Feroc which as L.7045 resided at Martlesham during 1938/9. This installation was between the cylinder blocks of the engine with the muzzle of the gun in the airscrew hub. The 20mm Hispano cannon designed by the Hispano Automobile and Aero Engine Company of Paris was then examined together with several other foreign-made cannons which had been acquired for comparision trials. Operated by three actions, Recoil, Gas and Blow-Back, this large but efficiently simple piece of mechanism seemed the best of the weapons evaluated and although modifications would be necessary to use it as a wing-mounted remotely controlled fire-arm, it was decided to go ahead with its procurement. Manufacture in England was placed with the British Marco Company of Grantham, Lincolnshire, who also did the conversion work to change the feed from one of a 60 shell drum to belt feed for aircraft use. During 1939, a Spitfire, L.1007 was tested with 2 - 20mm Hispano cannons in the wings, but double-feed stoppages made the tests not too successful. However, as a long term policy, a new factory was built to produce these cannons under licence, with a production rate of 250 units per month, soon raised to 750 units per month. The Hispano 20mm Cannon Mk.I suffered from unreliable feed mechanism and an unsatisfactory ejector caused jamming. After tests with deflectors, slight improvements were obtained although the original trouble persisted. Pilots reported that when one cannon jammed, it was difficult to sight the remaining one owing to the off-set recoil. The firing time of 6 seconds was also at first considered too short for real operational use. Although the larger gun had more hitting power, it did not have the spread of fire of the 8 guns, and greater accuracy of aiming was required.

In looking through the aircraft lists of Martlesham for the years 1938 and 1939, the reader will note the many and varied aircraft in the Armament Testing Flights and this will give a good idea of the tremendous amount of work being carried out by this Section. The Hurricanes and Spitfires had standardised on the 8-gun wing mounted layout, Brownings, followed by the Fairey Fulmer for the Navy with the same fire-power. During 1939, a Hurricane L.1750, was temporarily armed with two Oerlikon, Swiss-made cannons fitted under the wings in connection with the trials for the Westland Whirlwind. During the Battle of Britain, as noted earlier, this aircraft remained on the ground and did not have the chance to prove its value against the enemy.

The Westland Whirlwind with its four cannons in the nose broke with tradition regarding armament, but was treated at first with much suspicion like so many other new things. As early as 1935, the need for heavy armament had been felt and it was revealed in the new specifications issued then which resulted in the Westland Whirlwind and the Bristol Beaufighter, each armed with 4 20mm cannons as main armament. The limiting factor appeared to be the lack of engine power to carry these heavy guns with their attendant ammunition. By March, 1938, however, no guns had been air-tested in a single engined aircraft, all testing been carried out on multi-engined aircraft of the "hack" variety, and so the new prototypes were built with batteries of Browning 0.303 guns.

We rather tend to think of aircraft armament rockets as something of the Second World War and associate them with the Hawker Typhoon, but many readers will no doubt be surprised to learn that the Sopwith Pups and Nieuport Scouts in the early days of the First World War carried them as armament,

Early rocket-gun installed in the front gun position of the Royal Aircraft Factory—built N.E.1 experimental night fighter. Observe the spare rocket carried on the fuselage side.   *Stuart Leslie*

machine guns as yet not being fitted to aircraft. They were attached to the interplane struts on crude rails and resembled very much in looks, the popular November the Fifth variety.

The early 1930's saw the first turret installed in a medium bomber, the Boulton and Paul Overstrand, and although nowadays it appears rather crude, powered by compressed air bottles instead of hydraulics, it was a start and showed what great advantages were to be gained from enclosing the gunner within the aircraft. The early bombers of the Expansion Schemes sported enclosed gun positions for the gunners, fore and aft, but these were not powered turrets, but merely "protected gun positions" with the guns still worked as free units by the gunners. The next step was the revolving, counter-balanced, manually operated types, soon replaced by the mechanically actuated, hydraulic powered ones with the guns also power operated. The armament of these turrets also stepped up from the single machine-gun to first two and then four guns, usually two in the front and four in the rear.

Several interesting experiments were carried out in connection with the under protection of bombers and retractable gun positions, affectionately known as "dust-bins" were installed in the Handley-Page Heyford and several other types. The cantilever monoplane tailplane with twin fins and rudders was also a step in the right direction as it now gave the mid-upper gunner a clearer field of fire over the stern which could be backed-up by the rear-gunner as well.

Hawker Demon 2 seat fighter experimental installation, showing Frazer-Nash "lobster-back" gunner's turret. J.9933.

Hawker Siddeley Aviation

It is interesting to note that until the middle 1930's the standard armament for light and medium bombers, notably the Hawker series of aircraft, was one or two fixed Vickers guns firing forward through the airscrew disc, and the usual single or double Vickers "K" guns, mounted on a Scarff ring for the gunner. The only real attempt to improve this situation was the introduction of the Frazer-Nash "Lobster-Back" shielded gun position on the Hawker Demon 2-seat fighter. Bristols tried a transparent canopy on their experimental Type 118 and Type 120 aircraft and these were purchased by the Air Ministry to carry out further tests at Martlesham into the possibilities of protecting the gunner from the airstream and also to achieve better sighting. Mr John North, the Chief Designer for Boulton and Paul Aircraft Limited, negotiated with the French firm, Societé d'Applications des Machines Motrices during 1935 to build a turret for his Company for use in the Overstrand. A little later he took up the licence of another design by the same French firm and developed it to fit a new 2-seat four-gun fighter he was in the process of designing. This aircraft eventually came into service with the R.A.F. as the Defiant, the turret being known as the SAMM. It will be recalled that the first Defiant Squadron was formed at Martlesham Heath, No. 264.

The large refrigerator built at the A & A.E.E. also played a big part in gun trials in the altitude and temperate tests. Temperatures could be lowered to -60° in 24 hours with adjustments to atmospheric pressure and humidity as well.

Early during the First World War the air drop bombs were in the main, merely converted hand-grenades, weighing about 4½ lbs. These were carried in the cockpits of aircraft and dropped overboard as the occasion arose. They were generally supplemented by steel darts, known as Rankin Darts or other missiles of the pilot's own choice, and all the above were normally dropped on land targets or enemy aircraft or airships. Progress was slow but the urgencies of war speeded up design and before long the weights had risen to 550 lbs. The weight composed, generally speaking, of about 30—35 per cent explosive, the balance being the weight of the casing.

De Havilland 9 bomber running up prior to take-off. Two bombs are on racks under the lower
mainplane. *M. Martin*

Bombs were mainly in two classes, those with large amounts of explosive and
known as "blast bombs" and those with heavy cases "fragmentation bombs". The
blast-bombs were used for the demolition of surface buildings by blast whereas
the fragmentation variety were used against deep targets and ships. Variations of
these types could be effected by the various types of fuses fitted, allowing
instantaneous detonation or internal or delayed action.

Incendiary bombs were also of crude design at first, and weighed about
2½ lbs. with an indifference performance. More success was obtained with
larger bombs of this type which weighed up to 20 lbs.

Bomb release gear was not deemed necessary in the early days as the amount
of lift available would not have allowed more than a few hand grenades or a light
bomb to be carried, coupled with a revolver or carbine for the pilot. As the
specially designed air bomb came into being, thought had to be given to aiming
them. At first this was a "chancy affair" usually carried out by "eye and rule of
thumb method" and at the best only aided by simple instruments. Captain Henry
Tizard whilst at Martlesham, developed, towards the end of the First World War,
a high altitude drift sight for use up to 17,500 feet. It had certain drawbacks but
was much better than anything then in existence.

During 1924 a new type of bomb-sight appeared, the Course Setting Sight
which allowed for wind vector on course and could be used in any direction, as
opposed to the drift-sight which could only be used up or down wind. The
early 1930's saw the introduction of the Tachometric Automatic Sight, a step
further allowing ground speed to be determined and further compensated for
drift angle. It was possible to calculate the correct release angle and was accurate
in good conditions. Further development of this instrument resulted in the
"Stabilized Automatic Bomb Sight" which gave even greater accuracy under most
conditions encountered during a bombing run-in.

During the post war years the bombs which the R.A.F. held were mostly
old stock of 1919 vintage. During 1921, attempts were made to design and

manufacture more up-to-date missiles, but these did not get under way until 1938. Production was slow and even by 1940 stocks were still very small.

These bombs were filled with Amatol, an explosive which had been used during the First World War although a new explosive R.D.X. had been in existence during the late 1920's. For some reason manufacture of this explosive had been stopped during 1932 and it was not until 1942 that the R.A.F.'s bombs were again filled with R.D.X. The Treasury apparently was the "stumbling block" who pointed out that as the planes were designed to carry 500 lb. bombs, 500 lb. bombs they would carry.

Work also began on designing armour piercing bombs for use against naval vessels, and these were in the 250 lbs. and 500 lbs. classes. The casing was cast in steel with a hardened front end and toughened gradually towards the tail-end in order to prevent breaking up on impact. It was estimated that a bomb of the 250 lb. variety would pierce 3½ inches of steel armour plating when dropped from a height of 6/7000 ft. General purpose bombs were also developed also with cast steel cases which could be fitted with instantaneous or delayed action fuses. Unfortunately in this case, also, the explosive content was small compared with the weight of the bomb.

Various explosives were experimented with and useful research carried out for efficiency coupled with economy and ease of manufacture. The ideal was to find a compound which embodied lower and safer handling sensitivity but at the same time exerted the necessary action to make it effective. Two such compounds experimented with were Trinitrotoluene (T.N.T.) and Dinitrobenzine (D.N.B.) but these were expensive to produce owing to the large quantities of raw materials required for their manufacture. From these two came Amatol which was a mixture of T N.T. and Ammonium Nitrate and later Boratol, but these two had disadvantages in that Amatol does not store for long periods, whilst Boratol requires considerably more volume of weight in order to achieve the same effect as Amatol. The later R.D.X became the filling but once again has the disadvantage as a peace-time requirement of being expensive to manufacture.

Small hexagonal incendiary bombs invented by Squadron Leader C. Cransford A.F.C. were packed in bundles and used for "scatter release". Dropping trials were carried out at Martlesham Heath by an Armament Flight Officer; Flight Lieutenant Davies who used to amaze the assembled onlookers by getting right into the trials dropping zone to observe the flight and scatter of the dummies used in these tests.

Although not able to show its wares as openly as the Performance Testing side of the business, the Armament Testing Section worked along steadily all the while hoping that their preparations would not be wanted, but if they were indeed called upon, then they would have the best to offer.

CHAPTER EIGHT

Reports. 1917—1939

SINCE it carried out its first test, Martlesham Heath reported on all aspects of the work performed, and so from its earliest days of 1917 until its move to the West Country during 1939, a steady flow of these technical and illuminating reports were prepared to help aviation, and armament technology. Over the years "Martlesham Reports" were continually referred to in the world of aircraft performance and were regarded with the highest esteem by all concerned.

To illustrate the detail contained in the reports of aircraft or armament under test a few examples are given to give the reader an idea of the tremendous amount of work involved in their preparation. The first ones deal with First World War aircraft. First of all weekly reports:

HANDLEY-PAGE BOMBER WITH 4-200 h.p. HISPANO MOTORS.

The strength of the engine mountings has been examined and found satisfactory. Some figures have been obtained but the trials are not yet completed. Trouble has been experienced with one of the engines which has since been changed.

SOPWITH PUP.

The designer has been interviewed on the subject of fitting a 170 h.p. A.B.C. Wasp into a machine of this type. Work is proceeding on an estimate of performance.

R.A.F. F.E.2.B.

Drawings have been called for to carry out strength calculations on the machine with a 220 h.p. B.H.P. engine. The estimate of comparative performance for this machine with the 220 h.p. B H.P. instead of the 160 h.p. Beardmore has been submitted.

R.A.F. R.E.9.

Calculations of longitudinal stability have been delayed owing to the drawings having been withdrawn.

Two heavy bombers on test during 1918. Nearest the camera is the Handley-Page 0/400 and in the distance the second prototype Vickers Vimy FB.27.

HANDLEY-PAGE BOMBER.

Report on the strength of the box-spars has been delayed pending receipt of the necessary drawings from the makers.

HANDLEY-PAGE BOMBER WITH 2-200 h.p. FIAT ENGINES.

This machine has not been removed to Martlesham Heath from Hendon owing to bad weather during the past few days. Two new propellers of Air Board Design have been fitted in place of the two Lang propellers, which proved unsatisfactory. The machine will be flown to Martlesham Heath as soon as possible.

And now a more fuller report on propeller types.

REPORT BY EXPERIMENTAL STATION, MARTLESHAM HEATH, ON TRIALS OF PROPELLERS ON SOPWITH DOLPHIN No. 3 FITTED WITH 200 H.P. HISPANO SUIZA (BRAZIER) No. 16136.

Below are given the results of tests which have been carried out on the above machine with the undermentioned propellers:—

(a)   Marked D.R.G. L.2610 L.H.
     200 h.p. Hispano Suiza Sopwith Dolphin D.2590. F.2240. L/14357.

(b) Marked D.R.G. L.3800 L.H.
200 h.p. Hispano Suiza Sopwith Dolphin D.2670. P.2450. L/17566.

These propellers have been measured with the following results:—

	L.3610.	L.3800.
Type	2 bladed tractor airscrew.	
Diameter	2595 mm.	2673 mm.
Pitch (2/3 radius)	2190 mm.	2360 mm.
Maximum blade width	232 mm.	236 mm.
Weight	25½ lbs.	26½ lbs.
Makers	Lang	Lang

SPEEDS AT HEIGHTS

	L.3610.		L.3800.	
Standard Height.	Speed M.P.H.	R.P.M.	Speed M.P.H.	R.P.M.
10,000 Feet.	120	2105	—	1970
13,000 Feet.	117.5	2075	—	1945
15,000 Feet.	114.5	2045	—	1915
17,000 Feet.	110	1995	—	1870

Only one set of speeds was done with propeller L.3800 (owing to a connecting rod breaking) the results of which were not very satisfactory but tend to show that speeds obtained with this propeller were practically the same as with L.3610.

It will be noted that the speeds obtained on this machine are 8—10 m.p.h. more than those obtained with Dolphin 11 which was fitted with a Peugot Hispano (No. 115037) gear ratio 2000/1170 and propeller L.3500.

Further tests will be done with these two propellers on C.3778 Dolphin as soon as possible.

TESTS ON D.H.4 WITH B.H.P. (SIDDELEY) 200 h.p. PROPELLER 4-BLADED BY WESTLANDS No. W.A.1038. DIAMETER 2674 MM PITCH 2520 MM.

Number of Crew.	Two.
Military Duty.	Bomber.
* Total Military Load.	545 lbs.
Speed at 10,000 feet.	114 m.p.h. Revs. 1355.
Speed at 15,000 feet.	106 m.p.h. Revs. 1310.
Climb to 10,000 feet.	19 mins. 10 secs. Revs. 1235.
Climb to 15,000 feet.	37 mins. 55 secs. Revs. 1220.
Calculated Ceiling.	About 20,000 feet.
Air Endurance.	About 4½ hours at full speed at 10,000 feet. (including climb to 10,000 feet)

Total weight of machine.　　3,234 lbs.
Fully Loaded.

* Total Military Load is made up of the following items:—

Pilot	180 lbs.
Passenger	180 lbs.
Vickers Gun	35 lbs.
Lewis Gun	16 lbs.
Deadweight	134 lbs.
Total	545 lbs.

NOTES ON ABOVE AIRCRAFT

UNDERCARRIAGE

The deeper undercarriage seems to be in every way an improvement. There is no sign of any defect developing. The machine is, if anything, easier to land in normal circumstances, but it is distinctly better for a forced landing as the tail can be got further down before the wheels touch. The machine pulls up a little sooner after landing.

COWLING

The pilot's view is distinctly worse in this machine than it was with the original B.H.P. machine. Full advantage is not taken of the narrowness of the engine at the top, the fairing in front of the pilot being about semi-circular.

The forward view would be much improved if this fairing were narrowed down so as to conform with the shape of the radiator. There is apparently no reason why the wider fairing should have been adopted, except to standardize this machine as far as possible with the Rolls-Royce and the D.H.4's.

PILOT'S GUN

This is placed on the top of the cowling as in the case of the Rolls-Royce machine. It would have been easier for a pilot to get at it if it had been fixed inside the cowling just underneath the exhaust manifold, a hole being made in the radiator for the gun to fire through. This would have also materially improved the pilot's view and reduced head resistance.

RADIATOR

The water gets too hot climbing in warm weather. This would probably be improved a little if the cowling were not bent round the front edge of the radiator so far. About an inch of the radiator all round is completely screened and it is possible that the effect of the curved surface of the cowling is to screen a good deal more than this inch of radiator. The radiator should certainly be worked with blinds but there is not sufficient clearance to fit the standard blinds on the R.A.F. and Roll-Royce D.H.4's.

REPORT BY EXPERIMENTAL STATION, MARTLESHAM HEATH, ON RADIATOR TESTS ON D.H.9 No. A.7559 WITH SIDDELEY DEASY ENGINE No. 5094.

1.   The radiator fitted to this machine was a 7 mm honeycomb radiator.

The following report deals with the temperature tests of this machine and a hexagonal tube radiator, tube diameter about 13 mm. No. 2 radiator which is similar to No. 3 but with 10 mm tubes could not be tested as it was leaking badly in about fifty places. Both No. 2 and No. 3 are narrower and have different outlet and inlet pipes than No. 1. The reason for this is probably that D.H.9 No. 7559 is not a standard machine and the radiator fittings are different to those of the production machines.

PRELIMINARY REPORT ON PERFORMANCE OF S.E.5A WITH 180 h.p. HIGH COMPRESSION HISPANO SUIZA ENGINE No. 717223. W.D. A.8292.

Full tests of this machine have been delayed owing to failure of the radiator which is very badly supported and has developed bad leaks during each flight. A new radiator has been obtained from the Royal Aircraft Factory today and the full trials will be pushed forward as quickly as possible. The radiator support brackets are strengthened here. The preliminary results of these trials are very good indeed. The table given later gives the average results of two climbs. The climb is very nearly as good as that of S.E.5A A.4563, the French 200 h.p. Hispano Suiza engine and is very considerably better than the performances of S.E.5a's with Wolseley Hispano Suiza engines.

The speed when flying level is also very considerably better, but cannot be given with accuracy as no opportunity has yet occurred of calibrating the airspeed indicator over the speed range.

The engine has been running very well. The carburettor fitted is the standard 200 Zenith carburettor and will therefore require modifications.

Here followed a series of figures showing the comparative figures of the two aircraft.

MACHINE BEARDMORE No. W.B.11.

This has now been returned to Messrs Beardmore for partial rebuilding etc. It is hoped that the work will be completed during this week and then the machine will be returned to Martlesham Heath for further testing. Arrangements have been made to obtain easier access to the magnetos by means of doors fitted in the cowling.

Vickers Vimy FB.27 B.9952 with French Hispano motors. This was the Vimy prototype proper.
Wing Commander A. Boeree

VICKERS THREE SEAT BOMBING MACHINE FB 27 No. 9952.

Two 220 h.p. French Hispano engines have been installed in this machine but certain small defects in the installation have been pointed out to the makers and are now being rectified. A further inspection of this machine is being made.

SOPWITH DOLPHIN

The second machine has arrived at Martlesham Heath. The report of the pilot who flew it is unfavourable. The radiators in the top plane of this second Sopwith Dolphin have not proved entirely satisfactory as the engine still overheats considerably. Owing to the necessity of avoiding the wing bracing it is not possible conveniently to enlarge the size of these radiators. It is proposed to try radiators fitted to the side of the fuselage.

SOPWITH CAMEL

This machine fitted with 100 h.p. Monosoupape engine has arrived at Martlesham. This machine is tail heavy and it is doubtful if this defect can be overcome easily, as it is due to the fitting of the lighter engine.

SOPWITH 1½ STRUTTER

The first Sopwith 1½ Strutter fitted with 110 h.p. Le Rhone engine for the Roumanian Government has been finally inspected and is undergoing trials at Martlesham Heath.

BRISTOL FIGHTER F.2.B.

The short span tailplane for this machine has been found satisfactory and has been made standard for this type.

Running alongside the airframe testing were the engine tests and a few words of these once again shows the tremendous amount of work involved, even in these early days, these reports being dated 1918.

SILENCERS.

A visit has been made to the Experimental Station and tests carried out on the instrument devised at the Research Laboratory, South Kensington, for indicating the magnitude of aeroplane noise. This instrument is designed to work at distances up to 200 yards from the source of the noise. It is an open question whether or not a comparison of noises made by this instrument would be the same as a comparison of the limits of audibility made by a human ear. It is, of course, the audibility of the aeroplane to the human ear that is of importance. It is satisfactory to find that on a comparative test between the instrument and three observers the measure of noise given by the instrument corresponded exactly with the measure of audibility to the ear given by three observers. Further tests at Orfordness are proceeding after several days' delay due to storms.

SOPWITH F.1 MACHINES FITTED WITH 110 h.p. LE RHONE ENGINES.

It has been ascertained from Messrs Sopwith that as the number of Le Rhone engines fitted by them in F.1 machines is to date only six, they have continued to fit the standard cowl as used for the Clerget engines, but are of the opinion that they had slightly modified the exhaust outlets in the cowl to suit the Le Rhone engine. Several F.1 machines fitted with these Clerget cowls and also some D.H.5 machines with Le Rhone with similar cowls have been inspected after the engines had been run and it was observed that the cowling was "blued" due to the exhaust gases discharging directly on the cowl. This matter has been fully investigated by Testing Squadron, Martlesham Heath, and modifications made to the cowl which have proved satisfactory.

Further work has been carried out on the drawings and report on the 220 h.p. 8-cylinder Mercedes engine, also the 260 h.p. Mercedes and the 230 h.p. Benz. (It is interesting to note that these tests were on captured German motors).

SOPWITH F.1 MACHINES FITTED WITH 150 h.p. MONO ENGINE.

It is reported that the revolution counter drive reduction gear was incorrect, the reason for this being that the drive is taken from a spindle on the new type selector box. This defect is being remedied by Testing Squadron. At present the speed of the engine is controlled, firstly by means of a selector, and secondly by the use of the petrol needle valve. In connection with the latter control, a suggestion has been made that a screw-down cock be inserted in the petrol pipe in order to avoid disturbing the setting of the needle valve. It is understood that this will be tried. Up to the present it has been found that the machine can only be flown using a fuel feed pressure of 4½ lbs. per square inch, the results being unsatisfactory if a lower pressure is used.

Experiments are to be made to ascertain if it is possible to obtain the required engine speed with a much lower pressure and to do this the engine driven petrol pump will be temporarily disconnected from the petrol feed pipe.

BEARDMORE W.B.11 MACHINE WITH 200 h.p. FRENCH HISPANO ENGINE.

This machine has been at Martlesham Heath before, but was returned to Messrs Beardmore's Works to be rebuilt. The long exhaust uptake pipes have now been deleted and stack pipes substituted. The air intake to the carburettor which previously came through the cowl has been cut back and a hole in the cowling blanked off. It was noted during the inspection that the suction pipe from the oil tank to the pump has not been connected up. The single type of radiator is still being used although it is understood that much trouble has been experienced with this type of radiator in the past. A ground test was made with the engine and 1750 revolutions were obtained. The machine was flown a few minutes and the revolutions in the air, climbing, were 1950.

The Beardmore WB II after rebuilding and return to Martlesham. The final design was not accepted.
Stuart Leslie

SOPWITH PUP.

It is reported that the rear engine bearer is too weak and broke in the event of the machine standing on its nose. Investigation showed that this was, if nothing, a fault on the right side, as it helped to avoid damage to the entire engine in such a case.

SOPWITH CAMEL.

Reports have been received that the oil tanks in Sopwith Camels give trouble through bursting. A new modification has been issued showing the new tank made of sheet steel in lieu of aluminium.

From the foregoing the reader will see that when Martlesham Heath made a recommendation the makers carried them out and it was this co-operation over the years that enabled the British Aircraft Industry to produce such fine aircraft. And so from the early days with trials carried out with somewhat primitive instruments to one of the last aircraft to be evaluated at Martlesham Heath. This aircraft, of American manufacture, only stayed at the A & A.E.E. for a few days, and was not evaluated for R.A.F. service, but the tests were just as thorough and comprehensive, although all the lists, graphs and drawings are not shown in this condensed example.

SEVERSKY N.X.2586. TYPE P.A. Model 202.
A & A.E.E. REF. M.H. 93/39 A.T.134

In accordance with instructions given in Air Ministry letter dated 1st March, 1939 brief performance and handling trials have been completed on the above named aeroplane. Comments on the radio and armament installation are also given.

Comments on trials.

The performance trials were all made with Major Seversky as pilot; an observer was carried on some of these tests. The aeroplane was flown by pilots of the A & A.E.E. for the handling trials.

It should be noted that the two fixed firing guns were not fitted, and a fairing was fitted over the spaces normally occupied by the guns.

General Description.

The Seversky Type A PA.A. is a two seat fighter, full cantilever, low wing monoplane with a retractable undercarriage. With the exception of the control surfaces which are fabric-covered, the aeroplane is of all metal construction.

It is powered by a Pratt and Whitney 14 cylinder air-cooled radial engine driving a three-bladed constant speed airscrew.

Seversky Type 2 P.A. Model 202, NX 2586, 2-seat fighter, the subject of the printed report.

Ministry of Defence

Construction

(i) *Wings and ailerons.* The basic aerofoil section is the Clark C.Y.H., but the actual leading edge appeared rather sharper than usual. The wing is full cantilever all metal construction and tapers in plan form and thickness. It is made up of a centre section and two outer panels. The structure consists of five main spars with fore and aft ribs. The top metal skin covering is made up in two layers, the inner being corrugated.

A unique feature of the wing is the integral fuel tank which is formed by the structure of the centre section itself.

Split trailing edge flaps extending from aileron to aileron are fitted to the wing.

Ailerons, of the Frise type, are metal constructed and fabric covered. A fabric covered trimmer tab is inset in the trailing edge of the port aileron.

(ii) *Fuselage.* The fuselage is circular in cross-section, and is of all metal construction of the semi-monocque type. The structure consists essentially of continuous longitudinal stringers and frames or former rings. Four box-section longerons at the front take the engine mounting.

(iii) *Tailplane and fin.* The tailplane and fin are of fixed cantilever type of all metal construction with metal covering. The elevators and rudder are also all metal with fabric covering. Two trimmer tabs are inset in the trailing edges of the elevators and one in the trailing edge of the rudder.

(iv) *Undercarriage.* The undercarriage, each leg of which consists of a single oleo unit, retracts backwards under the wing. In the retracted position the landing gear is proud of and rests against the wing. Should an emergency landing be made with the wheels up, the structure is so arranged to take the landing loads, through pads in the wing structure.

(v) *Tailwheel.* The tailwheel is of the steerable type interconnected with the rudder and fully retractable. Retraction is by the same mechanism as used to retract the undercarriage, but is connected through a friction clutch, so that in the event of the tailwheel sticking it would not effect the operation of the undercarriage. With the tailwheel retracted the steering control is disengaged and the rudder operates independently.

(vi) *Engine Installation.* The engine installation is very neat with ample access for maintenance purposes. It is designed as a unit complete with oil tank and coolers so that a corresponding alternative unit complete with different type of engine could be changed over in a matter of an hour or so. An unusual feature was that controllable cooling gills were confined to the sides and bottom of the fuselage instead of all the way round.

General. The detail design, general finish and workmanship were of a very high standard. As an instance of this the flush rivetting in the leading edge of the planes has been effected practically without any dimpling or waving of the sheet metal.

Here followed some six pages giving full dimensions of the aircraft with areas and weights of components.

Engine Particulars. The information given in the log-book was very meagre. The following has been compiled from data given in the log-book and the descriptive notes for the aeroplane.

Engine	Pratt & Whitney Wasp R.1830. S.3.C.
Type	14 cylinder. Air cooled radial
Number	33857
Gear reduction	16 : 9

Horse Power Rating	B.H.P.	R.P.M.	Ht. Ft.
Maximum (Military Rating)	1100	2700	9000
Cruising (maximum)	700	2325	14000
Fuel		100 Octane	

Here followed full particulars of the airscrew, and full weights and unloaded and separate weights of all components such as radio, guns, ammunition etc., amounting to another 3 pages.

Take-off at 7,630 lbs. The following is the result of a single take-off. Repeats were not practicable because a considerable expenditure of fuel was necessary before landing. In this case, the pilot, Major Seversky, concentrated mainly on the distance to the 50 foot screen. A previous test showed that the take-off run could be reduced, but only at the expense of increasing the distance to clear a 50 ft. screen. The wing flaps were not used.

	Corrected to zero wind and standard atmosphere	Under conditions of test Wind: 10.5 m.p.h. Pressure: 20.86 Hg. Temp: +10°C
Take-off run (yards)	510	400
Distance from rest to clear 50 ft. screen	760	625
Take-off speed (by panoramic camera) m.p.h.		105.5
R.P.M. at take-off		2700
Boost (absolute) at take-off "Hg.		48

CLIMBING TRIALS

Weight — 6140 lbs.

Weight — 7658 lbs.
(Deduced from results at 7150 lbs.)

Standard Hr. Ft.	Rate of Climb ft/min	Time Mins.	A.S.I. m.p.h.	R.P.M.	Boost "Hg Absolute	Rate of Climb ft/min	Time Mins.	A.S.I. m.p.h.	R.P.M.	Boost "Hg Absolute
5000	2690	1.9	120.5	2700	41.5	2270	2.5	130	2700	45
*FTH	2900	3.4	120.5	”	41.5	2480	3.5	130	”	45
10000	2780	3.7	120.5	”	40.5	2150	4.6	125	”	42
15000	2200	5.7	111	”	35	1490	7.4	116	”	35
20000	1620	8.4	101	”	30					
25000	1050	12.2	90.5	”	24.5					
30000	460	19.2	85	”	19					

Service Ceiling:— 33,100 feet.
Estimated absolute ceiling:— 34,000 feet.

*Full throttle height for boost of
41.5 "Hg = 9,000 feet.

This climb was made to 15,000 feet only and it is not possible to accurately estimate the ceiling.
*Full throttle height for boost of
45 "Hg = 7,600 feet.

An A & A.E.E. observer and barograph were carried for the climb at the heavy load and a barograph at the light load.

Here followed several more graphs relating to performance in the climb and the ceiling, but the above example gives a good idea of the work involved — compare with the First World War graph on previous pages.

Fuel consumption. The fuel consumption was measured by tankage at two speeds on the same flight. Before flight, the two wing tanks were drained completely and then each refuelled with 30 Imperial gallons of fuel. The refuelling was done by 5 gallon drums and checked by the weight difference before and after refuelling.

The procedure for the flight was to fly at one speed on one wing tank until the engine cut, and then at the second speed on the other tank until the engine cut. The residue of the fuel from these tanks were drained after flight, this amounted to a total of ¾ Imperial gallons. The fuel from the main tank was used for warming up, take-off, climb to height, etc. An A. & A E.E. observer was carried.

Here followed another series of graphs recording fuel consumption.

HANDLING

(1)   Pilot's and observer's cockpits.
Ease of entry and exit, comfort etc.   The cockpits are completely enclosed by sliding hoods, operated manually by handle controls on the right of the cockpit. They can be locked in any one of several intermediate positions. The cockpits are roomy, and entry to and exit from either cockpit by way of the sliding hoods is easy.

The seats are comfortable and there is ample room for large occupants dressed in full flying gear.

Cockpit heating is provided. The aeroplane was not flown by A & A.E.E. pilots at low air temperatures, but an observer from the A & A.E.E. when flying at 15,000 feet, air temperature $-19^{\circ}C$, with Major Seversky as pilot, complained of cold with the heat off, but was quite comfortable with the heat on. The pilot was understood to state that his cockpit was stuffy with the heat on.

The above comments are only one example of remarks about all aspects of the aeroplane, the full report running into some 56 pages of foolscap paper, and a full collection of descriptive photographs of almost every component of the aircraft.

All Martlesham Reports carried the pre-fix "M" and should the reader in further readings come across this code, he or she will know that the aircraft was tested at Martlesham Heath in pre-war days.

Civil aircraft went through the same procedure in order to gain their Certificate of Airworthiness (C. of A.) without which, of course, they were unable to operate.

The weighing of the aircraft on the large scales in "B" Flight Hangar could be a lengthy operation and one or two of the larger specimens such as the Handley-Page H.P.42 and the Armstrong-Whitworth Ensign caused much effort in order to carry out this procedure.

As noted above, the measuring of fuel for trial purposes also posed a problem overcome in the main, by using 5 gallon drums, more easily weighed and using only sufficient fuel in order to carry out a specific test. It will be noted in the case of the Seversky that in order to get the full fuel load take-off weight, after take-off the pilot had to fly around for some considerable time in order to consume fuel to reduce the landing weight, the aircraft not being able to land again carrying the full fuel load. Modern aircraft are, of course, equipped to jettison their fuel load should this become necessary.

Mention in the Seversky Report of the 50 foot screen, is also interesting as this was the same procedure as used in the Air Ministry Civil Aeroplane Competition during 1920, the aircraft's ability to land and take-off over the screen and its run before and after being judged as its best performance.

Normally an aircraft would be able to complete its trials at Martlesham Heath in one session, but on many occasions, either due to recommendations from A & A.E.E. pilots or engineers, it would return for further tests. Quite often a prototype would visit the A & A.E.E. several times after it had passed the first time in order to clear manufacturer's further modifications which they wished to incorporate in production machines, in this manner saving them time by using the "hack" aircraft. A notable example of this procedure was the prototype Hawker Hart, which not only served to cover modifications in its own design, but also became the prototype for at least two other types in the Hart series of aircraft.

Always of interest to observers of the A & A.E.E. were the "foreign" aircraft which visited and these either fell into the category of imported machines for evaluation, or British aircraft sold to an overseas buyer and therefore unfamiliar in their new markings or registration.

In the first category were the French war-time aircraft, and then the post-war French Breguet, the German Dornier Komet and later Heinkel, the Dutch Fokker, and the American Northrop and Chance-Vought aircraft, together with the Seversky which were tested and evaluated.

In the second class were the Furies for Persia with American Pratt and Whitney radial motors, Harts for Iraq with Pegasus motors, Bulldogs for Finland,

Furies for Spain and Yugoslavia, and the reader will note, even in the early days, Sopwith 1½ Strutters for Roumania.

The reports on the "other side of the business" were more confidential, but nevertheless make interesting reading, as one early example shows:—

REPORT ON TRIALS OF A, B AND C TYPES OF KN 17 MK. VIIS A. BALL FOR USE WITH INTERRUPTER GEARS

TEST ONE. "A" TYPE

(a) GROUND TRIALS

50 rounds of this type were put through in a hand Vickers, rate of fire developed approximately 550 rounds per minute. The firing was rated to be very irregular. During this burst two distinct "hang-fires" were experienced. The cases and the caps were examined but no peculiarities were noticed.

(b) AERIAL TRIALS

Machine — Sopwith Pup (Mono engine) fitted with C.C. Gear. Engine revs 1200. Height 10,000 feet.

This gear was thoroughly overhauled and tested before ascent and operated perfectly efficiently. 250 rounds were loaded up and fired after considerable trouble due partly to weak charger.

Propeller blades holed in 4 places, three in one blade and one in the other.

Pilot reported irregular firing. Gear was checked and found to be in perfect order. The holing of the propeller was without doubt due to "hang-fires" in the ammunition as the gear was above suspicion.

TEST TWO. "B" TYPE

(a) GROUND TEST

100 rounds were put through in two bursts of 50 rounds each. No "hang-fires" were experienced, gun firing with remarkable regularity, approximate rate developed 580 rounds per minute. During the second 50 rounds one miss-fire was experienced, this being directly due to a "deep set cap".

(b) AERIAL TRIALS. 10,000 Ft.

1,000 rounds were fired in four flights. Pilot reported that gun developed a good even and high rate of fire. During these tests no gun trouble of any nature was experienced. Gun and gear checked after each flight of 250 rounds and found correct. During this test no damage was recorded on the propeller.

TEST THREE. "C" TYPE

(a) GROUND TEST

100 rounds fired in two burst, a miss-fire was experienced during the first burst due to "deep-set cap" otherwise regularity of fire good.

(b) AERIAL TEST. 10,000 Ft.

500 rounds fired, pilot reported good gun speed and even rate of fire, no trouble experienced and no damage to propeller.

During the third 250 rounds one hole was registered in the leading edge of one blade. The pilot reported that the gun developed a good even rate of fire with no gun or ammunition trouble experienced during flight. The gear was then subjected to a superficial examination and timing checked and found to be perfectly correct. No alterations or adjustment to gear carried out. The machine was then loaded up with 100 rounds of "B" Type ammunition and the entire lot fired in one burst at 3,000 feet. No damage was recorded on the propeller and gun and gear worked perfectly.

It is therefore considered that the holing of the propeller would be safely accounted for by a distinct "hang-fire".

It was then decided to fire a further 500 rounds of this type thoroughly to test out the reliability of this ammunition. Two belts of 250 rounds were fired at the same altitude as in the previous shoots, no trouble being experienced of any nature. It is of interest to note that throughout the "C" tests, no alterations or adjustments were made to gear other than checking the line for air.

Conclusion

"A" type is not considered sufficiently reliable for use with interrupters.
"B" type is thoroughly recommended and is the most reliable for every use.
"C" type except for the one "hang-fire" experienced in 1500 rounds is proved as
   an ammunition quite satisfactory.

Once again, a Martlesham Report left no stones unturned, no matter what the subject, and this principle was applied to all tests. Thus it was that over the years Martlesham Heath became a standard that was trusted and respected, and if Martlesham approved, then it was good, and this tradition is still carried on as the standards that were laid down originally still hold good although the means of testing have now changed completely from the days when the A & A.E.E. were "on the Heath".

List of Commanding Officers

Captain G. B. Stopford assumed command on 6th May, 1915 and the Testing Squadron moved to Martlesham Heath on 16th January, 1917. Very soon after the move Major G. D. Mills took over command.

Major T. B. O'Hubbard.	16.7.1918.
S/Ldr. A. Shekleton.	31.5.1919.
S/Ldr. A. C. Maund.	2.1921.
W/Cmdr. Napier Gill.	3.1922.
W/Cmdr. H. Blackburn, M.C., A.F.C.	9.1924.
G/Capt. V. O. Rees, O.B.E.	25.11.1924.
W/Cmdr. R. M. Field.	17.9.1931.
G/Capt. H. L. Reilly, D.S.O.	7.1.1932.
G/Capt. A. C. Maund, C.B.E., D.S.O.	26.9.1933.
G/Capt. H. G. Smart, O.B.E., D.F.C., A.F.C.	28.1.1937.
S/Ldr. A. B. Luxmore ⎫ No.4 R.T.P. S/Ldr. B. D. Brice, A.F.C. ⎭	17.9.1939.
W/Cmdr. W. E. Smann.	20.10.1939.
W/Cmdr. L. Martin, A.F.C.	8.11.1939.
W/Cmdr. A. D. Farquhar, D.F.C.	14.4.1940.
W/Cmdr. V. S. Parker, D.F.C., A.F.C.	9.3.1941.
W/Cmdr. A. M. Wilkinson, D.S.C.	16.6.1941.
S/Ldr. Ogier. (Handed over to USAAF L/Col. Rau.)	1.11.1943.
W/Cmdr. Hawkins.	4.1944.
W/Cmdr. W. H. Costello.	3.1.1945.

U.S.A.F. COMMANDERS

L/Col. H. J. Rau.	9.2.1943.
Col. Einar A. Malmstrom.	28.11.1943.
Lt/Col. P. E. Turkey, Jnr.	24.4.1944.
Lt/Col. D. A. Baccus.	3.11.1944.
Col. P. E. Turkey, Jnr.	11.1.1945- 10.11.1945.

BLIND LANDING EXPERIMENTAL UNIT
(under R.A.F. Felixstowe. G/Capt. Welch. 1.6.1946)

W/Cmdr. P. C. Lambert.	7.1947.
W/Cmdr. J. Clift, O.B.E., D.F.C.	29.9.1947.

B.L.E.U. & B.B.U. — A.I.E.U.

S/Ldr. A. L. Law.	3.1950.
W/Cmdr. W. G. Oldbury, D.F.C.	21.4.1950.
W/Cmdr. E. A. Johnson.	28.4.1953.

Some Organisational Dates and Typical Flying Hours

January	1920	In No. 3 Group, Spittlegate, Grantham, Lincolnshire.
1 April	1920	Establishment. 17 Officers and 284 men.
June	1921	A.E.S. Orfordness closed.
August	1921	In No. 1 Group, Kenley.
July	1922	To Coastal Area.
September	1922	Establishment of 2 Home Defence Squadrons.
May	1923	To No. 3 Group.
		No. 22 Squadron formed at Martlesham Heath.
March	1924	Headquarters and No. 1 Flight, No. 15 Squadron.
May	1924	2nd Flight, No. 15 Squadron formed.
		Orfordness reopened. Armament ranges.
April	1925	Rebuilding of Station begun.
July	1926	To. No. 2 Group, Inland Area.
March	1931	W/T Test Flight formed.
May	1934	Personnel of No. 22 Squadron to Performance Squadron.
June	1934	Personnel of No. 15 Squadron to Armament Squadron.
July	1934	To Direct Inland Area.
October	1934	Both Squadrons renamed Sections.
May	1935	Station first opened to the public. Empire Air Day.
July	1936	To Training Command.
July	1937	To No. 24 Group.
August	1938	Experimental Co-op Flight renamed "D" Flight, Performance Testing Section.
June	1939	Station Badge presented.

TYPICAL FLYING HOURS

	1927	1928	1929	1930	1931	1932	1933	1934	1935	1936	1937
No. 15 Sqdn.	481	782	570	906	1055	1158	1289	1453	1601	1196	1356
No. 22 Sqdn.	1670	1967	1799	1578	1393	1558	1707	1885	1708	1660	1742

Aerodrome Lease

When the emergency of the First World War was over, thought was given to the leasing of the site on a more permanent basis, the establishment of boundaries and the passing of bye-laws for the protection of all parties.

Meetings were held and finally a lease was taken out on 14th November, 1921 with the Rt. Hon. Ernest George Pretyman, M.P. of Orwell Park, Nacton, as the lessee and the President of the Air Council, the lessor. The lease was to run for 5 years* at a yearly rental of £200, to be paid in two equal half-yearly instalments, 1st May and 1st November.

The lessee had certain rights, in particular the right to shoot, fish, hunt, course and sport, subject to conditions imposed by the Officer Commanding, and also the right to fell timber-like trees, the cutting of bracken and the grazing of sheep on the demised land. The lessee also had the mineral rights, but any tunnels or excavations or workings required to extract the said minerals had to surface a set distance from the aerodrome boundary. The boundaries were set:—

ON THE EAST

By a line commencing at the North-East extremity of Martlesham Heath at the junction of Sandy Lane with the Woodbridge-Felixstowe Road, by Mill Cottages, and running in a South-Easterly direction along the West side of Spratt's Plantation and thence continuing due South passing the West end of Swale Plantation for a distance of 1,030 yards.

ON THE SOUTH

By a line running in a Westerly direction along the North side of Welham's Plantation to its extreme Western point, thence following a line of fence running in a North-Westerly direction for a distance of 480 yards and thence in a Westerly direction along a line of fence to the Western end of Long Strop.

ON THE WEST

In a line following the boundary of Foxhall Parish, and continuing along a North-West boundary of Brightwell Parish to Dobb's Corner, thence in a Northerly direction as far as the road leading to Hall Farm, thence skirting the edge of Martlesham Heath in an Easterly direction for about 310 yards and thence in a Northerly direction to the Ipswich-Woodbridge Road.

ON THE NORTH

By a line skirting the Ipswich-Woodbridge Road in an Easterly direction for a distance of 830 yards and thence skirting the edge of Martlesham Heath onwards to the starting point at Mill Cottages.

The aerodrome area covered approximately 830 acres.

The Secretary of State surrendered the lease, which still had 959 years to run, during 1963 to the present holders, the Bradford Property Trust Limited, and the property is administered by Bidwells Limited of Cambridge.

*Shortly afterwards extended to nine hundred and ninety nine years.

Operational Squadrons. 1939—1945

Listed herewith are the Squadrons which served at Martlesham Heath during the period 1939 to 1945 and are those which were, as far as can be ascertained, on a semi-permanent basis or a detachment from a nearby Station, and not just visiting units. Some dates are approximate and the names of the Commanding Officers could have been different whilst the Unit was at Martlesham.

No. 1 Squadron (F) Coded J X	S/Ldr A. Zweigburgh	February 1944 to April 1944. Hawker Typhoon 1B's. Shipping strikes. Typical aircraft. JP 685 J X - O.
No. 3 Squadron (F) Coded Q O	S/Ldr R. F. Aitken	April 1941 to June 1941. Hawker Hurricane 11B's and 11C's. East Coast shipping patrols. Typical aircraft. Z.2865 Q O - F.
No. 17 Squadron (F) Coded Y B	S/Ldr C. Walter S/Ldr G. C. Tomlinson S/Ldr A. G. Miller	December 1939 to May 1940. October 1940 to February 1941. March 1941 to April 1941. Hawker Hurricane 1's and 11's. Interceptor roles Dunkirk and Battle of Britain. Typical aircraft. P.3878 Y B - W.
No. 25 Squadron (F) Coded Z K	S/Ldr J. R. Hallings-Pott, D.S.O.	October 1939 to January 1940 "A" Flight. June 1940 to September 1940. Bristol Blenheim 1's. Night-fighter and radar roles. Typical aircraft. L.1257 Z K - I.
No. 29 Squadron (F) Coded R O	S/Ldr P. S. Gomes S/Ldr J. S. McLean	October 1939 to April 1940. May 1940 to June 1940. Bristol Blenheim 1's. Night fighter roles. Typical aircraft. V.8324 R O - B.
No. 41 Squadron (F) Coded E B	S/Ldr C. J. Lee	June 1942. Supermarine Spitfire Vb's. Coastal patrol and standby fighter duties. Typical aircraft. AD.504 E B - W.
No. 54 Squadron (F) Coded K L	S/Ldr N. Orton, D.F.C.	August 1941. Supermarine Spitfire Va's. Fighter sweeps and interception duties. Typical aircraft. W.3332.
No. 56 Squadron (F) Coded U S "Punjab Squadron"	S/Ldr E. V. Knowles S/Ldr P. Hanks, D.F.C. S/Ldr G. L. Sinclair, D.F.C.	October 1939 to February 1940. June 1941 to August 1943. October 1943 to February 1944. Hawker Hurricane 1's. Shipping patrols. Typical aircraft. P.2970 U S - X. Hawker Hurricane 11B's. Patrols and interception. Typical aircraft. Z.3324 U S - F. Hawker Typhoon 1B's. Fighter sweeps. Typical aircraft. EK.268. Later Typhoon bomber duties.

No. 64 Squadron (F) No pre-war code	S/Ldr P. J. R. King	September 1936 to May 1938. Hawker Demon turret fighters. Worked up for Air Defence of Great Britain.
Coded S H	—	July 1942. Supermarine Spitfire IX's. Used as forward base for operations.
No. 65 Squadron (F) Coded Y T "East India Squadron"	S/Ldr A. C. Bartley, D.F.C.	June 1942. Supermarine Spitfire Vb's. Offensive sweeps and bomber escorts. Typical aircraft. EN.849 Y T - X. Mostly Empire pilots.
No. 71 Squadron (F) Coded X R	S/Ldr W. E. G. Taylor S/Ldr C. G. Peterson, D.F.C.	April 1941 to June 1941. December 1941 to May 1942. Hawker Hurricane 1's. Typical aircraft. V.6919 X R - T. Supermarine Spitfire Vb's. Aircraft W.3171. Became first Eagle Squadron, later No. 334 Squadron, U.S.A.A.C.
No. 85 Squadron (F) Coded V Y	S/Ldr P. W. Townsend, D.F.C.	May 1940 to June 1940 as detachment. June 1940 to August 1940. Hawker Hurricane 1's. Typical aircraft. V.7240 V Y - M. Coastal patrols and interception. Supermarine Spitfire Vb's. July 1942.
No. 111 Squadron (F) Coded J U	S/Ldr A. C. Bartley, D.F.C.	September 1942. Supermarine Spitfire Vb's. Fighter sweeps and bomber escort duties. Typical aircraft. AB.330.
No. 121 Squadron (F) Coded A V	S/Ldr H. C. Kennard,	Detachment April 1942. Supermarine Spitfire Vb's. Typical aircraft W.3240. Fighter sweeps and offensive patrols. Second Eagle Squadron, later No. 335 Squadron U.S.A.A.C.
No. 122 Squadron (F) Coded M T "Bombay Squadron"	S/Ldr Prevot S/Ldr J. R. C. Killian	June 1942 to July 1942. September 1942 to October 1942. Supermarine Spitfire Vb's. Typical aircraft. BM.352 M T - Z. Fighter sweeps and offensive patrols.
No. 124 Squadron (F) Coded O N "Baroda Squadron"	S/Ldr T. Balmforth, D.F.C.	Detachment June 1942. Supermarine Spitfire Vb's. Typical aircraft. AA.733 O N - K. Fighter sweeps and wing sorties.
No. 132 Squadron (F) Coded F F "City of Bombay Squadron"	S/Ldr J. R. Ritchie	September 1942 to October 1942. Detachment October 1942 to March 1943. Supermarine Spitfire Vb's. Typical aircraft. AB.925 F F - C. Used for fighter escorts sweeps and "Rhubarbs".
No. 151 Squadron (F) Coded D Z	S/Ldr E. M. Donaldson	Detachment May 1940. Full squadron May 1940. Hawker Hurricane 1's. Typical aircraft. L.1754 D Z - E. Interception roles.

No. 165 Squadron (F) Coded S K "Ceylon Squadron"	S/Ldr H. J. L. Hallowes, D.F.C.	Detachment August 1942 to March 1943. Supermarine Spitfire Vb's. Typical aircraft AB.818 S K - Z. Convoy patrols and offensive sweeps.
No. 182 Squadron (F) Coded X M	S/Ldr T. P. Pugh, D.F.C.	Formed at M/H 1st September 1942 with Hawker Hurricanes and Typhoons. September 1942 to December 1942. January 1943 to March 1943. Hurricane 1. Typical aircraft. AG.232. Typhoon 1. Typical aircraft. R.8979 X M - D. Used in offensive roles over Europe.
No. 198 Squadron (F) Coded T P	S/Ldr J. Manak	June 1943 to August 1943. Hawker Typhoon 1B's. Typical aircraft. JR.197 T P - T. Used on offensive fighter-bomber roles over Europe.
No. 222 Squadron (F) Coded Z D "Natal Squadron"	S/Ldr E. J. F. Harrington S/Ldr G. J. Stonhill, D.F.C.	April 1943 to December 1943. Supermarine Spitfire IX's. Typical aircraft. BS.314 Z D - A. Engaged on "Rodeos" over Europe as well as interception and bomber escort duties.
No. 242 Squadron (F) Coded L E	S/Ldr D. R. S. Bader, D.S.O., D.F.C.	December 1940 to April 1941. Hawker Hurricane 1's and 11B's. Typical aircraft. P.3054 L E - N. Limited night fighter duties, mainly massive sweeps and convoy patrols. Empire pilots.
No. 257 Squadron (F) Coded D T "Burma Squadron"	S/Ldr R. R. Stanford-Tuck, D.F.C.	September 1940 to October 1940. Hawker Hurricane 1's. Typical aircraft. V.7137 D T - G. Fighter interception.
No. 258 Squadron (F) Coded Z T	S/Ldr W. G. Clouston, D.F.C. S/Ldr Cooke	July 1941 to October 1941. Hawker Hurricane 11's. Typical aircraft. Z.2353. Used on fighter sweeps, "fighter-nights" and "Rhubarbs".
No. 264 Squadron (F) Coded P S "Madras Presidency Squadron"	S/Ldr S. H. Hardy S/Ldr P. A. Hunter, D.S.O.	December 1939 to May 1940. Detachment August 1940 to October 1940. Boulton-Paul Defiant 1's. Typical aircraft. L.6957 P S - T. (1st squadron equipped with this aircraft). Day fighter roles.
No. 266 Squadron (F) Coded U O	S/Ldr J. W. A. Hunnard S/Ldr T. B. de la Beresford	March 1940 to May 1940. September 1941 to October 1941. Supermarine Spitfire 1's and 11B's. Typical aircraft. N.3178 U O - K. Coastal patrols and offensive strikes.
No. 278 Squadron (ASR) Coded B A	—	1942 until 1944. Walrus, Defiant, Lysander, Spitfire 11, Anson and SSea Otter aircraft. Engaged on Air Sea Rescue operations over the North Sea.

No. 303 Squadron (F) Coded R F "Kosciusco Squadron"	S/Ldr Z. Bienkowski, K.W.	March 1943 to April 1943. Supermarine Spitfire Vb's. Typical aircraft. AB.376 R F - B. Enemy interception and patrol duties. Polish personnel.
No. 306 Squadron (F) Coded U Z		October 1942 to November 1942. Supermarine Spitfire IX's. Offensive patrols. Polish personnel.
No. 310 Squadron (F) Coded N N	S/Ldr F. Weber	June 1941 to July 1941. Hawker Hurricane 11B's. Typical aircraft. Z.3325. Used for offensive attacks on North Sea shipping. First Czech Squadron formed in R.A.F.
No. 312 Squadron (F) Coded D U	S/Ldr A. Vasatko, D.F.C.	July 1941 to August 1941. Hawker Hurricane 11B's. Typical aircraft. Z.4994. Used on daylight bombing raids. Coastal patrols. Second Czech squadron formed in R.A.F.
No. 317 Squadron (F) Coded J H "Wilno Squadron"	S/Ldr Z. Czaykowski	April 1943 to June 1943. Supermarine Spitfire Vb's. Typical aircraft. AA.672 J H - W. Bomber escort and offensive patrols. Formerly the Wilenski Squadron of the Polish Air Force.
No. 350 Squadron (F) Coded M N	S/Ldr D. A. Guillaume, D.F.C.	June 1942 to July 1942. Supermarine Spitfire Vb's. Typical aircraft. AA.833 M H - E. Used for offensive sweeps and escort duties. First Belgian Squadron formed in R.A.F.
No. 401 Squadron (F) Coded Y O "Ram Squadron"	S/Ldr A. G. Douglas S/Ldr E. L. Neal, D.F.C.	July 1942 to August 1942. July 1943. Supermarine Spitfire IXb's. Typical aircraft. BR.589 Y O - A. Wing sweeps and bomber escort duties. Originally No. 1 Squadron, Royal Canadian Air Force.
No. 402 Squadron (F) Coded A E "Winnipeg Bear Squadron"	S/Ldr V. B. Corbett	June 1941 to July 1941. Hawker Hurricane 11a/s. Typical aircraft. Z.2426. Used for East Coast shipping patrols. August 1942. Supermarine Spitfire IX's. Offensive patrols. Originally No. 2 Squadron, R.C.A.F.
No. 403 Squadron (F) Coded K H "Wolf Squadron"	S/Ldr A. G. Douglas S/Ldr A. C. Deere, D.F.C. and Bar	October 1941 to December 1941. June 1942. Supermarine Spitfire Vb's. Typical aircraft. AD.114. East Coast shipping patrols. Canadian pilots.
No. 411 Squadron (F) Coded D B	—	October 1942 to November 1942. Supermarine Spitfire Vb's. Offensive patrols and fighter sweeps.

No. 412 Squadron (F) Coded V Z "Falcon Squadron"	S/Ldr R. C. Weston	May 1942 to June 1942. Supermarine Spitfire Vb's. Typical aircraft. W.3380. Working up to operational status with new aircraft. Royal Canadian Air Force Squadron.
No. 416 Squadron (F) Coded D N "City of Oshawa Squadron"	S/Ldr L. V. Chadburn, D.F.C.	July 1942 to September 1942. November 1942. Supermarine Spitfire Vb's. Typical aircraft. W.3128. Coastal convoy patrols. Destroyed Dornier 217 on first patrol. Royal Canadian Air Force Squadron.
No. 452 Squadron (F) Coded U D	S/Ldr Bungey, R.A.A.F.	November 1941. Supermarine Spitfire Vb's. Bomber escort duties. Typical aircraft. W.3821 U D - D. Royal Australian Air Force Squadron.
No. 453 Squadron (F) Coded F U	S/Ldr R. J. Ratten	November 1942 to December 1942. Supermarine Spitfire Vb's. Typical aircraft AA.936 F U - B. Working up to operational status. Royal Australian Air Force.
No. 485 Squadron (F) Coded O U		October 1942. Supermarine Spitfire Vb's. Offensive patrols and sweeps over Europe.
No. 501 Squadron (F) Coded S D "County of Gloucester Auxiliary Squadron"	S/Ldr B. Barthold	May 1943 to June 1943. Supermarine Spitfire Vb's. Typical aircraft. EN.974 S D - D. Engaged on escort duties, sweeps, scrambles.
No. 504 Squadron (F) Coded T M "County of Nottingham Auxiliary Squadron"	S/Ldr F. Y. Beamish	Detachment October 1939 to May 1940. Hawker Hurricane 1's. Typical aircraft. P.3774 T M - V. Working up exercises and air firing practice.
No. 604 Squadron (F) Coded N G "County of Middlesex Auxiliary Squadron"	S/Ldr R. A. Budd	Detachments September 1939 to January 1940. Bristol Blenheim 1's. Typical aircraft. L.8607 N G - A. Shipping patrols off East Coast and working up for night fighting duties.
No. 605 Squadron (F) Coded U P "County of Warwick Auxiliary Squadron"	S/Ldr C. R. Edge, D.F.C.	February 1941 to March 1941. Hawker Hurricane 11B's. Typical aircraft. Z.3099. Bomber escort and offensive sweep duties.
No. 607 Squadron (F) Coded A F "County of Durham Auxiliary Squadron"	S/Ldr C. G. Craig	August 1941 to October 1941. Hawker Hurricane 11B's. Typical aircraft. BE.403. Working up for duties as Hurribomber unit with 250 lb. bombs.
No. 610 Squadron (F) Coded D W		October 1942 to November 1942. Supermarine Spitfire Vb's. Offensive and coastal patrols.

No. 1488 Fighter Gunnery Flight		Spring and Summer 1943. Westland Lysander and Boulton-Paul Defiant aircraft. Sleeve target towing for fighter firing practice.
No. 2735 Squadron Royal Air Force Regiment		Stationed at Martlesham Heath for aerodrome defence.

UNITED STATES AIR FORCE SQUADRONS

No. 359th Squadron No. 356th Wing 8th Air Force Coded O C	Major White Major Richard A. Rane	November 1943 to April 1945. Republic Thunderbolt P.47. Converted to North American Mustang P.51.D.
No. 360th Squadron No. 356th Wing 8th Air Force Coded P I	Col Claiborne Kinnard Lt/Col Joe E. Williams	Bomber escort duties and then on conversion, long range strike sorties over Europe.
No. 361st Squadron No. 356th Wing 8th Air Force Coded Q I		As above.

Aircraft, Military and Civil, Tested. 1917—1939

The following lists of aircraft have been compiled from reliable sources and photographic evidence and they give some idea of the numbers of machines which visited Martlesham Heath over the years for testing and evaluation. Some aircraft may appear which in fact only made fleeting visits, and some may have made visits and not been recorded.

Maker and name of aircraft	Serial No.	Date of visit	Remarks
		1917	
Albatross D.V	D.2129/17 G.56	November	Captured German aircraft.
Armstrong Whitworth FK.8	B.215	May	Engine Trials.
	N.513	April	Engine Trials.
	A.2696	April	Performance Trials.
Armstrong Whitworth FK.10	B.4000	March	Airframe trials.
Austin Ball ARB 1	None	July	Handling trials.
Austin Ball AFT 1	None	—	Rebuilt aircraft.
Avro 529	3694	June	Crashed at M.H.
Avro 529A	3695	November	Crashed at M.H.
Avro 530	1811	—	Motor trials.
B.E.2.D.	—	June	Development aircraft.
Beardmore W.B.II	None	December	Cleaned up B.E.2.C.
Bristol M.I.B	—	March	Developed in M.I.C.
Bristol M.I.C	C.4902	December	Production aircraft.
	C.4908	December	Production aircraft.
Bristol F.2.B	A.7183	July	Engine trials.
	B.1181	December	Engine trials.
De Havilland (Airco) 4	N.5960	—	First R.N.A.S. aircraft.
	A.7532	July	Armament trials.
	A.7446	August	Engine trials.
	A.2148	—	Engine trials.
	A.8083	—	Engine trials.
	A.7673	November	Armament trials.
	A.2129	March	Engine trials.
	A.2128	March	Engine trials.
De Havilland (Airco) 5	A.9186	July	Production aircraft tests.
De Havilland (Airco) 6	—	June	Production aircraft tests.
De Havilland (Airco) 9	A.7559	November	Prototype trials.
	C.6051	December	First production aircraft.
F.E.2.B	—	April	Production aircraft tests.
Halberstadt D.II	G/5BDE/22	October	Captured German aircraft.
Handley-Page 0/400	C.9681	August	Handling trials.
Martinsyde F.1	A.3933	July	Handling trials.
Martinsyde F.2	None	May	Handling trials.
Martinsyde F.3	B.1490	November	Handling trials.
Martinsyde R.G	None	February	Handling trials.
	None	July	Revised airframe.
Martinsyde G.102 Elephant	None	January	Trials aircraft.
N.E.I	B.3971	November	Night fighter trials.

Nieuport Scout	5173	February	French aircraft trials.
Nieuport Triplane	A.6686	March	French aircraft trials.
Parnall Panther	N.91	--	Shipboard aircraft tests.
Pfalz D.IIIA	4184/17 G.141	November	Captured German aircraft.
Port Victoria P.V.8	N.540	October	Light fighter tests.
The Eastchurch Kitten			
R.E.8	B.2251	September	Handling trials.
Rumpler C.V	C.8500/16	November	Captured German aircraft.
S.E.5	A.4845	March	Prototype trials.
	—	June	Engine trials. (British)
	—	September	High compression motor tests.
	A.8916	November	Wolseley Viper motor tests.
S.E.5A	A.4563	May	Developed S.E.5 aircraft.
	B.4862	July	First Viper engined aircraft.
	B.4899	December	Second Viper engined aircraft.
	B.4875	December	Triple gun mounting tests.
Siddeley R.T.I	B.6625	December	Prototype aircraft trials.
	B.6626	December	Modified airframe trials.
Sopwith Pup	—	March	Production aircraft trials.
	A.653	May	Experimental motor trials.
Sopwith Camel F.1/3	—	March	Prototype aircraft trials.
	—	March	Experimental motor tests.
	—	July	Experimental motor tests.
F.1/1	—	July	Motor and handling trials.
	N.6336	May	Motor trials.
	—	May	Tapered wing trials.
F.1.AR.I.	N.518	May	Bentley A.R.I. motor tests.
F.1.F.I.	B.3751	June	1st production motor trials.
	—	July	Motor trials aircraft.
F.2.F.I.	—	March	Performance trials.
2.F.I.	N.5	July	First R.N.A.S. aircraft tests.
	—	June	R.N.A.S. performance tests.
	—	August	Bentley B.R.I. motor tests.
1.F.I.	B.3851	August	Motor trials.
	B.3888	August	Motor trials.
	B.3835	August	Motor trials.
	—	October	Aircraft for U.S.A.S.
	—	December	Gnome Monosoupape trials.
	—	August	Gnome Monosoupape trials.
Sopwith 1½ Strutter	A.8194	July	Trials aircraft.
	B.762	August	Single seat fighter trials.
Sopwith Snipe	B.9963	December	1st prototype aircraft trials.
	B.9964	December	3rd prototype aircraft trials.
Sopwith B.I	B.1496	April	Handling and bombing trials.
Sopwith Dolphin 5.F.I	—	June	Prototype fighter aircraft tests.
	—	August	2nd Prototype fighter aircraft tests.
	—	September	3rd Prototype fighter aircraft tests.

	—	September	4th Prototype fighter aircraft tests.
	C.3777	November	1st production aircraft tests.
S.P.A.D. S.7	A.8965	August	French aircraft trials.
Vickers F.B.12.C	A.7351	May	Engine trials aircraft.
	A.7352	June	Anzani engine trials aircraft.
Vickers F.B.14.D	None	March	Handling trials.
Vickers F.B.19.F Mk. II Bullet	A.5225	May	Handling trials.
Vickers F.B.14.D	C.4547	March	General handling trials.
Vickers F.B.16.A	A.8963	May	Handling and engine trials.
Vickers F.B.25	—	May	Crashed at M.H.
Vickers F.B.26 Vampire I	B.1484	July	Extended handling trials.
Wight Quadraplane	N.546	February	Handling trials.

1918

Austin AFT.3 Osprey	X.15	March	Experimental triplane tests.
Austin Ball A.F.B. I	—	July	SPAD type wings trials.
Boulton and Paul Bobolink P.3	C.8655	March	Evaluation trials.
Boulton and Paul Bourges P.7 Mk. II. Later K.129/G-EACE	F.2903	—	Bomber trials.
British Air Transport FK.22/2 Later Bantam	B.9945	January	Fighter prototype trials.
British Air Transport FK.23 Bantam Mk. I	None	October	Developed prototype tests.
British Air Transport FK.23	F.1654	November	Revised airframe trials.
B.E.2.E	—	July	Production aircraft trials.
B.E.12.A	C.3188	July	Experimental fighter trials.
	A.591	December	Modified aircraft trials.
Beardmore W.B. IV	N.38	July	Shipboard fighter trials.
Blackburn Blackburd	N.113	June	Crashed at M.H.
	N.114	October	Re-designed aircraft evaluated.
Blackburn Kangaroo	B.9970	January	Comparison trials with Avro 529.
Bristol F.2.B	—	January	Falcon engined trials.
	B.1200	October	Wolseley Viper motor trials.
	B.1201	January	Hispano Suiza motor trials.
	B.1201	September	R.A.F.4D motor trials.
	B.1204	March	Sunbeam Arab motor trials.
	B.1206	February	Siddeley Puma motor trials.
	C.4654	September	H.C. Siddeley Puma motor tests.
Bristol Braemar Mk. I	C.4296	September	Triplane bomber trials.
Bristol Scout F	B.3989	March	Fighter tests. Motor trials.
Bristol Scout F.I	B.3991	September	Developed F. Handling trials.
Caudron G.IV TWIN	B.8822	December	Tests with Orfordness.
De Havilland (Airco) 9	C.6052	January	Trials with Fiat A.12 motor.
	C.2207	May	Siddeley Puma motor trials.
	C.6051	January	Siddeley Puma motor trials.

De Havilland (Airco) 9A	B.7664	March	Handling trials.
De Havilland (Airco) 10 Amiens I	C.8658	April	Handling and bomber trials.
De Havilland (Airco) 10 Amiens II	C.8659	July	Bombing and R.R. Eagle motor tests.
De Havilland (Airco) 10 Amiens III	C.8660	July	Liberty motor and bombing tests.
	C.4283	August	Re-designed motor nacelle tests.
De Havilland (Airco) 10A Amiens IIIA	F.1869	September	Revised airframe. Handling tests.
Fairey IIIA Later G-EALQ	N.10	July	Airframe and engine trials.
Fiat Scout S.V.A.	6758	August	Captured Italian aircraft trials.
F.E.2.H	A.6545	August	Rebuilt FE2D. Handling trials.
Fokker D.VII	2009/18	October	Captured German aircraft trials.
Grain Griffin	N.100	April	Performance trials.
	N.101	June	Bentley BR 2 motor trials.
	N.102	June	Sunbeam Arab engine trials.
Handley-Page 0/400	—	May	Sunbeam Maori engine trials.
	—	May	R.R. Eagle VIII motor trials.
	—	July	Bombing trials.
Handley-Page V/1500	B.9463	September	Heavy bomber handling trials.
L.V.G. C.II	G/5BD E./18	August	Captured German aircraft trials.
Martinsyde F.4 Mk. I Buzzard	D.4256	June	Airframe and engine trials.
	D.4211	August	Airframe and engine trials.
Martinsyde F.3	B.1490	May	R.R. Falcon motor trials.
N.E.I	B.3973	April	Armament trials.
	B.3975	April	Armament trials.
Nieuport BN.I	C.3484	March	Fighter handling trials.
R.A.E. Ram (A.E.3)	B.8781	July	Handling trials.
R.E.9	A.3561	May	Performance and motor trials.
S.E.5A	—	December	Parachute trials aircraft.
	—	February	Sunbeam Arab II engine trials.
Short Shirl	N.110	June	Torpedo bomber handling trials.
	N.III	September	2nd prototype handling trials.
Sopwith B.I	B.1496	May	Handling trials with modified aircraft.
Sopwith Bulldog 2F RA Mk. I	X.3	April	2nd prototype evaluation.
Sopwith Camel	B.3835	August	Handling trials.
1.F.1	B.2541	April	Motor trials.
	F.6394	August	Clerget motor trials.
2.F.1	N.6812	August	Shipboard aircraft from Felixstowe.
1.F.1	B.6329	August	Motor and gunnery trials.

Sopwith Dolphin Mk. I	—	February	Crash pylon tests.
Mk. II	—	February	Armament trials.
Mk. III	D.3615	October	Hispano-Suiza motor trials.
Mk. III	C.8194	October	Motor and handling trials.
	D.6567	May	First aircraft for America.
Sopwith Hippo. 3.F.2	X.10	January	Prototype handling trials.
Sopwith Rhino. 2.B.2	X.7	January	Bombing and handling trials.
Sopwith Salamander T.F.2	E.5431	June	2nd prototype trials.
Sopwith Scooter	None	June	Rebuild of Camel as monoplane.
Sopwith Snail 8F Mk. I	C.4288	June	Fighter and engine trials.
Mk. II	C.4284	May	Fighter and engine trials.
Sopwith Snipe 7.F	B.9965	January	Prototype evaluation.
	B.9966	June	5th prototype modified trials.
	E.7987	August	1st production aircraft tests.
	E.8083	August	Tailplane trials aircraft.
	E.8006	August	Trials aircraft.
	—	November	Long-range trials aircraft.
	E.8068	December	Trials for use with Fleet.
	E.8089	December	Bomber escort trials.
Sopwith Swallow	B.9276	October	Experimental monoplane trials.
Sopwith Buffalo	H.5893	November	Evaluation and trials aircraft.
Sunbeam Bomber	N.515	August	Long range bomber trials.
Vickers Vimy FB.27	B.9952	January	1st bomber prototype aircraft.
	B.9953	April	Crashed at M.H. Engine failure.
	B.9954	August	Crashed at M.H. Engine failure.
	F.9569	October	4th Prototype. Handling trials.
	F.701	September	Fiat A.12 motor trials.
Vickers FB.26. Vampire Mk. I	B.1484	January	Developed aircraft trials.
Westland Wagtail RAF Type 1	C.4293	July	Fighter trials. Motor tests.
	C.4291	August	Fighter evaluation trials.

1919

Alliance P2 Seabird	G-EAOX	October	C of A trials.
Avro 533 Manchester Mk. II	F.3492	January	Bomber and motor trials.
Avro Manchester 533 Mk. I	F.3493	October	Modified airframe trials.
Austin Greyhound	H.4317	May	Airframe and motor trials.
Austin Whippet	K.158/G-EAGS	August	Lightplane C of A trials.
Armstrong Whitworth Ara	F.4971	—	Prototype fighter trials.
	F.4972	—	2nd prototype fighter trials.
B.E.2.E	C.6980	August	Metal wing trials aircraft.
Blackburn Kangaroo	G-EADG	September	C of A performance trials.
Boulton and Paul Bourges 1A	F.2903	August	ABC Dragonfly motor trials.

Boulton and Paul Bourges 1B	—	October	Gull-wing trials aircraft. Atlantic.
Bristol Badger F.2.C. Mk. II	F.3496	September	Airframe and motor evaluation.
Bristol Fighter F.2.B	E.2400	February	300 hp Hispano motor trials.
	C.9883	August	Sunbeam Arab motor trials.
	D.7968	August	Sunbeam Arab motor trials.
	E.2306	August	Sunbeam Arab motor trials.
Bristol Braemar Mk. II	C.4297	July	Performance trials. Later crashed.
British Air Transport. FK.25	F.2907	—	2nd prototype aircraft trials.
Basilisk	F.2908	—	1st prototype aircraft trials.
Central Centaur IV	K.108/G-EABI	—	C of A performance trials.
De Havilland (Airco) 4	A.7446	August	R.R. Eagle VIII motor tests.
De Havilland (Airco) 9	C.6078	January	Prototype Napier Lion motor tests.
	D.5792	July	Silencer trials with Puma.
	C.2207	August	Trials with H.C. Puma motor.
	D.5625	May	Engine trials and tests.
	D.3010	July	Engine trials and tests.
De Havilland 16	K.130	—	C of A performance trials.
Grahame-White E.IV Ganymede later G-EAMW	C.3481	September	Bomber trials and tests.
Handley-Page V/1500	—	June	Trial aircraft.
Martinsyde Buzzard	—	May	Evaluation and trials aircraft.
Nieuport Nighthawk	F.2910	June	Airframe and engine trials.
S.E.5A	C.8735	June	Standard aircraft. Engine tests.
	C.9117	August	Standard aircraft. Fuel tests.
	F.5696	June	Parachute development aircraft.
Short Shirl	N.112	—	Further prototype trials.
Siddeley R.T.1	B.6630	March	Motor and radiator trials.
Siddeley Deasy SR 2 Siskin	C.4541	July	Fighter and motor trials.
Sopwith Bulldog	C.4543	August	3rd prototype for evaluation.
Sopwith Camel	F.6394	August	180 hp Clerget motor trials.
Sopwith Buffalo	H.5893	February	2nd prototype for evaluation.
Sopwith Cobham Mk. II	H.671	August	Bomber and bombing trials.
Sopwith Dragon	E.7990	February	Trials aircraft.
	F.7017	August	Modified airframe for test.
Sopwith Snapper RAF Type 1	F.7031	September	Airframe and armament trials.
Sopwith Snark	F.4068	November	Type test and engine trials.
	F.4070	November	3rd prototype for evaluation.
Sopwith Snipe	E.8089	—	Revised tail surfaces trials aircraft.
Westland Limousine 1	G-EAFO	—	C of A performance trials.
Westland Limousine 11	G-EAJL	—	Revised tail unit for test.
Westland Weasel	F.2912	April	Airframe and Dragonfly motor tests.
	F.2914	November	Airframe and Jaguar motor tests.

Austin Greyhound	H.4317	April	Engine and airframe trials.
	H.4318	April	Service trials.
	H.4319	August	Performance trials.
Austin Kestral	G-EATR	March	A.M. Competition trials aircraft.
Avro 504K	H.2431	March	Fuel consumption tests.
	D.6308	March	100 hp Mono motor. Metal wings.
	H.2041	March	Propeller trials.
Avro 547A	G-EAUJ	August	A.M. Competition aircraft.
Beardmore W.B. X	G-EAQJ	August	A.M. Competition aircraft.
Boulton and Paul P.7 Bourges	F.2903	January	Propeller trials.
Bristol F.2.B. Mk. II	J.6790	September	Undercarriage trials. Existed as G-ACCG until 1939.
	F.4864	October	Fuel consumption trials.
Bristol Badger	F.3495	January	Rudder modifications.
	F.3497	April	Engine change. New rudder.
Bristol Braemar II	C.4297	January	Full load performance trials. 4-Libertys fitted 2.20.
Bristol Pullman	C.4298	September	C of A performance trials. G-EASP
British Air Transport FK.23 Bantam	F.1661	May	Civil performance trials.
Central Centaur IIA	G-EAPC	June	A.M. Competition aircraft.
De Havilland (Airco) 4A	F.5764	June	C of A trials. Later G-EAWH.
De Havilland (Airco) 9	E.8903	February	Altitude control tests.
De Havilland (Airco) 9A	E.753	April	Napier Lion engine trials. Later G-EAOH
	F.979	June	R.R. Eagle engine tests.
	E.9697	June	R.R. Eagle engine trials.
De Havilland II Oxford	H.8591	September	Performance and engine trials.
De Havilland 15 Gazelle	J.1937	May	Performance and engine trials.
De Havilland 18	G-EARI	March	Civil performance trials.
	G-EAWX	—	Civil performance trials.
Fairey IIIC	N.2246	July	Performance trials.
Handley-Page V/1500	J.6573	June	High altitude, 28,000 ft. trials.
Martinsyde F.4 Buzzard	H.7716	July	Calibration tests.
	H.7781	October	Fuel consumption trials.
Martinsyde Semiquaver	G-EAPX	March	Speed record aircraft. 161.43 m.p.h.
Nieuport & General Aircraft Goshawk	G-EASK	June	Speed record aircraft. 166.5 m.p.h.
Nieuport & General Aircraft London Mk. I	H.1740	June	Bomber performance trials.
Nieuport & General Aircraft Nighthawk	H.8533	December	Badly damaged on arrival. Never flew.
	J.2403	February	Unreliable Dragonfly motor. Scrapped after 43 hours flying.

Parnall Panther	N.7516	July	Performance trials for R.N.A.S.
S.E.5.A	E.5923	April	Experimental tail unit.
	F.9097	December	Consumption trials.
	D.7018	June	Trials aircraft.
S.E.5.B	A.8947	June	Comparison trials with D.7018.
Siddeley Siskin SR.2	C.4541	January	Engine and performance trials.
	C.4542	January	Engine trials. Burnt out.
	C.4543	March	Performance trials.
Sopwith Cuckoo T.1	N.8005	June	Parachute development aircraft.
Sopwith Cobham Mk. I	H.672	May	2nd Prototype. Performance trials.
	H.671	July	Fitted with Puma motors. Trials.
Sopwith Grasshopper	G-EAIN	May	C of A performance trials.
Sopwith Scooter	G-EACZ	July	Civil evaluation trials.
Sopwith Snark	F.4068	March	Dragonfly re-engined trials.
	F.4069	April	Performance trials.
	F.4070	October	Performance trials and tests.
Vickers Vimy	F.3175	January	Armament performance trials.
	H.5081	January	Fitted with 37 mm C.O.W. Gun. Trials.
Westland Walrus	N.9500	May	Trials for Fleet Air Arm.
	N.9523	April	Performance trials.
	N.9515	August	Modified wing trials.
Westland Weasel	F.2913	September	3rd prototype for performance tests.
	J.6577	July	Jaguar engined prototype for trials.
	F.2914	November	Stability tests. Crashed.

Also during this year were all the civil aircraft taking part in the Air Ministry Civil Aeroplane Competition as described in a previous chapter.

1921

Air Navigation & Engineering Ltd. A.N.E.C. 1A	J.7506	May	Ex G-EBIL. Evaluation trials.
Armstrong Whitworth Siskin 1	C.4541	August	Re-engined prototype for trials.
	C.4541	June	Jupiter engined trials aircraft.
Armstrong Whitworth Siskin II	J.6583	March	First all metal airframe.
Avro 504K	H.2401	November	Propeller trials.
B.E.2.E	C.6980	January	Metal winged aircraft for evaluation.
Blackburn Dart	N.140	October	Fleet Air Arm performance trials.
Blackburn Swift Mk. I (G-EAVN)	N.139	December	Fleet Air Arm performance trials.

Boulton and Paul Bourges Mk. II	F.2905	March	Performance trials with full load.
Bristol Badger II	J.6492	June	4th prototype performance trials.
Bristol F.2.B Fighter	F.4819	June	Metal propeller tests.
	H.1436	June	Parachute development aircraft.
	H.1559	March	Dual control aircraft. Parachute work.
Mk. II	J.6586	January	Full performance trials.
	J.6753	July	Radiator performance trials.
Bristol Ten-seater	G-EAWY	July	Performance trials.
British Air Transport FK.23 Bantam	J.6579	February	Wasp engine trials.
De Havilland 9A	H.3629	May	Fuel system trials.
	J.597	January	Last Norwich built aircraft for test.
De Havilland 10	E.6041	May	Fuel consumption trials.
De Havilland 10A	F.8423	February	Performance trials. Wrecked 3.21
De Havilland 14 Okapi	J.1938	March	Performance and engine trials.
	J.1939	August	Armament performance trials.
De Havilland 18B	G-EAWW	August	Civil evaluation trials.
"City of Brussels"	G-EAWX	November	3-bladed airscrew trials.
De Havilland 29 Doncaster	J.6849	September	Aerodynamic research trials.
Fairey IIID	—	March	Performance and armament tests.
Gloucestershire Aircraft Co. Mars 1 Bamel	G-EAXZ	December	Speed record aircraft 196.4 m.p.h.
Gloucestershire Aircraft Co. Mars VI	H.8534	May	Performance and motor trials.
Handley-Page 0/100	G-EAKG	—	Civil performance trials.
Handley-Page 0/400	Several Aircraft	—	Weighing procedures for C of A
Junkers J.1	G/3 BDE/31	April	German aircraft on trial. Destroyed in hangar fire.
Martinsyde F.4. Buzzard 1A	H.6542	June	Long range experimental aircraft tests.
Nieuport & General Aircraft Co. London	H.1741	January	Full performance trials.
Nieuport & General Aircraft Nighthawk	H.8534	May	First Jaguar engined aircraft tests.
	J.2405	June	Modified A.B.C. Dragonfly engine.
	J.2416	January	Parachute development aircraft.
Nieuport & General Aircraft Co. Nightjar	H.8535	May	Full performance trials.
Nieuport & General Aircraft Co. Sparrowhawk	JN.400	May	Trials for Japanese Navy.

Parnall Possom	J.6862	July	Experimental Mail Plane Trials.
Sopwith Snark	F.4070	February	3rd prototype. Engine trials.
Sopwith Snipe	E.8137	January	General performance trials.
	E.7534	March	General performance trials.
Vickers Vernon ex G-EAUY	J.6864	August	Performance trials as bomber.
Vickers Vimy Ambulance (Vernon)	J.6855	March	Evaluation and performance.
Westland Wagtail	C.4292	July	General performance trials.
	J.6581	January	Dragonfly and Wasp motor trials.
	J.6582	February	Dragonfly and Lynx motor trials.
Westland Weasel	J.6577	November	Fitted with Jaguar AS.2 motor.

1922

Armstrong Whitworth Siskin II	G-EBEU	March	C of A trials with 2 seater aircraft.
Avro Aldershot Mk. I	J.6852	May	Full performance trials.
Avro Bison	N.153	August	1st prototype. Performance trials.
	N.154	September	2nd prototype. Performance trials.
Avro 504K (later N)	E.9265	July	Trials with Lynx engine.
	E.9261	July	Extended engine trials.
	H.2202	September	Carburettor trials aircraft.
Beardmore W.B.IIB	G-EARY	April	C of A Performance trials.
Blackburn Dart	N.141	January	Comparison trials.
	N.142	February	Full performance trials.
	N.9542	August	7th production aircraft trials.
	N.9545	November	Production aircraft proving trials.
Blackburn Blackburn	N.150	August	Handling trials. Performance tests.
	N.151	September	Radiator and engine trials.
	N.152	September	Full performance trials. Destroyed in hangar fire.
Boulton & Paul P.15	J.6584	October	Full evaluation testing.
Bristol Bullfinch Type 52	J.6901	May	Performance and engine trials.
Bristol Type 62	G-EAWY	—	C of A Performance trials.
Bristol M.I.C.	G-EASR	September	C of A Trials of ex-service aircraft.
Bristol F.2.B. Fighter Mk. II	J.6790	March	Used for drop tests.
	J.6800	January	Long range trials aircraft.
De Havilland (Airco) 9A	H.3657	February	Oleo undercarriage trials.
De Havilland 18	G-EAWX	January	3-bladed airscrew tests.
De Havilland 27 Derby	J.6894	November	Performance trials.
De Havilland 29	G-EAYO	September	Civil Doncaster for C of A trials.

De Havilland 34	G-EBBQ	July	C of A trials of 9 seater aircraft.
	G-EBBN	July	C of A trials of 9 seater aircraft.
"City of Glasgow"	G-EBBR	April	Performance trials.
Fairey IIID	N.9451	July	R.R. Eagle engined version trials.
Gloucestershire Aircraft Co. Mars 1 Bamel	G-EAXZ	November	Modified aircraft for performance tests.
Gloucestershire Aircraft Co. Mars IV Nighthawk	J.2405	August	Jupiter III engined version. Tests.
	H.8534	September	Siddeley Jaguar IV AS 4 engine tests.
Handley-Page Hanley Mk. I HP 19	N.143	April	Modified aircraft for trials. 3 visits.
Handley-Page Hanley Mk. III HP 19	N.145	April	Developed aircraft. Performance trials.
Handley-Page W8B HP 18	G-EBBG	April	C of A Performance trials.
Handley-Page W18/G "Bombay" later "Princess Mary"	—	—	Revised airframe for C of A trials.
Hawker Duiker	J.6918	—	Evaluation trials.
Nieuport Nightjar Mars X	H.8535	May	Prototype aircraft for test. Damaged.
Parnall Pixie	G-EBKM	June	C of A trials. Single-seat lightplane.
Parnall Plover	N.160	April	Fleet aircraft performance trials.
	N.162	July	3rd prototype. Structural failure.
Vickers Vernon	J.6884	February	1st production aircraft. Range trials.
	J.6879	March	Undercarriage trials.
Vickers Viking V	N.156	August	Land trials of amphibian. M.A.E.E.
Vickers Virginia Type 57	J.6856	December	Full load trials with propeller tests.
Vickers Vulcan Type 61	G-EBBL	October	C of A performance trials.
	G-EBEJ	November	Further civil trials.
	G-EBEC	November	Engine trials for C of A.
	G-EBEK	December	Freight version for A.M. Underpowered.
Westland Wagtail	J.6582	October	Revised airframe tests. Lynx motor.
Westland Weasel	J.6577	March	Performance trials with Jaguar motor.

1923

Armstrong Whitworth Awana	J.6897	October	Troop carrier performance trials.

Armstrong Whitworth Wolf. AW18	G-EBHI	February	Civil version of RAF trainer. Tests.
Armstrong Whitworth Siskin III	J.6921	March	Trials and performance aircraft.
	J.6583	June	First steel aircraft. Performance trials.
	J.6982	December	Aerobatic strength trials.
Avro Aldershot Mk. III	J.6952	January	Trials with lengthened fuselage.
	J.6953	January	Tailplane modification trials.
Avro Bison	N.154	September	Double bay wings and Lion motor. Tests.
	N.155	June	Single bay wings. Propeller tests.
Avro 504K	—	April	Fitted with Lucifer radial motor.
Avro 504N	E.9261	June	Trials aircraft.
	J.733	August	Developed "K" with Lucifer motor.
	J.750	October	Developed "K" with Lynx motor.
	G-EADA	June	Flying test-bed for Bristol motor.
Blackburn Blackburn Mk. I	N.9581	April	Torpedo and armament trials.
Boulton and Paul Bodmin	J.6910	—	Bomber performance trials.
Boulton and Paul Bugle Mk. I P25	J.6984	September	Type tests. Heavy controls.
Bristol Bullfinch. Type 51	J.6903	April	Lower wing fitted to mono aircraft.
Bristol Jupiter Fighter	G-EBEF	—	Civil Demonstrator for export.
Bristol Taxiplane Type 73	G-EBEW	April	Civil C of A evaluation.
		August	Further load tests.
Bristol Trainer	G-EBFZ	July	2 seat trainer for C of A Trials.
	G-EBGE	July	2 seat trainer for C of A Trials.
De Havilland (Airco) 9A	J.6957	April	Lion engined aircraft for trials.
De Havilland Doncaster	J.6849	September	Full load and vibration tests.
	G-EAVO	June	Civil version. Little flown.
De Havilland Dormouse	J.7005	November	Type trials. Jaguar motor trials. Trials with engine bearers.
De Havilland 37	G-EBDO	July	C of A Trials. Performance tests.
Dornier Komet 1	J.7276	April	German aircraft purchased for trials.
English Electric Wren	J.6973	July	Ultra lightplane for evaluation.
Fairey Fawn II	J.6908	March	Revised production aircraft trials.
	J.7198	April	Production trials.
Fairey Fawn Mk. III	J.6907	June	Developed Mk. II for trials.

Gloucestershire Aircraft Co.	J.6969	June	Fighter performance trials.
Nighthawk. Grebe prototype	J.6970	July	Fighter performance trials.
Gloucestershire Aircraft Co. Grebe II	J.7283	October	1st production aircraft trials.
Gloucestershire Aircraft Co. Mars X Nightjar	J.6941	May	Trials aircraft. To R.A.F. Leuchars.
Gloster Bamel 1	J.7234	December	High speed aircraft trials.
Handley-Page HP 19 Hanley 11	N.144	September	Fleet aircraft performance trials.
Handley-Page HP 21	—	June	Fleet fighter for U.S. Navy. Crashed.
Handley-Page Hyderabad HP.24	J.6994	October	Heavy bomber trials. Armament tests.
Hawker Duiker	J.6918	December	Army Co-op trials aircraft. Little flown.
Hawker Woodcock Mk. I	J.6987	August	Wing flutter trials. Performance.
Junkers J.10	—	June	All metal German aircraft for trials.
Nieuport Nighthawk	J.6925	February	Experimental metal aircraft trials.
	J.6941	April	Bentley BR 2 motor trials.
Parnall Pixie I	—	June	S/Seat ultra lightplane. Trials.
Parnall Pixie II	—	August	S/Seat ultra lightplane. Increased motor power.
Parnall Plover	N.162	May	Jaguar engined aircraft for trials.
	N.160	December	Jupiter engined aircraft for trials.
Parnall Possum	J.6862	—	Experimental Postal Aircraft.
Short Springbok Mk. I S.3	J.6974	April	Performance trials. Crashed.
	J.6975	May	Trials with new wings.
Short Springbok Mk. II S.3A	J.7295	July	Trials with lighter wing.
	J.7296	July	Performance trials.
	J.7297	August	Modified tailplane trials.
Supermarine Seagull II	N.158	January	Revised Mk. I for performance trials.
Vickers Vanguard Type 62	J.6924	April	Troop-carrier trials.
	G-EBCP	June	Civil performance trials.
Vickers Vernon II	J.6976	May	1st production aircraft. Fuel tests.
Vickers Victoria II Type 56	J.6861	February	Troop carrier performance trials.
		September	Fuel and endurance trials.
Vickers Viking IV Type 60	G-EBED	July	Civil amphibian performance trials.
Vickers Virginia	J.6856	April	Armament trials.
	J.6857	July	Modified nacelle trials. Later Mk. VII

Vickers Vimy	F.9176	October	Tests on rebuilt aircraft.
	F.9158	June	Undercarriage and brake tests.
Vickers Vixen I Type 71	None	March	Private Venture aircraft. Trials.
Vickers Vulcan	G-EBEC	March	C of A performance trials.
	G-EBFC	April	Further C of A trials.

1924

A.N.E.C.1	J.7506	August	Lightplane performance trials.
Armstrong Whitworth Siskin III	J.6981	June	1st metal aircraft. Performance trials.
	J.7148	April	Comparison motor trials. Crashed.
	G-EBJS	April	Civil aircraft. Increased tankage.
Armstrong Whitworth Awana	J.6898	February	2nd prototype for evaluation.
Armstrong Whitworth Wolf	J.6921	February	Performance trials.
Avro 560	J.7322	April	Evaluated as light trainer aircraft.
Avro 561 Andover	J.7261	August	Ambulance duties performance.
Avro 555A Bison	N.154	August	Fleet Air Arm trials.
Bison Mk. II	N.9844	October	Production trials.
Beardmore Wee Bee WB XXIV	G-EBJJ	July	2 seat lightplane trials.
Blackburn Cubaroo	N.166	—	Performance and motor trials.
Boulton and Paul P.25 Bugle Mk. I	J.7235	July	Re-engined and modified aircraft.
Bristol Bloodhound Type 84	G-EBGG	January	Evaluation trials.
Bristol Brownie	G-EBJL	November	Evaluated for lightplane use.
	G-EBJK	December	Larger span wooden wings.
Bristol Trainer	G-EBCE	—	Return visit. Load trials.
Bristol Taxiplane	G-EBEY	January	Tested as 3 seater. Failed.
Bristol Type 75	—	May	C of A performance trials.
Cranwell C.L.A.2	G-EBKC	May	Performance trials. Crashed.
De Havilland 18B	G-EAWW	May	Used for flotation trials.
De Havilland Dingo 1. D.H42A	J.7006	June	General Purpose Trials. Crashed.
De Havilland Dormouse.			
DH.42	J.7005	May	Performance trials.
DH.42B Dingo II	J.7007	July	Steel tubular fuselage trials.
Fairey Fawn II	J.7184	November	Production aircraft trials.
Gloucestershire Aircraft Co. Grebe III	J.7519	July	Tested as 2-seat trainer.
Gnosspelius Gull	No. 19	—	Ultra lightplane. Performance.
Handley-Page W.8F Hamilton	—	—	C of A trials. 3 engined aircraft.
Handley-Page Hendon HP.25	N.9724	—	Rebuild of Hanley. F.A.A. trials.
Hawker Hedgehog	N.187	September	F.A.A. Evaluation. Cancelled.
Hawker Woodcock II	J.6988	August	Night fighter trials.
Martinsyde F.4	—	May	Jaguar engined civil aircraft trials.

Parnall Pixie III	—	May	Lightplane performance trials.
Parnall Plover	N.9608	July	Trials aircraft.
Raynham Monoplane	J.7518	August	Performance trials. Lightplane.
Supermarine Seagull II	N.158	June	Amphibian for land trials.
Vickers Venture Type 94	J.7277	June	Revised Vixen II. Performance.
Vickers Virginia I	J.6856	April	Condor engined aircraft for trials.
Vickers Vixen II. Type 87	G-EBEC	May	General purpose aircraft trials.
Vickers Vixen III	G-EBIP	May	Cleaned-up Mk. II. Performance.
Westland Pterodactyl Mk. 1A	J.8067	—	Tail-less monoplane for trial.
Westland Widgeon Mk. I	—	—	2 seat club plane for trials.

1925

Airdisco Avro	—	March	504K fitted with RAF motor.
Airdisco Martinsyde	—	June	F.4 Buzzard with Jaguar motor.
Avro Ava Mk. I Type 557	N.171	May	Large bomber performance trials.
Avro Avis	—	June	2 seat ultra lightplane. Trials.
Avro Andover Type 563	G-EBKW	April	Civil Andover for Imperial Air.
Armstrong Whitworth Atlas	G-EBLK	November	Prototype Army Co-op aircraft. Trials.
	J.8777	July	2nd prototype. Performance.
Armstrong Whitworth Siskin III	J.7552	May	2 seat trainer performance tests.
IIIDC	J.7000	June	Performance trials.
II	G-EBHY	June	Civil Demonstrator. Trials.
Armstrong Whitworth Ajax	G-EBLM	May	Army Co-op aircraft for evaluation. Later J.9128
Beardmore W.B.26	None	January	2 seat fighter for Latvia.
Boulton and Paul Bugle Mk. II	J.7266	—	Modified Mk. I Armament trials.
Blackburn Blackburn Mk. II	N.150	May	Modified Mk. I. Raised tailplane.
	N.9589	—	Trainer Version for trials.
Blackburn Cubaroo	N.167	July	2nd aircraft for Service trials.
Breguet 19	J.7507	January	French aircraft for extended trials. Written-off during trials.
Bristol Berkeley Type 90	J.7403	March	Comparison trials aircraft.
Bristol Bloodhound Type 84	J.7248	March	Trials aircraft.
	J.7236	June	Performance trials.
	G-EBGG	June	C of A Trials. Civil version.
Bristol Boorhound Type 93	G-EBLG	August	Comparison trials aircraft.
Bristol Brandon Type 79	J.6997	April	Performance trials as transport.
Bristol Fighter F.2.B. Mk. III	J.8251	June	Army Co-op trials aircraft.
De Havilland 53 Humming Bird	J.7268	May	Lightplane for Service trials.
	J.7325	October	Special aircraft for airship trapeze use.

De Havilland 60A	G-EBKT	May	2 seat light club trainer. C of A.
	J.8030	June	Service trials. Slotted wing tests.
De Havilland Moth 60 X	J.8820	September	Genet I engined version. Trials.
	J.8816	September	Service trials aircraft.
Fairey Fawn III	J.7768	May	Napier Engine trials. (Lion)
Fairey Ferret Mk. I	N.190	October	First Fairey all-metal aircraft. Trials.
Fairey Fox	J.7941	June	2 seat bomber evaluation trials.
Gloucestershire Aircraft Co.	J.7497	May	Prototype fighter evaluation.
Grebe II. Later Gamecock	J.7756	June	2nd aircraft with Jupiter motor.
Mk. I	J.7757	September	3rd aircraft for armament trials.
	G-EBNT	October	Civil demonstrator.
Hawker Cygnet I	G-EBMB	—	Ultra lightplane for C of A.
Hawker Cygnet II	G-EBJH	—	Ultra lightplane for C of A.
Handley-Page HP.22/23	J.7265	—	Lightplane for Service trials.
Handley-Page W.9 Hampstead	—	—	Civil C of A Performance trials.
Handley-Page Handcross HP.28	J.7498	September	Light bomber Service trials.
	J.7500	December	All-metal for trials.
Hawker Hedgehog	N.187	February	Drooping aileron trials.
Hawker Horsley	J.7511	February	Day Bomber Service trials.
	J.7721	May	2nd prototype for trials.
Hawker Woodcock Mk. II	J.7512	June	Trials aircraft. Extended Tests.
	J.7513		
	J.7514		
	J.7515		
	J.7516		
	J.7517		
	J.7594	August	Night flying trials.
Parnall Pixie III	G-EGJG	September	Tested with detachable upper wing.
Raynham Monoplane	J.7518	May	Further Service evaluation.
Short Springbok II.S.3A	J.7295	April	Further Service trials.
Vickers Vernon Mk. II	J.7548	March	Armament trials.
Vickers Vespa Mk. I Type 113	None	June	General purpose evaluation.
Vickers Venture II	J.7282	All year	Used as Station "hack".
Vickers Virginia VIII	J.6856	March	Armament trials. Gun positions on trailing edge of upper wing.
	J.6993	April	Full trials as Mk. VII.
Westland Westbury	J.7766	February	Trials with C.O.W. Guns.
Westland Widgeon Mk. II	—	May	Light civil aircraft for trials.
Westland Yeovil Mk. I	J.7508	August	Day bomber evaluation trials.

During this year comparison trials were held at the A & A.E.E. With the following aircraft participating.

Air Ministry Specification No. 26/23

Bristol Berkeley
Handley-Page Handcross
Hawker Horsley
Westland Yeovil

Hawker Horsley gained production contract.

Air Ministry Specification No. 8/24

Bristol Bloodhound
Armstrong Whitworth Atlas
De Havilland Hyena
Vickers Vespa

Armstrong Whitworth Atlas gained production contract.

Air Ministry Specification for light single-seat aircraft for training.

De Havilland Humming Bird
Avro 560
Parnall Pixie III

De Havilland Humming Bird gained production contract.

1926

Avro Ava Mk. I	N.172	June	Metal version for performance trials.
Avro Avenger Type 566	G-EBND	August	Fighter for evaluation trials.
Avro Avian	G-EBOV	May	C of A evaluation for club aircraft.
Avro Buffalo Type 571	G-EBNW	August	Fleet Arm Air trials aircraft.
Armstrong Whitworth Argosy	G-EBLF	June	Large airliner for C of A trials.
Armstrong Whitworth Atlas	G-EBLK	June	Prototype for further tests.
	G-EBNI	February	C of A for civil version. Demonstrator.
Armstrong Whitworth Siskin IIIB	J.8627	April	Modified aircraft for evaluation.
IIIA	J.7001	January	Prototype aircraft. Further trials.
IIIA	J.8428	February	Further trials aircraft.
Armstrong Whitworth Siskin V	None	June	Export aircraft for trials. Rumania.
Blackburn Airedale	N.189	June	Deck land trials for F.A.A.
Blackburn Blackburn Mk. I	S.1056	October	Performance trials.
Blackburn Ripon Mk. I. T.5	N.203	August	Evaluation as torpedo bomber.
Blackburn Spratt TR.I	N.207	May	Advanced trainer for evaluation.

Aircraft	Serial	Month	Notes
Boulton and Paul P.29 Sidestrand	J.7938	March	Prototype 3 seat bomber trials.
	J.7939	June	2nd prototype for trials.
Bristol F.2.B Mk. IV	F.4587	May	Developed aircraft with H.P. slots.
Bristol Boorhound	G-EBLG	July	Revised prototype. Load tests.
Bristol Brownie	G-EBJK	August	Rebuilt lightplane with metal wings.
Cranwell C.L.A. 4	G-EBPB	June	2 seat lightplane for trials.
De Havilland 9A	J.6957	May	Re-engined Lion trials aircraft.
De Havilland 9 AJ Stag	J.7028	May	Jupiter engined DH.9 for G.P. use.
De Havilland 9J	G-AARS	April	Jaguar engined 9A with short fuselage. Evaluation trials.
De Havilland 54 Highclere	G-EBKI	June	C of A trials for 14 seat airliner.
De Havilland 56 Hyena	J.7780	July	Performance trials with Jaguar III
	J.7781	August	Performance trials with Jaguar IV
De Havilland 66 Hercules	G-EBMW	May	Airliner C of A performance trials.
Fairey IIIF Mk. IV.M	J.9053	September	R.A.F. Version of IIIF GP aircraft.
	N.198	May	Prototype for load trials.
	N.225	August	2nd prototype for type trials.
G.P.	J.9164	October	Long range trials aircraft.
Fairey Fawn III	J.7978	July	1st aircraft of last production batch.
Fairey Ferret II	N.191	February	Fleet performance trials.
	N.192	March	2 seat aircraft for G.P. trials.
Fairey Firefly I	—	June	P.V. fighter for performance trials.
Fairey Fox	J.8427	May	Further performance trials.
Fokker F.VIIA/3m	J.7986	May	Dutch aircraft for cantilever wing test.
Gloucestershire Aircraft Co. Gamecock Mk. I	J.7891	August	1st production aircraft for performance test.
Handley-Page W.10	G-EBMM	April	C of A for civil airliner.
Handley-Page Hamlet HP 32	G-EBNS	May	Experimental high wing monoplane.
Handley-Page Harrow HP 31	N.205	October	Fleet performance trials.
Hawker Cygnet	G-EBJH	June	Ultra lightplane for trials.
Hawker Heron. Later G-EBYC	J.6989	May	Load tests of steel fuselage.
Hawker Hornbill	J.7782	July	S/Seat fighter for performance tests.
Hawker Horsley Mk. I	J.8006	August	Components trials.
	J.8007	August	Tyre burst investigations.
Parnall Perch	N.217	January	Fleet evaluation trials.
Parnall Pixie III	G-EBJG	February	Return visit further performance trials.

Vickers Vendace Mk. I	N.208	August	Advanced trainer for evaluation.
Vickers Vespa Type 113 Mk. I	G-EBLD	September	Armed aircraft for trials.
Vickers Victoria III Type 56	J.7921	February	Swept wing version for test.
Vickers Virginia Mk. VI	J.7558	February	Performance trials with Lion motors. Later built as Mk. IX.
	J.7717	October	Performance trials with Lion motors. Later built as Mk. X.
Vickers Vivid Type 146	G-EBPY	July	G.P. aircraft for evaluation.
Vickers Vixen Type 148	G-EBIP	March	Modified aircraft for performance trials.
Westland Wizard Mk. II	J.9252	June	Fighter monoplane for performance trials.

During the year the following Contract Competitions were held.

Air Ministry Specification 7/24	Avro Avenger
	Gloster Gorcock
	Hawker Hornhill

None of the aircraft were accepted.

Air Ministry Specification 21/23	Avro Buffalo
	Blackburn Ripon
	Handley-Page Harrow

Blackburn Ripon gained contract.

Air Ministry Specification 5A/24	Blackburn Spratt
	Vickers Vendace
	Parnall Perch

No contract placed as requirement not fulfilled.

The De Havilland 66 Hercules tested during this year was so named after a competition had been run in the June 1926 Meccano Magazine to find a name for this three-engined airliner for Imperial Airways.

1927

Armstrong Whitworth Atlas ex G-EBLK	J.8675	November	Tests with new wings.
Armstrong Whitworth Siskin	J.7180	May	Dual control trainer aircraft for test.
Armstrong Whitworth Starling L.	J.8027	June	Prototype fighter for evaluation.
Boulton and Paul P.31 Bittern	J.7936	March	Armament and performance trials.
Bristol Beaver Type 93A	G-EBQF	April	Redesigned Boorhound for trials.
Bristol Badminton Type 99A	G-EBMK	July	C of A trials for rebuilt Type 99.
Bristol Bulldog 1	None	June	S/s fighter evaluation trials.
Cranwell C.L.A.4A	G-EBPB	April	C of A Performance trials.
De Havilland 65A Hound	G-EBNJ	April	G.P. Trials. Wooden structure rejected.

De Havilland 71 Tiger Moth	G-EBQU	July	C of A performance trials.
Fairey IIIF Mk. IV CM	—	March	Special evaluation aircraft.
Fairey Fox Mk. IA	J.9026	June	Re-engined aircraft for trials.
Gloster Gamecock Mk. I	J.7910	May	Flutter trials and aileron tests.
	J.8075	July	Mercury IIa motor trials.
Gloster Goldfinch G.23	J.7940	May	S/S fighter for performance trials.
	—	August	Extended fin trials. Metal aircraft.
Gloster Goral G.22	J.8673	June	G.P. biplane for evaluation.
Gloster Gorcock G.16/16A	J.7501	May	S/S fighter evaluation. Lion IV motor.
	J.7502	June	Tests with Napier Lion VIII motor.
Halton H.A.C. I Mayfly	G-EBOO	June	Aeroclub built aircraft for performance trials.
Handley-Page HP.32 Hamlet	G-EBNS	February	Re-engined aircraft for further trials.
Handley-Page Hendon	N.9729	August	Service trials aircraft.
Handley-Page HP.33 Hinaidi I	J.7745	May	Rebuild of Hyderabad for trials.
Hawker Harrier Mk. I	J.8325	December	Performance trials and load tests.
Hawker Hawfinch	J.8776	July	S/S fighter for evaluation.
Hawker Horsley Mk. II	J.8932	May	Standard aircraft for performance trials.
	J.8612	May	Standard aircraft for performance trials.
Parnall Imp	—	March	Revised aircraft for test.
Short Chamois S.3B.	J.7295	April	Converted Springbok II for performance tests.
Vickers Type 131 Valiant	No. 11	June	G.P. aircraft for evaluation trials.
Vickers Virginia Mk. X	J.7439	August	1st aircraft with metal wings. Trials.
	J.7424	February	Auto pilot trials.
Mk. VII	J.7432	April	Slotted wing trials.
Mk. VII to Mk. X	J.7434	April	Auto pilot trials.
Vickers Vixen VI	G-EBEC	September	G.P. evaluation trials.

The Gloucestershire Aircraft Company changed its name on the 11th November, 1926 to the Gloster Aircraft Company, thus making a change in aircraft designation.

Contract Competitions held 1927

Air Ministry Specification F.20/27 (revised F9/26)   Bristol Bullpup Type 108A
Hawker Hawfinch
Boulton and Paul Partridge
Armstrong Whitworth XVI

Westland F.20/27
Gloster Goldfinch
Gloster SS.19
Bristol Bulldog

Bristol Bulldog awarded contract.

1928

Armstrong Whitworth Atlas	J.8675	February	Further trials with metal wings.
	J.8792	May	Dual control trainer trials.
Armstrong Whitworth Ajax	J.8802	September	Army Co-op evaluation aircraft.
Avro Type 583 Antelope	J.9183	September	2 seat day bomber evaluation.
Beardmore Inflexible	J.7557	February	Large research aircraft. Erected at M.H.
Boulton & Paul P.31 Bittern	J.7937	April	Modified prototype for trials.
Boulton & Paul P.33 Partridge	J.8459	June	Evaluation and comparison tests.
Boulton & Paul P.29 Sidestrand III	J.9176	February	1st production aircraft for testing.
Blackburn F.2 Lincock Mk. I	G-EBVO	July	S/Seat fighter evaluation.
Blackburn Turcock	G-EBVP	February	Export fighter. Crashed at M.H.
Bristol Bulldog Mk. II	J.9480	August	Developed Mk. I for performance trials.
Bristol Type 101	G-EBOW	July	C of A Trials.
De Havilland 60.G Gipsy Moth	J.9922	May	Trainer performance trials.
60.M	K.1227	August	Service trials.
De Havilland Type 65 Hound	J.9127	September	Rebuilt aircraft. Not tested.
De Havilland Type 65 Hound II	—	December	Revaluation for Australian Government.
Fairey Ferret III	N.192	March	Cleaned-up Ferret II for armament.
Fairey Flycatcher II	N.216	August	Redesigned Mk. I for evaluation.
Fairey Fox IIM	J.9834	June	Evaluation aircraft.
Fairey Long Range Monoplane I	J.9479	March	Experimental aircraft trials.
Gloster Gamecock Mk. I	J.8047	February	Aircraft for spinning trials.
	J.8804	July	Modified aircraft with Jupiter VI motor.
Gloster Gorcock	J.7503	September	3rd prototype. Performance trials.
Gloster Goring G.25	J.8674	March	Performance trials as day bomber.
Handley-Page HP 42	G-AAGX	—	C of A for large 4-engined airliner.
Handley-Page HP 35 Clive III	J.9126	May	Troop-carrier performance trials.

Handley-Page HP 34 Hare	J.8622	June	Performance trials as day bomber.
Hawker F.20/27	J.9123	May	Propeller trials.
Hawker Harrier Mk. I	J.8325	July	Further load trials.
Hawker Hart	J.9052	All year	Performance and extended trials.
Hawker Hoopee	N.237	May	Naval fighter for evaluation.
Hawker Horsley Mk. II	J.8606	May	Handling trials.
	J.8604		
	J.8610		
	J.8619		
	J.8620	February	Metal aircraft for evaluation.
	J.8612	July	Standard aircraft for performance trials.
Hawker Tomtit	J.9772	All year	2 seat trainer performance trials.
Parnall Imp	G-EBTE	—	Civil C of A trials with Genet II
Saro Windhover	G-ABJP	June	3 engined amphibian for C of A
Simmonds Spartan	G-EBYU	April	2 seat biplane for C of A Performance Trials.
Vickers Type 141	None	October	Converted Type 123. Performance tests.
Vickers Vellore Mk. I. Type 134	G-EBYX	October	Transport C of A Performance Trials.
Vickers Vendace Mk. II Type 133	G-EBPX	November	2 seat G.P. biplane Performance Trials.
Vickers Victoria Mk. III	—	March	Test vehicle for Virginia tail unit.
Vickers Victoria Mk. IV	J.9250	October	Performance trials. Known as Jupiter Victoria.
Vickers Vildebeest Type 132	N.230	September	Torpedo bomber evaluation trials.
Vickers Vireo	N.211	May	Metal Fleet fighter for performance tests.
Vickers Virginia Mk. IX	J.8236	September	Fitted French Gnome Rhone Jupiters.
Mk. X	J.7717	November	Armament testing.
Mk. IX	J.7715	May	Upgraded aircraft for trials.
Vickers Vixen Type 124 Mk. VI	G-EBEC	May	Further performance trials. Re-engined.
Westland Wapiti Mk. I	J.8495	June	2 seat G.P. biplane evaluation.
Westland Widgeon Mk. III	—	—	Civil monoplane C of A trials.
Westland Wapiti Mk. II	J.8492	August	Re-engined with Jupiter VIII tests.
	J.9238	December	Comparison trials.
Westland Witch Mk. I	J.8596	April	Bomber monoplane evaluation trials.
Wibault (Vickers) Type 122c2	J.9029	June	2 seat French built aircraft for test.

No. 15 Squadron had the following Hawker Horsley Mk. II's for bombing trials.
J.8604. J.8606. J.8610. J.8619.

1929

Armstrong Whitworth Argosy Mk. II	—	June	23 seat development of Mk. I C of A.
Armstrong Whitworth Siskin III DC.	J.9236	June	Trials for Royal Canadian Air Force.
Armstrong Whitworth Starling Mk. I	J.8027	August	S/S Interceptor evaluation trials.
Mk. II	J.8028	December	As above with alternative wings.
Avro 621 Trainer	G-AAKT	December	2 seat trainer for Service trials.
Avro 616 Avian IVa	G-AACV	March	Metal version of Mk. III. Trials.
	J.9783	July	Comparison trials with Tomtit.
Avro Avian 594B Mk. III	J.9182	May	2 seat trainer for standard testing.
Avro Avocet Type 584	N.209	April	Fleet fighter for trials.
	N.210	July	2nd aircraft for further trials.
Avro Gosport 504 R. ex G-EBUY	J.9175	April	Evaluation trials.
Blackburn Beagle	N.236	July	Evaluation and comparison trials.
Blackburn Bluebird IV	—	March	Development of earlier aircraft. C of A
Blackburn Nautilus 2F1	N.234	March	Evaluation for Fleet aircraft.
Bristol Bullpup	J.9051	May	Developed with Bulldog. Performance.
Clarke Cheetah	G-AAJK	August	C of A trials of civil aircraft.
Comper CLA Swift	—	April	Lightplane C of A performance trials.
De Havilland 71 Tiger Moth	—	March	Trials aircraft.
De Havilland 80 Puss Moth	G-AAHZ	June	Civil aircraft for C of A testing.
Desoutter IIIF	—	March	C of A certification trials.
Fairey III Mk. IV M/A	J.9164	—	Further developed IIIF Performance.
	J.9150	August	Fitted with Jupiter VIII motor.
Fairey IIIF Mk.3M	S.1354	September	Fitted with experimental tail unit.
Fairey Firefly Mk. IIM	—	May	S/seat interceptor. Performance trials.
Fairey Firefly Mk. IIIM	—	August	Naval version of above. Performance.
Fairey Fleetwing	N.235	June	Evaluation of 2 seat Fleet spotter.

Gloster AS.31 Survey	G-AADO	February	Civil survey aircraft. C of A trials.
	K.2602	May	Service version of above.
Gloster SS.18	J.9125	October	S/seat interceptor. Evaluation.
SS.18A	J.9125	December	Re-engined with Jupiter VIIF
Gloster SS35 Gnatsnapper	N.227	May	S/Seat fighter evaluation trials.
Hawker Harrier I	J.8325	January	Further load trials as bomber.
Hawker Hart	J.9052	January	Further extended trials.
Hawker Hornet. Later Fury	J.9682	May	S/Seat interceptor for evaluation.
Hawker Hoopee	N.237	February	Revised airframe for trials.
Hawker Horsley	J.8932	March	All metal airframe for testing.
Hawker Tomtit	J.9773	February	Service evaluation aircraft.
	K.1453	April	Production aircraft for testing.
Hawker G.22/26 Naval Hart. (Osprey)	J.9052	March	Original Hart with folding wings.
Hendy Hobo	G-AAJG	—	Light monoplane. C of A trials.
Henderson-Glenny Gadfly	G-AAEY	—	Civil aircraft for C of A trials.
Parnall Pippit	N.232	February	Fleet fighter evaluation. Crashed.
Parnall Elf	—	July	Civil lightplane for trials.
Saro A.10 F.20/27	None	April	S/Seat interceptor evaluation.
Short Gurnard II. S.10	N.229	May	2 seat Fleet spotter. Evaluation.
	N.228	June	As above with Jupiter motor.
Southern Martlett	G-AAII	August	Light aircraft for club use. C of A.
Vickers Vimy	F.9168	March	Fitted with Jupiter radials.
Vickers Type 141	None	January	Rebuild of previous aircraft for Navy.
Vickers Type 143	None	June	S/Seat Scout for Bolivian A.F.
Vickers Victoria Mk. V	J.9766	October	Performance trials with slotted wings.
Vickers Virginia Mk. IX	J.7562	October	Performance trials to Mk. X.
	J.7715	April	Performance trials to Mk. X.
Vickers Virginia Mk. IX	J.7720	July	Cockpit canopy trials.
Mk. X	J.8238	September	Lion XI engine trials.
Westland F.20/27	J.9124	May	S/Seat interceptor for performance trials.
Westland IV Later Wessex	G-EBXK	April	Original aircraft re-engined with Genet Majors.
Westland Wapiti Mk. II	—	April	Metal structured version. Performance trials.

1930

Aircraft	Registration	Month	Description
A.B.C. Robin AN.17	G-AAID	June	S/Seat lightplane for C of A trials.
Armstrong Whitworth Aries	J.9037	April	2 seat Army Co-op aircraft for evaluation.
Armstrong Whitworth Atlas	J.8792	May	Trainer version for evaluation.
	G-ABDY	September	Civil demonstrator C of A.
	G-EBYF	—	Civil Demonstrator. Trials aircraft.
Armstrong Whitworth XVI	S.1591	November	S/Seat interceptor. Evaluation trials.
Avro Avian 616 IVa.	VH-HAC	August	S/Seat version for overseas buyer.
Avro Tutor 621	K.1230	May	Performance trials.
	K.1237	July	A/S Mongoose IIIc motor trials.
	K.1797	October	Service trials for standard aircraft.
Blackburn Lincock III	G-AALH	February	Metal version of original aircraft. Performance.
Blackburn Ripon II T5A	S.1270	January	Developed Mk. I for evaluation.
T5B. Mk. IIA	S.1272	February	Production aircraft for testing.
T5B. Mk. IIC	S.1468	March	Mk. IIA modified for testing.
T5B.	S.1424	July	Production aircraft Service trials.
T5E. Mk. III	S.1272	October	Further modifications aircraft.
	S.1272	December	Revised upper mainplane tests.
Bristol Type 109	G-EBZK	September	C of A trials.
Bristol Bulldog IIA	K.1603	May	D.T.D. Trials aircraft.
Comper Swift CLA 7	G-AARX	August	Further trials of civil aircraft.
De Havilland 77 Interceptor	J.9771	September	S/Seat interceptor evaluation.
De Havilland 80A Puss Moth	K.1824	June	Investigation trials aircraft. Wing failure.
De Havilland 86	G-ACPL	January	C of A trials aircraft.
Fairey S.9/30	—	May	Evaluation of stainless steel frame.
Fairey Fox IIM. (G-ABFG)	S.1325	March	Extended trials for Fleet Air Arm.
Fairey IIIF Mk. IV C.R.	J.9154	August	Service trials as day bomber.
Gloster SS.18.B.	J.9125	February	Re-engined aircraft for evaluation.
Gloster SS.19	J.9125	October	Re-engined with Jupiter motor.
Gloster AS.31 Survey	G-AADO	January	Further C of A trials.
Gloster Gnatsnapper Mk. I SS.35	N.227	March	Developed Mk. I with Jaguar radial.
	N.254	April	2nd prototype with Mercury III.

Aircraft	Registration	Date	Notes
Mk. II	N.254	August	New tailplane and Jaguar VIII motor.
Handley-Page HP.38 Heyford	J.9130	March	Heavy night bomber performance trials.
Handley-Page Clive II	—	August	Metal version of Mk. I. Evaluation.
Hawker Hart	J.9933	All year	Extended performance trials.
Mk. I	K.1416	June	Service trials.
Hawker Hoopee	N.237	November	Re-engined aircraft with Jaguar III
Hawker Horsley	J.8606	April	Handling trials.
	S.1235	August	All metal torpedo bomber for performance.
Mk. II	S.1236	August	All metal bomber for performance trials.
Hawker Hornet	J.9682	June	Trials as Fury prototype, and Yugoslav sales tour.
Hawker Norn HN I	—	August	S/S Fleet fighter for trials.
Hawker Osprey	J.9052	September	Hart prototype as Osprey prototype.
Hawker Tomtit	G-AASI	February	Civil version of R.A.F. trainer.
Hawker F.20/27 Interceptor	J.9123	July	Original aircraft re-engined. Mishap.
Henderson HSF I	G-EBVF	March	6 seat civil aircraft for C of A trials.
Hendy 302	G-AAVT	—	2 seat cabin monoplane for C of A tests.
Parnall Elf I	G-AALH	May	2 seat biplane for C of A trials.
Robinson Redwing I	G-AAUO	—	2 seat biplane for club use. C of A.
Seagrave Meteor	G-AAXP	June	4 seat civil monoplane. Fuel trouble during C of A performance trials.
		October	Furthers tests for C of A.
Spartan Arrow	G-AAWY	May	2 seat civil biplane. C of A performance trials.
Vickers Vannock 195 Mk II	J.9131	March	Heavy bomber performance trials.
Vickers Type 151 Jockey	J.9122	April	Evaluation trials for interceptor.
Vickers Type 132 Vildebeest 1	G-ADGE	February	Private Venture torpedo bomber for performance trials.
	S.1707	April	Service trials with do.
Vickers Type 177	None	February	Shipboard fighter trials and performance tests. Forced landing at M.H.
Vickers Type 204 Vildebeest	0 — 1	August	Private Venture 2nd prototype. Evaluation.
Vickers Virginia Mk. X	J.7275	April	Lion engined. Armament tests.

	J.7421	October	Jupiter IX engined. Performance trials.
Westland Wapiti Mk. IIA	J.9328	August	Revised Mk. II as production aircraft. Performance.
	J.9247	September	Standard aircraft performance trials.
	K.1129	September	Long range trials.
Mk. I	J.9102	July	Oil pump trials. Ballast tests.

1931

Armstrong Atlas I	K.1540	April	Trials aircraft.
	G-ABIV	April	Clean-up civil version for trials.
	G-ABKE	March	Clean-up civil version for range tests.
Armstrong Whitworth Siskin III	J.7161	March	Experimental cockpit heating.
	J.9236	April	2 seat trainer fighter trials.
Armstrong Whitworth XVI	A − 2	June	P.V. fighter. Official trials.
Arrow Active I	G-ABIX	June	Civil aerobatic biplane. C of A tests.
Avro 618 Ten	K.2682	April	Evaluation as R.A.F. Communications aircraft.
Avro 620/Cierva C.19/111 ex G-ABCM	K.1948	March	Rotating wing autogiro for evaluation.
Avro Tutor Type 621	K.1237	July	Handling trials. Mongoose IIIC.
Avro 627 Mailplane	G-ABJM	August	C of A performance trials.
Blackburn Beagle	N.236	March	Re-engined with Jupiter XF. Performance trials.
Blackburn CA 18 Seagrave I	G-ABFP	February	Original Seagrave aircraft. C of A trials.
Boulton and Paul P.32	J.9950	March	Night bomber handling trials.
Bristol Bulldog IIIA	R − 5	April	Developed Mk. IIA for testing.
Bristol Type 119. Later K.2873	R − 3	July	General Purpose P.V. aircraft for evaluation.
De Havilland 60T Tiger Moth	E − 5	April	2 seat elementary trainer for evaluation.
Later G-ABNJ	G-ABPH	June	2nd prototype for evaluation.
De Havilland 82	E − 6	August	Trials and handling aircraft.
De Havilland 82 Tiger Moth	E − 6	September	Full Service aircraft for performance trials.
82A ex G-ABPH	K.4242	October	Shortened wing struts. Performance trials.
Fairey Flycatcher	S.1286	March	Service aircraft for testing.
Fairey Gordon	K.1697	August	2nd prototype for full handling trials.

Fairey Long Range Monoplane II	K.1991	April	Fuel tests on long range aircraft.
Gloster SS.19	J.9125	May	Armament trials with 6 guns.
Gloster SS.19A	J.9125	November	Lewis guns removed. Night flying tests.
Gloster Gnatsnapper III	N.227	June	Rebuild with R.R. Kestral IIS motor.
Handley-Page Heyford	K.3489	April	Non standard aircraft for trials.
Hawker Fury I	K.1926	May	Production aircraft for trials.
	K.1927	May	Production aircraft for trials.
	K.1928	May	Production aircraft for trials.
Hawker Fury IA Yugoslavia	N.F.1	August	Export aircraft for trials.
Hawker Hart	K.1416	January	Dive bombing trials.
	None	June	A/S Panther engine. Evaluation.
India Hart	K.2083	May	Special aircraft for tropical duties.
	K.1438	June	Hart modified to Audax standards.
	J.9933	August	Hart re-engined with Kestral IIS.
	J.9937	November	Further aircraft with same equipment.
Hawker Osprey 19/30	S.1677	June	First Osprey roper. Performance trials.
Hawker Horsley	S.1452	January	Target towing trials.
Monospar Wing Co. ST.3	G-AAHP	—	3 seat civil aircraft for performance tests.
Saro A.19 Cloud	K.2681	August	Amphibian trainer. Evaluated in conjunction with M.A.E.E. Felixstowe.
Saro A.21 Windhover	G-ABJP	January	Return visit of amphibian. Performance tests.
Short Gunard Amphibian	N.229	June	Tested in conjunction with MAEE
Vickers Type 161 COW Gun Fighter	J.9566	September	Pusher, biplane interceptor with COW gun. Performance and armament trials.
Vickers Type 172 Vellore II	G-AASW	May	Development of Vellore I. Performance trials.
Vickers Type 173 Vellore III ex G-ABKC	K.2133	August	Twin engined mailplane. Remained as Station "hack" after evaluation.
Vickers Type 195 Vannock II	J.9131	June	Rebuild of Type 150. Kestral III motors.
Vickers Jockey Type 151	J.9122	May	Modified aircraft with Jupiter VIIF motor.
Vickers Vespa VI Type 210 K.3588	G-ABIL	March	C of A certification for tour of China. Later World Altitude Record 43,976 ft.

Vickers Victoria Mk. V Type 169	K.2340	November	Jupiter engined aircraft for Service trial.
Vickers Vildebeest	N.230	June	Service trials and performance trials.
Westland F.29/27 COW Gun Fighter	J.9565	May	S/S interceptor with COW gun. Performance and armament trials.
Westland P.V.3. Later G-ACAZ and K.4048.	—	March	Private Venture torpedo bomber. First aircraft to fly over Mount Everest.
Westland Pterodactyl Mk. IV	K.1947	September	Tail-less 2 seat cabin research monoplane. Gipsy III motor.
Westland P.V.6 Wapiti V	G-AAWA	July	General Purpose biplane. Evaluation. Later used on Mount Everest flight.
Wapiti IIA	K.1380	—	Fitted with new elevators. Performance trials.
Westland Wapiti Mk. VII	K.3488	September	Rebuild of PV 6. Later Wallace. Performance.
Westland Wallace I	K.3562	October	Wapiti to Wallace standard.

1932

Airspeed Ferry S.4 "Youth of Britain II"	G-ABSI	April	Certification as 10 seat airliner.
Arrow Active II	G-ABVE	March	Developed Mk. I. C of A Performance trials.
Armstrong-Whitworth AV.XV Atlanta	G-ABPI	July	Certification as 17 seat airliner.
Armstrong Whitworth AW XVI	G-ABKF	September	S/S P.V. Interceptor. Engine trials.
		November	Maintenance Trials.
Avro 621 Tutor	K — 4	January	Original design revised for evaluation.
	G-AARZ	August	Further aircraft for evaluation.
	K.1797	November	Service trials.
	K.1237	November	Full performance trials.
Avro Type 626 Prefect	—	September	Service and C of A performance trials.
Blackburn B.2	G-ABUW	May	Elementary trainer for C of A Trials.
Blackburn CA.15C Biplane	G-ABKW	August	Evaluated with Blackburn Mono to A.M. specification. Brake troubles.
Blackburn CA.15C Monoplane	G-ABKV	August	Evaluated with above. Performance.
Blackburn Nautilas	N.234	April	Used as M.H. communications aircraft.
Blackburn Ripon Mk. IIC	S.1670	April	Production aircraft for testing.

Bristol Bulldog IIIA	R — 5	March	Prototype re-engined Mercury IVS2
Bristol Type 118A	K.2873	August	Modified Type 118 for testing.
Bristol Type 120. Later K.3587	R — 6	May	Development of 118. Armament trials.
Chance-Vought V.66E Corsair	K.3561	June	American dive-bomber for evaluation.
De Havilland 60G III Moth Major	—	September	Development of 60G. C of A Performance trials.
De Havilland 83 Fox Moth	—	July	Small 4 seat aircraft for civil C of A.
De Havilland 84 Dragon later G-ACAN	E — 9	February	6 seat airliner for C of A Performance tests.
Fairey Night Bomber 20/34. Later Hendon	K.1695	May	Heavy night bomber evaluation.
Fairey Seal	S.1325	August	Rebuild of IIIF Mk. VI. F.A.A. trials.
	K.3477	October	1st production aircraft for performance tests.
General Aircraft Ltd Monospar ST.4	G-ABUZ	June	4 seat twin-engined monoplane for civil certification.
Gloster FS.36 TSR 38	S.1705	April	2 seat fleet spotter. Evaluation.
Gloster TC.33 Transport	J.9832	October	4 engined troop transport for performance test.
Handley-Page HP.36 Hinaidi II	J.9478	June	Developed Mk. I. Performance trials.
Handley-Page HP.43	J.9833	May	Large 3 engined troop transport. Performance.
Handley-Page Heyford Mk. II	K.3503	June	Developed Mk. I with enclosed cockpit.
Hawker Audax I	K.1995	May	First Audax proper. Performance tests.
Hawker Demon	K.9933	June	2 seat fighter version of Hart. Performance.
Hawker Fury. Norway	401	September	Panther IIIa engined export fighter.
Hawker Hart	K.2083	February	Engine trials with Kestral V. Later Station Flight aircraft.
Hawker Hart	146	August	First aircraft for Estonia.
Hawker Hart Trainer	K.1996	May	1st prototype of Audax performance trials.
	K.3146	June	Full standard aircraft. Performance trials.
Hawker Nimrod I	S.1577	March	Propeller trials.
	K.2823	August	Mk. II prototype. Full performance trials.
Hawker Dantrop	201	September	Horsley for Royal Danish Naval Service

Heinkel HE 64C. Later K.3596	G-ACBS	July	German aircraft for flap and slotted wing performance trials.
Percival Gull PIA Mk. II	—	April	Javelin engined prototype for performance.
PIB Mk. II	—	July	Gipsy Major engined aircraft for performance.
Percival Gull Four P.I	G-ABUR	March	1st civil prototype for C of A trials.
Short Valetta	G-AAJY	July	Large civil monoplane for C of A.
Spartan Cruiser I	G-ABTY	May	Light civil airliner for C of A trials.
Vickers Type 151 Jockey I	J.9122	June	Continued trials. Crashed in spinning.
Vickers Type 163	O – 2	February	4 engined bomber trials. Performance.
Vickers 195, Vannock Mk. II	J.9131	September	Developed 150 and 163. Further evaluation bomber trials.
Vickers Type 207	S.1641	June	Torpedo bombing performance trials.
Vickers Vannox	O – 2	November	Further modified aircraft. Performance tests.
Vickers Type 173 Vellore IV	K.2133	April	2nd aircraft. Performance trials.
Vickers Victoria V	K 2340	February	Prototype Mk. VI aircraft. Pegasus test bed.
	K.2807	May	Modified wing structure tests.
Vickers Vildebeeste I	S.1707	September	Handling and type trials.
Westland Hill Pterodactyl Mk. V	K.2770	December	2 seat tail-less interceptor. Performance.
Westland Wapiti Mk. I	J.9084	October	Drop trials.
Mk. IIA	K.1129	August	Windscreen trials.
Mk. IIA	K.2262	February	Jupiter VIIIF and propeller trials.
De Havilland 82A Tiger Moth	K.2576	January	Performance trials.
	K.2579	January	Spinning trials.

The following Martlesham Heath aircraft took part in the 1932 Royal Air Force Hendon Display.

Gloster TC.33	J.9832	Blackburn Biplane	G-ABKW
Fairey Hendon	K.1695	D.H. Tiger Moth	K.2579
Vickers Jockey	J.9122	Handley-Page Heyford	K.3503
Boulton & Paul P.32	J.9950	Short Valetta	G-AAJY
Bristol Type 120	R – 6	Armstrong Whitworth Atlas	G-ABIV
Vickers Vildebeest	S.1707	Westland Wallace	K.3562
Hawker Hart	K.2083	Bristol Bulldog Mk. IIIA	R – 5

1933

Airspeed Courier AS.5	G-ABKN	June	Light civil cabin monoplane for C of A.
	K.4047	August	Trials for Service communication aircraft.
Armstrong Whitworth AW.XVI	A — 2	August	Re-engined aircraft with Panther VII. Performance.
Avro 621 Tutor	K.3189	November	Standard aircraft with modified controls.
	E.59	August	Trials for Greek Air Force aircraft.
Avro 626/637	G-ABJG	March	2 seat frontier patrol aircraft. Performance.
Boulton & Paul Overstrand	J.8175	All year	Armament trials.
Boulton & Paul P.64 Mailplane	G-ABYK	September	Performance trials. Crashed at M.H.
Blackburn TSR	B — 6	November	P.V. 2/3 seat torpedo aircraft Performance.
Blackburn Baffin	K.3546	December	1st production aircraft for testing.
	K.3589	April	Acceptance trials. Pegasus motor.
Blackburn M.1/30	S.1640	January	Fleet acceptance trials. Crashed.
Blackburn M.1/30A	B — 3	March	Revised M.1/30 for evaluation.
	K.3591	May	Above on R.A.F. Charge for tests.
		October	Control systems trials. Ditching trials at Felixstowe.
Blackburn Ripon	B — 4	February	Evaluated with Tiger motor.
	B — 5	February	Evaluated with Pegasus motor.
Blackburn Seagrave	—	March	Performance trials with civil aircraft.
Blackburn Biplane	G-ABKW	April	Returned for further performance trials.
Blackburn Monoplane	G-ABKV	April	Comparison trials with above.
Bristol Bulldog Mk. IIA Mod.	K.3512	May	Developed IIA for trials.
Mk. IIIA	R — 5	March	Performance trials. Crashed at M.H.
	R — 7	July	Replacement aircraft to continue trials.
Bristol Type 120	K.3587	March	Armament trials.
De Havilland 82A Tiger Moth II	G-ACDA	March	Service version for trials.
	K.2583	November	Mass balanced aileron trials.
De Havilland 85 Leopard Moth	G-ACHD	May	Civil C of A certification.
Fairey IIIF Mk. III	S.1847	June	Dual control aircraft for F.A.A. trials.
Fairey Fox I. (G-ACXO)	J.7950	May	Trials aircraft with Felix motor.

Fairey Fox III Trainer	G-ACKH	August	Trainer version of Fox III. Performance.
Fairey G.4/31 Mk. I	—	February	T.S.R. a/c for evaluation.
Mk. II	K.3905	July	2nd aircraft with Tiger motor. Performance.
General Aircraft Lt. Monospar	G-ACCI	May	Performance trials on civil aircraft.
Gloster SS.19B Gauntlet	J.9165	June	Final development of SS18. Propeller tests.
Gloster T.S.R. 38	S.1705	March	2nd visit for evaluation trials.
Handley-Page Heyford Mk. II	K.3489	February	1st production aircraft for acceptance.
Hawker Audax I (India)	K.4850	March	Gloster built aircraft for testing.
	K.3067	June	Fitted with Vickers K gun. Armament.
Persia	401	August	Fitted with Pratt & Whitney motor. For Persian Air Force.
Hawker Demon	K.9933	October	Developed aircraft with Frazer-Nash turret.
Hawker Fury Persia	203	March	Pratt & Whitney Hornet engined aircraft for Persian Air Force.
Hawker Fury II	K.1935	June	Trials aircraft for specification draft.
Hawker High Speed Fury	K.3586	August	Developed Fury. Full performance test.
Hawker Hart	K.2434	December	Test bed for Napier Dagger I motor.
	K.2969	July	Vickers built aircraft for testing.
	K.2967	July	Ballistic test aircraft.
Hawker Hart Trainer (Interim)	K.2475	February	Dual control trainer for trials.
	K.3146	July	Production aircraft for trials.
Hawker Hind	K.2915	March	Ex Hart tested with Kestral V.
Hawker Nimrod (Intermediate)	K.2823	February	Mk. II prototype. Swept wing performance test.
Hawker Osprey I	K.2776	March	Handling trials with enlarged rudder.
Spartan Clipper	G-ACEG	—	Seat civil monoplane for C of A.
Spartan Cruiser II	G-ACBM	—	Feeder airliner for C of A trials.
Supermarine Seagull V	K.4797	March	Amphibian flying boat for trials.
Vickers Valentia Type 264	K.3599	June	Performance trials as trooper.
	K.2344	September	Dunlop brake trials.
Vickers Vannock II Type 255	J.9131	March	Rebuilt aircraft with lengthened wing.
Vickers Type 259 Viastra X	G-ACCC	April	Civil aircraft for C of A certification.
	VH-UOO	June	Tested for Australian use.

Vickers Victoria V	K.2807	August	Performance trials and tail-wheel tests.
	K.2808	October	Performance trials. Experimental aircraft.
Vickers Vildebeest Type 244	S.1707	March	Trials with modified aircraft.
	S.1715	June	Evaluated as night bomber.
	K.2816	June	Trials and development aircraft.
	K.2819	June	Fitted Pegasus 11M3 and v.p. propellers.
Westland Wallace	K.3562	March	Type test and performance trials.
	K.3573	December	Rebuilt Wapiti J.9084. Performance tests.
	K.3673	December	Performance trials.
Westland Wapiti	G-ACBR	April	Prototype Wapiti with rear cabin.

1934

Airspeed Envoy AS.6	G-ACMT	September	Civil C of A Certification.
Armstrong Whitworth 19. A.3	K.5606	April	Torpedo bomber evaluation trials.
Armstrong Whitworth AW 35	G-ACCD	August	Civil Demonstrator performance trials.
Avro 636	A — 14	June	2 seat fighter trainer trials.
Avro 641 Commodore	G-ACNT	—	Civil certification of cabin biplane.
Avro 642	G-ACFU	January	C of A performance trials.
Avro 671 Cierva C.30A Rota I	K.4230	April	Autogiro for full performance trials.
Avro Tutor	K.1797	February	Fitted with Dowty wheels.
	K.3189	December	Fitted with metal wings.
Boulton & Paul P.71.A	G-ACOX	March	Airliner for C of A Trials.
Boulton & Paul Overstrand	J.9186	January	Extended armament trials.
Blackburn G.4/31	B — 7	February	Revised aircraft for evaluation trials.
Blackburn Baffin II	S.1665	April	D.T.D. Trials aircraft.
Blackburn Shark I	K.4295	September	Torpedo bomber for F.A.A. trials.
	K.4349	September	Torpedo bomber for F.A.A. trials.
Boeing 24TD. Later NC 11369	NC 257Y	—	Weighed-in at M.H. for Air Race.
British Aircraft Company Eagle	G-ACRG	March	Civil monoplane for C of A Trials.
Comper Kite	G-ACME	July	Civil monoplane for C of A Trials.
Comper Streak	G-ACNC	May	Civil monoplane for C of A Trials.

Comper Mouse	G-ACIX	May	Civil monoplane for C of A Trials.
De Havilland 60T Tiger Moth	K.2593	April	Cockpit heating trials.
De Havilland 82A Tiger Moth	K.4242	September	Full performance trials.
De Havilland 86	E2/G-ACPL	August	10 seat civil biplane C of A tests.
	VH-USF	December	Crash investigation tests.
De Havilland 87 Hornet Moth	E.6/G-ADIE	July	C of A and performance trials.
De Havilland 89 Dragon Rapide	E — 4	May	C of A of twin-engined airliner. Speed restrictions at M.H. owing to panels damage by airflow.
De Havilland T.K.I	E.3/G-ACTK	September	Light civil aircraft for C of A.
Douglas DC.2 "Ulver"	PH-AJU	—	Weighed-in for Air Race.
Fairey Hendon	K.1695	April	Comparison trials with Heyford.
Fairey T.S.R.2	K.4190	March	Revised TSR 1 for further trials.
Gloster Gauntlet I	—	December	Standard aircraft fitted with Mercury VI.
Gloster SS.37	G-37	November	Rebuilt Gauntlet to F.7/30 spec.
Handley-Page HP.47	K.2773	May	G.P. aircraft for trials. Twisted fuselage reported during M.H. trials.
Heinkel 70	G-ADZE	May	High speed German aircraft used by R.R. for Kestral engine trials.
Hawker Audax	K.5163	March	Avro built aircraft for trials.
Hawker Audax Persia		May	Export aircraft with Pegasus radial motor.
Hawker Fury Persia	203	October	Export aircraft with Mercury radial motor.
Hawker Fury Portugal	50	June	Export aircraft with Kestral 11S motor.
Hawker Hardy	K.3013	October	Modified Hart for new specification.
Hawker Hart I	K.2434	February	Trials aircraft. Dagger II motor.
	K.2466	January	Dive bombing trials.
Hawker Hart Swedish	1301	January	Export aircraft with Pegasus radial motor.
Hawker Hart Trainer	K.3743	July	Trials aircraft.
	K.3012	April	Trials aircraft. To Canada.
	K.3153	September	Trainer aircraft trials.
Hawker Hind	K.2915	May	Light bomber derived from Hart. Performance.
Hawker Nimrod II	K.2909	February	Developed Mk. I. Stainless steel frame.
Hawker Osprey Sweden	2401	October	Mercury engined aircraft for Sweden.

Miles M.3A Falcon Major	U.3/G-ACTM	April	Performance trials on civil aircraft.
Miles M.2F Hawk Major	G-ACTD	July	Performance trials on civil aircraft.
Northrop 2E	K.5053	June	American dive bomber for evaluation.
Parnall Heck. 3308	Class B	April	Civil aircraft for performance trials.
Percival Gull Six P.3	G-ADEP	April	Improved Gull 4. C of A Performance trials.
Percival Mew Gull I	G-ACND	May	S/Seat racing aircraft. C of A Trials.
Short Scion I	G-ACJI	January	Small feeder airliner. Performance trials.
Short Scylla	G-ACJJ	April	Large civil airliner. Certification.
Supermarine F.7/30. Type 224	K.2890	March	Interceptor performance trials.
Vickers Type 252 Vildebeeste XI	—	July	Developed aircraft. Evaluation trials.
Vickers Type 253	K.2771	August	Evaluation of 2 seat G.P. biplane.
Vickers Type 266 Vincent	S.1714	January	Rebuild of Vildebeest. Trials aircraft.
	K.4105	March	Further trials aircraft.
Vickers Valentia	K.3599	May	Propeller trials and brakes.
	K.3603	December	Handling trials. C of G tests.
Vickers Type 212 Vellox	G-ABKY	April	10 seat airliner C of A Certification.
Vickers Victoria VI	K.3168	January	Fuel system tests.
Vickers Virginia III	J.7130	January	Armament and engine trials.
Westland F.7/30	K.2891	May	Evaluation of s/seat interceptor.
Westland Wallace	K.3488	February	Gunner's cockpit trials.
(ex K.2245)	K.4010	October	Handling trials.

1935

Airspeed Convertible Envoy	—	February	Standard Envoy for military use.
Airspeed Envoy	G-ACVI	March	Wolseley engined aircraft. Flown to South Africa by S/Ldr E. Hilton.
Armstrong Whitworth 23	K.3585	June	Troop carrier for evaluation.
Armstrong Whitworth AW 35 Scimitar	405	August	Export aircraft for Norway. Performance tests.
	407	November	Further aircraft for performance tests.
	G-ACCD	September	Civil demonstrator for trials.
Avro C.30 Rota 1	K.4230	February	Autogiro for Army Co-op trials.

	K.4239	April	Performance trials.
	K.4775	November	Handling trials.
Avro 652 "Avalon"	G-ACRM	March	Feeder civil airliner. C of A tests.
Avro 652A Anson	K.4771	April	Extensive trials for maritime aircraft.
Avro 621 Tutor	K.3308	December	Extended performance trials.
Blackburn B.7	B — 7	May	Evaluation and performance trials.
Blackburn Baffin II	S.1665	June	Ripon aircraft to Baffin standard. Performance.
Blackburn T9A Shark II	K.5607	December	1st production aircraft. Performance tests.
	K.4295	July	Strengthened airframe tests.
Boulton & Paul P.75 Overstrand	K.4546	October	1st production aircraft for Service trials.
Bristol 130. Bombay	K.3583	March	Troop carrier for performance trials.
Bristol 142. "Britain First"	R — 12 G-ADCZ	June	Civil high performance aircraft for trials.
British Aircraft Company No. 3 Cupid	G-ADLR	August	Lightplane for performance trials.
British Aircraft Co. Swallow II	—	May	2 seat club and touring aircraft. Performance.
De Bruyre Snark	G-ADDL	April	Thick wing section performance tests.
De Havilland 86A. Later SU-ABV	E — 2	—	Modified airliner for evaluation.
De Havilland 88 Comet ex G-ACSS	K.5084	August	Service trials. Undercarriage failure. Winner of Melbourne Air Race.
De Havilland 89M	K.4772	April	Military version of airliner. Performance.
De Havilland 90 Dragonfly	—	June	5 seat light airliner. C of A Tests.
De Havilland T.K.2	E.3/G-ADNO	May	Racing aircraft. Range and performance tests.
Fairey G.4/31 Mk. II	K.3905	January	Rebuild of Mk. I. Performance trials.
Fairey Swordfish	K.4190	March	Original aircraft as production aircraft.
Fairey S.9/30	S.1706	July	Spotter for Fleet use. Performance tests.
Gloster Gauntlet I	K.4081	January	Handling and performance tests.
	K.4082	January	Production aircraft tests.
	J.9125	June	Prototype for production tests.
Gloster Gladiator G.37	K.5200	May	Cleaned-up prototype. Evaluation.
		October	Propeller trials.
Gloster T.S.R. 38	S.1705	June	Further performance trials.

General Aircraft ST.25 Monospar Jubilee.	—	September	Evaluation of 5 seat airliner.
Handley-Page 51	J.9833	March	Bomber transport for performance trials.
Heston Type I Pheonix	G-ADAD	August	5 seat civil monoplane. C of A.
Hawker Audax India	K.4850	March	Trials aircraft.
Hawker Audax Nisr Iraq	—	April	Export aircraft with Pegasus radial.
Hawker Audax I	K.5163	February	Avro built aircraft for trials.
	K.7380	July	Avro built aircraft for trials.
Hawker Demon	J.9933	March	Prototype Hart and Demon with turret.
Mk. II	K.3764	July	Evaluated Turret Demon. Armament.
Mk. I	K.5684	September	Evaluated Turret Demon. Armament.
	K.4496	All year	Frazer-Nash turret trials.
Hawker Fury Special	—	March	Lorraine engined aircraft. Export.
Hawker Fury II	K.7263	August	Engine trials with developed aircraft.
Hawker Fury Persia	203	February	Export aircraft with Mercury radial.
Hawker G.4/31 P.V.	K.6926	June	General Purpose aircraft for trials.
Hawker G.7/34 Hind	K.2915	May	General Purpose aircraft for trials.
	K.4636	June	Handling and performance trials.
Hawker GPDB IPV 4	K.6926	June	P.V. Dive Bomber for trials.
Hawker Hardy I	K.5919	May	Developed aircraft for desert tests.
Hawker Hart	K.2434	April	Napier Dagger test bed. Engine tests.
	K.3036	March	Rolls-Royce test bed. Engine trials.
Hawker Hartebeest	801	July	Performance trials on aircraft for S. Africa.
Hawker Nimrod Intermediate	K.2823	December	Standard aircraft with swept wing.
Hawker P.V.3	IPV 3	October	Experimental day and night fighter.
Martin Baker MB.I	G-ADCS	—	2 seat light civil aircraft for trials.
Miles M4A Merlin	U.8/G-ADFE	August	General purpose biplane for trials.
Percival Mew Gull Mk. II P.6	G-AEKL	June	Redesign of racing aircraft. C of A Certification.
Percival Vega Gull III	L.7272	April	Service light communication aircraft.

	G-AEAB	—	Performance trials.
	G-AFIE	—	Handling trials.
Short Scion II	G-ACUE	—	Developed Mk. I for performance trials.
Spartan Cruiser III	G-ACYK	June	Revised Mk. II with cleaned-up lines.
Supermarine Walrus	K.5772	February	Developed Seagull for Service trials.
Vickers Type 212 Vellox	G-ABKY	January	Further trials of civil airliner.
Vickers Vildebeeste Mk. III	K.4164	December	Mk. IV prototype trials.
Westland P.V.7	P.V.7	May	General Purpose aircraft for Test. Crashed.
Westland Wallace Mk. II	K.3488	April	Handling trials of Mk. II aircraft.
	K.4346	February	Weighing and handling trials.

During the year the following aircraft were evaluated in comparison trials.

Bristol 120	Westland P.V.7	Hawker P.V.4	Fairey G.4/31
Armstrong Whitworth A.W.19	Vickers 253	Parnall G.4/31	Handley-Page HP.47

None of the above aircraft were ordered into quantity production.

1936

Aeronca C.3	G-AEFT	May	Small civil aircraft of American design for C of A performance trials.
	G-ADSO	May	
Armstrong Whitworth AW 38 Whitley	K.4586	August	Prototype monoplane bomber. Performance trials.
Avro 652A Anson I	K.6152	October	1st production aircraft for Service trials.
	K.6228	November	Turret trials. Armament tests.
	K.6157	May	Trials aircraft.
Avro Tutor II	K.3308	July	Special aircraft. Double bay wings. Performance.
Avro Rota	K.4232	September	Civet engined autogiro. Performance tests.
	K.4236	May	Handling trials.
Blackburn Shark Mk. II	K.5607	January	Performance trials on 1st production aircraft.
Mk. III	K.4882	February	3rd production aircraft with Pegasus.
		June	Return visit for cockpit canopy.
British Aircraft Co. No. 4 Double Eagle	G-ADVV	July	6 seat civil aircraft for C of A tests.
	G-AEIN	July	Alternative engined version C of A.
Bristol 142M Blenheim I	K.7033	April	3 seat bomber for performance tests.
C.L.W. Curlew	G-ADYU	November	Civil aircraft performance trials.

De Havilland 86B ex G-ADYL	L.8037	October	Modified DH 86 for Service tests.
	G-ADYH	December	Rudder and aileron trials.
De Havilland 87B Hornet Moth	P.6785	February	Communication aircraft for performance tests.
	G-ADMS	February	Type test for civil aircraft.
De Havilland 89 Dragon Rapide	G-ADWZ	March	Modified 60th production aircraft. Weight trials for new all-up load.
De Havilland 90 Dragonfly	—	—	Type test of modified aircraft.
Fairey Battle	K.4303	November	Prototype light bomber trials.
Fairey Seafox	K.4305	August	Light Fleet aircraft. Service trials.
General Aircraft Co. Monospar ST.18 Croydon	G-AECB	June	Civil airliner C of A Trials.
Gloster Gauntlet I	K.4103	August	Flaps and oil cooler tests.
	K.4101	August	Low pressure tyres for test.
	K.4094	July	Trial Browning gun installation.
	K.4093	November	Tested with Mercury VIS
	K.5271	August	Evaluated as Mk. II. To Finland.
Hawker Audax	K.400	May	Panther engined aircraft for Egypt.
Hawker Fury Series II	4 — 1	June	Export aircraft for Spain.
Hawker Fury II	K.8232	May	General Aircraft built aircraft.
Hawker Fury Series II. Yugoslavia	—	October	Export aircraft for performance trials.
Hawker F.36/34 Hurricane	K.5083	April	S/Seat interceptor for trials.
	L.1547	October	Trials aircraft re-engined.
	L.1669	August	Service trials of production aircraft.
	K.5083	October	Merlin C engine trials.
Hawker Hart (T)	K.6426	March	C of G trials. Singapore aircraft.
Hawker Hector 14/35	K.3719	July	Prototype Army Co-op aircraft.
Hawker Hind	K.4636	January	Light bomber Service trials.
Handley-Page Harrow HP.54 later G-AFRG	K.6933	December	Performance and Handling trials.
	K.6934	December	Bomb sight trials. Armament.
Handley-Page HP 52 Hampden	K.4240	July	Medium bomber for performance tests.
Hillson Praga HA 12	G-AEEU	May	2nd prototype civil aircraft C of A of Czech design.
	G-AEPN	September	Civil aircraft C of A Czech design.
Lockheed 10	G-AEPN	September	American airliner evaluated.
Miles Falcon M.3	K.5924	June	Civil monoplane for Service test.

Miles Hawk Major	K.8626	February	Civil monoplane for Service test.
Miles M.II Whitney Straight	G-AECT	May	Civil aircraft for C of A Certification.
Parnall Heck IIC	K.8853	March	Armament trials aircraft.
Short Scion Senior	G-AECU	July	4 engined development of Scion. C of A certification tests.
Supermarine Spitfire	K.5054	September	Prototype aircraft for handling tests.
Vickers Type 279 Venom	PVO-10	May	S/Seat interceptor for trial.
Vickers B.9/32 Type 271	K.4059	April	Prototype bomber trials. Crashed.
Vickers G.4/31. Type 287 Wellesley I	K.7556	March	Monoplane bomber for evaluation.
Westland Lysander Mk. I	K.6127	July	Army Co-op aircraft evaluation tests.
	K.6128	July	2nd prototype for handling.

For the next three years the lists of aircraft are in slightly different format and as numbers became greater, they have been divided into their respective Sections, Performance and Armament Testing.

1937

PERFORMANCE TESTING SECTION

Airspeed Envoy (King's Flight aircraft)	G-AEXX	Fairey Battle	K.7558
		Fairey Hendon	K.5085
Airspeed Oxford I	L.4534		K.5086
Armstrong Whitworth Whitley I	K.7183	Fairey Seal	K.4779
		Fairey Swordfish	K.5660
	K.4587	Forster Wickner Wicko	G-AEZZ
Avro Anson	K.4771	Gloster Gauntlet II	K.5271
British Aircraft Double Eagle	ZS-AIY	Gloster Gladiator	K.7964
Blackburn Shark II	K.8902	Handley-Page Harrow	K.6933
Blackburn Skua 0.27/34	K.5178	Handley-Page Hampden	K.4240
Blackburn Monoplane	K.4241	Hawker Demon I (Turret)	K.4496
Boulton-Paul Defiant	K.8310	Hawker Hardy	K.5919
Bristol Blenheim (DC)	K.7034	Hawker Hector	K.8090
Bristol Bolingbroke	K.7072	Hawker Hind (Portugese)	
Bristol Bombay	K.3583	Hawker Hind	K.4636
C.W. Cygnet	G-AEMA		K.6770
De Havilland 85A	G-ADUE	Hawker Hurricane	K.5083
De Havilland 86B	G-ADUH	Hawker Nimrod	K.2823
	G-AENR	Hawker P.4/34 Henley	K.5115
De Havilland T.K.4	G-AETK	Miles Kestrel M.9	N.3300
De Havilland 93 Don	L.2387	Miles Magister	L.5912
	L.2391		L.5933
De Havilland 91 Albatross	G-AEVV		L.5934
De Havilland 94 Moth Minor	G-AFSD	Miles Mentor	L.4392

Miles Nighthawk	L.6846
Moss Brothers M.A.I	G-AEST
Parnall Heck II	K.8853
Percival Mew Gull X2	G-AFAA
Percival Q.6	G-AEYE
Vickers B.9/32	K.4049
Vickers Vannox III B.19/27	—
Vickers P.V. F.5/34 Venom	O – 10
Vickers Viastra	L.6102

Vickers Vildebeest I	K.2819
Vickers Vildebeest IV	K.6408
	K.8087
Vickers Wellesley I	K.7713
	K.7756
	K.7729
Vickers Wellington I	L.4212
	K.4049
Westland Lysander I	K.6128

ARMAMENT TESTING SECTION

Boulton & Paul Overstrand	K.8175
Bristol 120	K.3587
Bristol Bulldog IIA	K.1691
Bristol Bulldog II	K.9567
Dewoitine 510 (French)	L.4760
Fairey P.4/34	K.7555
Fairey Battle	K.7577
Gloster Gladiator	K.7919
	K.7939
	K.7922
	K.5200
Handley-Page Harrow	K.6934
Mk. II	K.6983

Handley-Page Heyford Mk. I	K.4029
Mk. II	K.3503
Mk. III	K.6902
Hawker Hart	K.2967
	K.2968
	K.2740
Hawker Hind	K.2915
Supermarine F.7/30	K.2890
Supermarine Spitfire	K.5054
Vickers Valentia	K.3603
Vickers Vildebeest	S.1715
Vickers Virginia X	J.7130

GENERAL DUTIES AIRCRAFT

Avro Tutor	K.6116
	K.3308
Avro Rota I. (Autogiro)	K.4232
Bristol Bulldog IIA	K.4189
De Havilland Moth 60M	K.1227

De Havilland 82A Tiger Moth	K.4281
Gloster Gauntlet	K.4103
Hawker Fury II	K.1935
Hawker Osprey IV	K.5742
Parnall G.4/31	K.2772

1938

AIRCRAFT IN PERFORMANCE TESTING SECTION

Airspeed Oxford I	L.4534
Armstrong Whitworth Ensign	G-ADSR
Armstrong Whitworth Whitley	K.7217
II	
I	K.7183
II	K.7208
Avro Anson I	L.7928
	L.6231
Boulton-Paul Defiant I	K.8310
Blackburn Shark	K.4882
Blackburn Skua	K.5179
Bristol Beaufort	L.2867
	L.4441

Bristol Blenheim I	K.7034
	L.6594
	L.1424
	K.7109
	K.7168
	L.6595
Bristol Bolingbroke	K.7072
Bristol Bombay	L.3583
Bristol Type 146	K.5119
C.W. Cygnet	G-AEMA
De Havilland Albatross	G-AEVV
"Faraday"	
"Frobisher"	G-AFDI

253

De Havilland Don I	L.2388	Heston Aircraft T.1/37	L.7706
	L.2391	Hillson Praga	G-AEYL
Fairey Albacore	L.7074	Lockheed 14	G-AFGN
	L.7075	Martin Baker M.B.2	G-AEZD
Fairey Battle	K.7558	Martin Baker Interceptor	P.9594
	K.9281	Miles Magister	L.5933
	L.4935		L.6905
Fairey Seal	K.4203		L.8168
Fairey Swordfish	K.5660	Miles Master I	N.7510
General Aircraft Monospar	K.8307	Miles Mentor	L.4392
Gloster Gladiator	K.8039	Miles Nighthawk	L.6846
	K.8049	North American Harvard I	N.7000
	K.7964	Phillips & Powis P.V. Trainer	U – 5
Gloster Gladiator (Portuguese)	—	Percival Q	G-AEYE
Handley-Page Hampden I	K.4240		VH-ABL
	L.4032	Short M.4 (½ scale Stirling)	S.31
	L.4033	Supermarine Spitfire	K.9787
	L.4035		K.9788
	L.4037	Tipsy "B"	G-AFGF
Handley-Page Harrow	K.6934	Vickers Vildebeest I	K.2819
Handley-Page Heyford II	K.3503	Vickers Vildebeest IV RNZAF	K.6408
Hawker Turret Demon I	K.4496	Vickers Wellesley I	K.7729
Hawker Hardy	K.5919	Vickers Wellesley	K.7724
Hawker Hart	K.3031		K.7740
Hawker Henley	K.5115	Vickers Wellington I	L.4212
Hawker Hind. (Iran)	601	Westland Lysander I	K.6127
Hawker Hind	K.4635	Westland Lysander I	K.6128
Hawker Hind Mk. Trainer	K.5387		L.4673
Hawker Nimrod	K.2823		L.4674
Hawker Hurricane	L.1547	Westland Whirlwind	L.6844

AIRCRAFT IN ARMAMENT TESTING SECTION

Airspeed Oxford I	L.4540		K.9231
	L.4543		K.7577
Armstrong Whitworth Whitley	K.7183		K.9221
Boulton & Paul Overstrand I	K.8175		K.7682
Boulton-Paul Defiant I	K.8310		K.9227
Blackburn Skua	K.5178	Fairey P.4/34	K.7555
Bristol Blenheim I	K.7034	Fairey Fantome/Feroc	L.7045
	K.7044	Gloster Gladiator	K.7919
	L.1113	Handley-Page Harrow II	K.7031
	L.1201	Handley-Page Heyford	K.4029
	K.7150	Handley-Page Heyford	K.3503
	L.1253	Hawker Demon	K.3764
	L.1424	Hawker Fury	K.2082
Bristol 148. A.39/34	K.6551		K.2876
Dewoitine 510 (French)	L.4670	Hawker Hardy	K.3013
Fairey Battle	K.9281	Hawker Hart	K.2967
	K.9223		K.2968

Hawker Henley	K.1416	Supermarine Spitfire I	K.5054
	L.3243		K.6788
	L.3247	Vickers Valentia	K.3603
Hawker Hind	K.2915	Vickers Vildebeest I	S.1715
Hawker Hurricane I	K.5083	IV	K.8087
	L.1562	Vickers Virginia X	K.7130
	L.1574	Vickers Wellesley I	K.7556
	L.1695		K.7791
	L.1696	Vickers Wellington I	L.4212
Parnall Heck IIC	K.8853	Westland Wallace II	K.3673

AIRCRAFT IN GENERAL DUTIES SECTION

Avro Tutor	K.3308	Hawker Fury II	K.1935
	K.6116	Hawker Hardy	K.5919
Bristol Bulldog	K.4189	Hawker Hind Trainer	K.4636
De Havilland Moth II 82A	K.4281	Parnall Heck IIC	K.8853
Gloster Gauntlet	K.4103	Vickers Vildebeest II	K.2819

AIRCRAFT IN EXPERIMENTAL CO-OPERATION FLIGHT
(this was the radio-location aircraft experimental unit)

Avro Anson	K.8758	Fairey Battle	K.9230
	K.6260	Miles Magister	L.8168
Fairey Battle I	K.9207	De Havilland 60M Moth	K.1876
	K.9208	Handley-Page Harrow	K.7021

1939

January 1st to September 1st

AIRCRAFT IN PERFORMANCE TESTING SECTION

Airspeed Oxford I	L.4560		L.6625
Armstrong Whitworth Whitley	K.7208		L.6626
	K.9836		L.6627
Armstrong Whitworth Ensign	G-ADSW	Bristol Bombay	K.3583
"Eddystone"			L.5808
Avro Anson	K.8758	Bristol Beaufort	L.4441
	K.6260	Fairey Battle	K.7605
	N.4871		K.9281
Avro Tutor	K.6116		L.4935
Blackburn Skua	K.5178		K.9207
	L.2871		K.9208
	L.2888		K.9230
Blackburn Roc	L.3058		K.7577
	L.3059		L.8662
	L.3057		L.8689
Blackburn Botha	L.6104	Fairey Swordfish	L.9776
Bristol Blenheim	L.6594	Gloster Gladiator	K.8039
	L.6622	Handley-Page Harrow	K.7021
	L.6623		K.6934
	L.6624	Handley-Page Hampden I	L.4033

Handley-Page Hampden I	L.4035		N.7013
	L.4037	Phillips & Powis T.1/37	L.7714
	L.4032	Phillips & Powis M.18	U — 2
Handley-Page Hereford I	L.7271	Parnall T.1/37	J — 1
Hawker Hardy I	K.5919	Reid & Sigrist Snargasher	G-AEOD
Hawker Hart	K.2968	RS.I	
Hawker Henley	L.3243	Seversky	NX.2586
Hawker Hurricane	L.1547	Supermarine Spitfire	K.9788
	L.1696		K.9787
	L.1702		K.9793
Heston Aircraft T.1/37	L.7706		K.5054
Hendy Heck IIC	K.8853	Vickers Vildebeest	K.2819
Lockheed Hudson I	N.7205	Vickers Wellington	L.4221
	N.7207		L.4223
	N.7208		L.4212
Miles Magister	K.8168		L.4213
Miles Mentor	L.4393		L.4302
Monospar ST.25 Jubilee	K.8307		L.4335
North American Harvard I	N.7000	Westland Lysander	L.4673
	N.7001		

AIRCRAFT IN ARMAMENT TESTING SECTION

Armstrong Whitworth Whitley	K.7183	Handley-Page Harrow	K.6934
Avro Anson	K.6152	Hawker Demon	K.3764
Avro Tutor	K.6116	Hawker Fury	K.2082
Blackburn Skua	L.2868		K.2876
Blackburn Roc	L.3058	Hawker Hardy	K.3013
	L.3069	Hawker Hart	K.2968
Bristol Blenheim I	L.1201		K.1416
	K.7044	Hawker Henley	L.3247
	L.1495	Hawker Hind	K.2915
	L.1253	Hawker Hurricane	L.1574
De Havilland Moth	K.4281		L.1695
Fairey Battle	K.9221	Lockheed Hudson I	N.7206
	K.9231	North American Harvard I	N.7001
	K.9223	Supermarine Spitfire I	L.1007
Fairey Fantome/Feroc	L.7045	Vickers Valentia	K.3603
General Aircraft Monospar	L.4671	Vickers Virginia X	J.7130
Gloster Gladiator	K.7964	Vickers Wellington	L.4212
	K.6129		L.4221
		Westland Lysander	L.4739
Handley-Page Hampden	L.4035		

An unusual type based for a while at Martlesham Heath early 1940 was the one and only British Burnelli OA-1 flying wing aircraft. G - A F M B.

In the last year of the A & A.E.E. at Martlesham Heath, the reader will note the large numbers of aircraft of one type which visited the Establishment for various tests, thereby cutting the time needed to evaluate completely an aircraft type.

The following list is of aircraft, mainly Handley Page types, found since publication of the original edition to have been tested at Martlesham Heath. The information on Handley Page aircraft became available following the release of historical information by the liquidators of this former company.

		1917	
Handley Page 0/100	3142	July	Tested for Russia. Crashed.
Handley Page 0/100	3138	September	Prototype for 0/400.
		1918	
Handley Page 0/400	C.9681	March	Trials aircraft.
Handley Page 0/400	C.9713	July	Aerodynamic trials.
Handley Page V/1500	B.9464	August	Trials aircraft.
Handley Page V/1500	J.1935	October	Ex-B.9464 for trials.
Handley Page V/1500	J.1936	December	Ex-Orfordness trials aircraft.
S.E.5A	B.4862	January	Radiator trials.
S.E.5A	B.4898	February	Sunbeam Arab engine trials.
		1919	
Handley Page 0/400	C.9713	—	Trials aircraft for V/1500.
		1920	
Handley Page 0/400	—	All year	Armament trials.
Handley Page V/1500	J.6573	June	Trials aircraft.
		1921	
Handley Page 0/400	—	All year	Armament trials.
Handley Page V/1500	J.6573	Six months	Trials with Napier engines.
		1922	
Handley Page 0/400	—	All year	Armament trials.
		1923	
Handley Page Handley HP.19	N.145	April	Evaluation.
		1924	
Handley Page Hanley I	N.9724	August	Armament trials.
Handley Page HP.21. S.2	—	February	Fighter trials.
Handley Page HP.22/23	J.7265	February	Not flown.
		1925	
Handley Page Handcross	J.7499	October	Armament trials.
Armstrong Whitworth Siskin V	No.10	December	Aircraft for Rumania.
		1926	
Handley Page Handcross	J.7499	All year	Armament trials.
Handley Page Harrow	N.206	December	Service trials.
		1927	
Handley Page Hinaidi I	J.7745	June	Trials aircraft.
Handley Page Handcross	J.7499	All year	Armament trials.
Handley Page Harrow	N.205	All year	Service trials.
Handley Page Harrow	N.206	June	Service trials.
		1928	
Handley Page Hinaidi I	J.9033	All year	Wireless trials.
Handley Page Handcross	J.7499	All year	Armament trials.
Handley Page Harrow II	N.205	January	Service trials.
		1929	
Armstrong Whitworth Siskin IIIB	J.8627	January	Evaluation trials.
Avro 504R	J.9175/G-EBOY	—	Mongoose engine trials.
		1930	
Handley Page Hare	J.8622	September	Engine trials.
		1931	
Handley Page Hare	J.8622	June	Engine trials.
Handley Page H.P.42	G-AAGX	April	C. of A. trials.
		1933	
Miles M.1 Satyr	G-ABVG	February	C. of A. trials.
		1935	
Handley Page Heyford II	K.4029	May	Service trials.

General Index

(For Aeroplanes and Zeppelins see separate index)

Index for Aeroplanes and Zeppelins

(Excluding Appendices IV and V.)

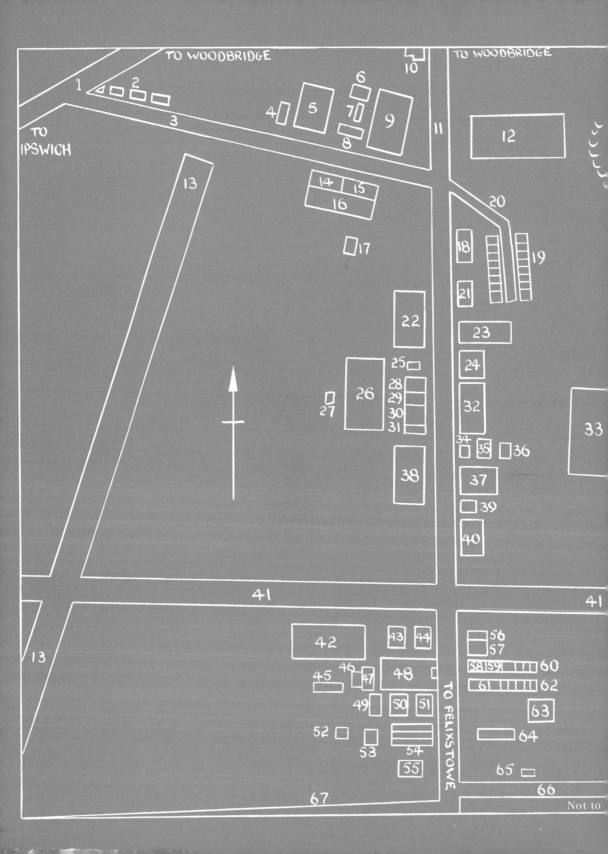